Thank You, Guru Dutt!

Lata Jagtiani

Edited by
Manek Premchand

ISBN
Paperback 979-8-89610-314-1
Hardcase 979-8-89632-381-5

This book is dedicated to
Shree Ramana Maharshi

Contents

SECTION TWO
Guru Dutt's Family and Friends

Introduction

'Thank You, Guru Dutt!' is my humble effort to share what I have understood about the actor, producer, story-writer and director Guru Dutt. Guru Dutt is acclaimed by the world as one of the greatest filmmakers from India, sharing the honours with fellow Indian Satyajit Ray. Both of them raised the bar for their peers. Many of us recognise that Satyajit Ray is for Bengali cinema what Guru Dutt is for Hindi films. While both were humanists, their handling of their plots was different: Ray, with his artistic but stark realism, was worlds apart from Dutt's romance and melodrama. Yet, they were both masters in characterization and their control and understanding of all aspects of filmmaking was rare, if not unique.

I have lost count of the number of times I have seen Guru Dutt's films. The delicious flavour of Aar Paar is nothing like the intense sadness of Kaagaz Ke Phool; the impishness of Mr. & Mrs. '55 is miles away from the intensity of Pyaasa, and the romance of

C. I. D. is the opposite of the loneliness of Sahib Bibi Aur Ghulam. Yet these films are magnets for us, drawing us to them because they bear the unmistakable stamp and signature of Guru Dutt.

When we study Guru Dutt's cinema, we realise that his films ran parallel to his personal life. These movies were like pearls strung together to form a necklace, but running through them was the strand of this giant's personal life. The stories of his films portrayed characters who underwent what the emotional Guru Dutt was then going through in his life. When love delighted or failed him, when society accepted or rejected him, or when thoughts of life's meaninglessness flooded his mind, he remembered all these emotions and presented them aesthetically in his cinema. In that sense, his films can be regarded as semi-autobiographical.

In Guru Dutt's short life span of thirty-nine years, he showed us how cinema could be artistic, and also, how emotions and situations can be conveyed beautifully through brilliant direction. Unlike many others who were filmmakers to obtain fame and profits, for Guru Dutt, filmmaking was an art to which he was one hundred per cent committed. Of course, he had to keep the financiers happy, so along the way, he heeded their counsel, tweaking this, adding that, and so on. Despite these interferences, he managed to create films that are now recognised as classics.

When Suresh Sinha, the protagonist of Kaagaz Ke Phool, walks slowly into the film studio, he appears like a poor, old man with sorrow written on his face. Through Guru Dutt's brilliant direction, viewers sense that this man is done with life. His quiet and slow walk up the stairs tells us that we do not need words from him. It is all in his body language and eyes: he is returning, not to his studio, but to his grave. I am reminded of Washington Irving's words, "Nothing impresses the mind with a deeper feeling of loneliness than to tread the silent and deserted scene of former flow and pageant." Guru Dutt returns to the studio to show us Sinha's loneliness, but, perhaps, his real impetus is to share his own. When Sinha revisits his past and dies, we are not aware that Guru Dutt, through his cinema, is writing his own obituary. It seems as if his future is written on destiny's cards and he has, somehow, managed to read them. He saw it all, his rejection and loneliness and, finally, a quiet slipping away from life...

Kaagaz Ke Phool had such a strong grip on me that, three years back, after some vacillation, I began to work on this book. Then, when I learnt a few things about him, I was shaken and, I must admit, I felt too emotionally engaged with him to continue writing the book with any semblance of objectivity. After a while, I gathered my wits about me, and quietly returned to my desk to honour the promise I had made to myself. I was being encouraged and motivated by some driving force that is still beyond my comprehension.

I would like to share that when I read these Bertrand Russel lines, I found them to be so true about Guru Dutt too: "Three passions, simple but overwhelmingly strong, have governed my life: the longing for love, the search for knowledge, and the unbearable pity for the suffering of mankind." I am sure if Guru Dutt were to read this, he would wrinkle up his forehead, and ask me with an impish smile, "But what about my passion for flying kites?"

'Thank You, Guru Dutt!' is a research-based study of Guru Dutt which attempts to understand the genius and offers a structured analysis of his life, his times and his career as a filmmaker and actor. The biography begins with a chapter which is an overview of Guru Dutt where I offer my understanding of his work and his unfortunate death. This is followed by two chapters, his timeline which consists of his historical data, and his filmography as producer, director and actor.

After these three general chapters, the book is divided into three sections. Section One has a chapter each on the most significant 14 films of his life, many of which he either directed or produced. Since Guru Dutt's epic trilogy of Pyaasa, Kaagaz Ke Phool and Sahib Bibi Aur Ghulam have come to be identified as his best cinema, their chapters are longer than the others.

Section Two deals with the people who were part of his personal and professional universe and who, over time, contributed their insights about him. This section includes, amongst others, chapters devoted to his wife Geeta Dutt, Abrar Alvi, Waheeda Rehman and Dev Anand; all of them provide us with an understanding of Guru Dutt's character and expertise, whether at home or at work. Also included in this section is a guest essay by film and music historian Manek Premchand on Guru Dutt's favourite cinematographer VK Murthy.

Section Three has six chapters that focus on the magical music of Guru Dutt's cinema. Four chapters focus on his work with composers and lyricists OP Nayyar, SD Burman, Ravi, Hemant Kumar, Majrooh Sultanpuri, Sahir Ludhianvi, Kaifi Azmi and Shakeel Badayuni. Two subsequent chapters offer statistics and data about all Guru Dutt's singers and the several songs with their different themes.

The book ends with a concluding chapter titled The Last Word.

A picture, it is said, is a thousand words, so there has been an effort to include relevant photographs in each chapter. While a few photographs are originals, some are screen grabs from his films and some from the web. The idea, firstly, was to provide readers with a structured book on the genius, and secondly, to write it in simple English so that readers did not need a dictionary to understand its content.

I have been extremely blessed to have had the help of many people during this three-year struggle to write about Guru Dutt. Manek Premchand, my husband who is an ace Hindi music historian and author of several invaluable books, not only stood by me while I struggled with the research, but he offered to edit it too. I can't thank him enough. My mother, Mira Madnani, has been the picture of patience and love and has understood my need to be involved with the book. From time to time, she sent me steaming dabbas of delicious food, accompanied by nutritious fruits, just to ensure that, in my effort to remember Guru Dutt, I did not forget myself! I am, of course, always indebted to my late father Keshowdas Madnani who was a cinema buff and who made sure we caught every new film in town and took us on Monday evenings for a film-and-dinner outing. More delicious than the Kwality restaurant dinners was the brainstorming about the film through dinner!

I would also like to thank the beautiful Chhaya Arya for her wonderful inputs on Guru Dutt whom she knew in London, Bombay and Lonavala. This was when she was signed on for the role of Chhoti Bahu, a role which was finally portrayed by Meena Kumari. Several friends, namely MN Sardana, Ajay Kanagat, Falguni Upadhyay, Nikhil Iyer, Antara Nanda Mondal, Sundeep Pahwa, Vineesh Vedsen, and Yogesh Kamdar offered their help when I reached out to them.

Very importantly, I would like to acknowledge two of my dear friends who have left this world but who put me on this path to write about Guru Dutt. One was my dear friend, the late music composer OP Nayyar whose incredible association with Guru

Dutt is well known, and the other is my writing guru, the Padma Bhushan awarded journalist MV Kamath who believed in me and encouraged me to continue writing till I dropped dead!

I would like to end with words from the author Arun Khopkar who summed it up so beautifully, "A work of art takes us away from our daily life for some time. On returning to life, it is not easy to discover and measure the change that the work of art has wrought in us. Yet, it is precisely the extent and quality of this change that gives us a measure of the extent of the truth that exists in the work of art."

I hope this book meets your expectations and I am able to enhance your love and understanding of the genius Guru Dutt. If you wish to reach out to me with your feedback, do email me, I would be delighted to hear from you!

Once you have finished reading this book, I do hope that, like me, you, too, will exclaim, "Thank You, Guru Dutt!"

Lata Jagtiani
latajagtiani@gmail.com

Guru Dutt, The Genius

"It is just because a director has something to say that he finds the form, the skill, and the technique to bring it out. If you are concerned only with how you say something without having anything to say, then even the way you say something won't come to anything. Techniques do not enlarge a director. They limit him. Technique alone, with nothing to support its weight, always crushes the basic idea, which should prevail."

– Akira Kurosawa, Japanese filmmaker of world-class cinema.

Through his roles as producer, director, actor and story-writer, Guru Dutt expressed what he understood of life in Hindi cinema. Many of his early films were different from the other movies of the time. His films had a new look about them; they were quick, slick and magnetic. These films were brilliantly picturised cinema noir thrillers. They had attractive protagonists and catchy melodies, there was suspense and superlative cinematography and, best of all, they had state-of-the-art editing. Songs that were called 'cigarette songs' (boring songs that made viewers step out for a cigarette/ toilet break) did not exist in Guru Dutt's cinema. Instead, his songs were not only catchy and melodious, they also helped move the plot forward. The audience, thrilled with foot-tapping music, would clap and whistle, sometimes even taking to dancing in the aisles. There was never a dull moment in a Guru Dutt film. In short, although his cinema was Indian and it was placed in an Indian ethos, Guru Dutt's films were breezy and possessed international class.

Guru Dutt was fascinated by books and international cinema. Right from age four, he had been a voracious reader. Now, as a director and producer, he read books that would help keep his creative juices flowing. As a youth, he had watched films of the world's top directors and was deeply influenced by them. Not surprisingly, therefore, when he began to direct, he did not want to be like every other Hindi film director. He raised the bar for himself, and in doing this, he also raised it for Hindi cinema as a whole. He was aiming for the stars. Yes, it was risky, but then Guru Dutt always believed in taking risks.

His films became a craze. Viewers exiting the theatres after seeing these cinema noir films would rush to the ticket counter to book tickets for another show, only to find, to their dismay that the whole week, from Friday to Thursday, was already sold out. There were black market touts hanging around selling tickets at double the marked price! These early films of his became big money-spinners because the risk-taker in Guru Dutt had pushed the envelope in a creative direction. Because his finger had been on the audience's pulse, viewers returned the favour by rewarding him generously. He was in step with the audience, not a minute too early or too late.

Later, when his films failed to impress the very same audience (especially Kaagaz Ke Phool and Sahib Bibi Aur Ghulam), it was not because Guru Dutt had failed at his craft and art. A study of his cinema shows that he had improved over time. His failure was because he had, once again, pushed the envelope, but this time he had been way ahead of his time. In the world of the creative arts, the cliché 'timing is everything,' rules. In his essay re-published in Nasreen Munni Kabir's biography, Guru Dutt, A Life in Cinema, Guru Dutt wrote about this difficulty while making a motion picture:

"If a classic in literature, poetry or painting, goes unclaimed and unrewarded momentarily, it is more a reflection on the public which is supposed to patronize it, and not on the accomplished genius who created it. The same is true of a film. If it is really a classic and fails to bring in the expected returns, the blame may not lie entirely with its creator. This means that the financial failure or success often depends on the whims, aesthetic standards and the intellectual caliber of an eternally capricious public."

Guru Dutt quoted examples of geniuses who had been recognised after they had passed on, such as Homer, Goldsmith, Johnson, Van Gogh, Swami Tulsidas, etc. He added that even Satyajit Ray was similarly neglected in India until his films received international recognition and awards. The point he was making was that several artists had been discovered as geniuses too late for them to taste the joys of recognition. Yet, despite knowing of this thorny path, Guru Dutt would not rest. He had decided to be the change he was seeking. He was a man in a hurry, a restless iconoclast keen to make his mark in the world of cinema. Luckily, after his initial successes, he was in a position to attract financiers and get funding for his pet projects. He could call the shots after the blockbuster success of his films Baazi, Aar Paar and Mr. & Mrs. '55. He desperately wanted to convert the novel he had authored Kashmakash to cinema. His peers understood what he was doing but they feared for him. He was so committed to art that even his friend Dev Anand observed that Guru Dutt had a "tremendous ambition to fight against the stereotyped, set conventionalism of the early fifties, to be original and different."

Yet, nobody can stop a genius when he decides to blaze forward on the road not taken by others. His mother, Vasanthi Padukone, wrote in her memoirs that Guru Dutt would not listen to anyone if his mind was made up. He wanted to tell his story in his way, to share his beliefs and thoughts through entertaining moving images; and through that entertainment he wanted his viewers to step out of their comfort zones. He wanted them to examine the story, examine the twisted values and beliefs they had, and then, hopefully, to examine themselves.

He was not a mere stylist, someone who says a lot and, in the end, says nothing. He was a romantic who wanted to change mind-sets through cinema; he wanted people to evolve and reject their comfortable beliefs that hurt the innocent. His films were melodramatic morality plays. Satyajit Ray, in his book Our Films, Their Films, aptly observed, "For the truly serious, socially conscious filmmaker, there can be no prolonged withdrawal into fantasy. He must face the challenge of contemporary reality, examine the facts, probe them, sift them and select from them the material to be transformed into the stuff of cinema." A serious filmmaker like Guru Dutt was certainly not going to hide his head in the sand while the world around him was, like him, in pain. Thus, we could not escape the moral messaging beneath the entertainment. Sometimes though, he went too far and the audience refused the sugarless bitter medicine he was offering. Of course, he was aware of the danger he was courting, yet he went ahead. His sense of responsibility to art made him forget that cinema did not have such broad shoulders. But it hurt him to acknowledge a fact that Arun Khopkar, in his book on Guru Dutt, 'A Tragedy in Three Acts' has so succinctly stated about romantics like Guru Dutt,

"The romantics believe that there exists between the artist and society an eternal conflict. When such experiences find expression in the artist's work, society is disconcerted by its unfamiliarity…society thrives on the daily monotony of routine, fearing the unknown. If society needs an artist, it is as an image, a name that must be worshipped. It needs him for the touch of the exotic that he brings into their insipid lives. Society is not the least bit interested in understanding him or in understanding itself better through his work. It would rather distance him by worshipping him in order to avoid facing the unpalatable truths about itself that his work may reveal."

Perhaps society was telling Guru Dutt to face the reality that it owed him nothing. It was advising the physician in Guru Dutt to heal himself. It was what it was, and Guru Dutt needed to stop trying to force it to change. Perhaps, all this was a bit too overwhelming for Guru Dutt.

Today, several decades after Kaagaz Ke Phool was released, we appreciate it, we gasp when we see the artist at his intense best in this film. He reflects our angst persuasively because we see how authentic he is.

The cinema of Guru Dutt was unsparing and cruel because it insisted on showing us the passion and pain of love; that while superficial civility oils our lives, hidden in the crevices of our minds is the darkness that must be acknowledged. Guru Dutt's failure was because, at that time, he went too deep into our psyches. When he was asking us to look into a mirror, he wanted us to really see ourselves. He thought he was making his cinema for grown-ups, but we preferred to hide under our beds if there was a monster in the room. We were ready to pay for escapist cinema, and we preferred the pleasant lie over the unpleasant truth. Escapism and not reality was what we, the audience, sought. Life was hard enough, why add to the pain of existence?

Yet an artist like Guru Dutt is driven, so he has to respond to the call of creativity. An artist might even choose to alienate the world if he wants to obey his inner self. Guru Dutt lived for perfection, for excellence. Perhaps, it was this very pursuit of excellence that, in the end, made life unbearable for him. After Sahib Bibi Aur Ghulam's failure to make a mark at the Berlin film festival in June 1963, he had, perhaps, already packed his bags. He realised that his best was behind him, and that he no longer understood how to communicate effectively with his audience. He had surrendered to art at a huge price. His personal life was in a mess, and he was surrounded by many false friends. He could not get sleep, but he didn't enjoy being awake either.

The Artist and His Angst

Some critics, taken in by Sahir's poem Jinhe naaz hai Hind par woh kahaan hai in Pyaasa, conclude that Guru Dutt was Left-leaning. To my mind, socialism was a convenient platform from which Guru Dutt could adequately express his artistic oeuvre; since this socialist platform was the popular medium in post-Partition India of the 50s, it was safer for him to employ it as a means to an end. To put it another way, socialism was the moving truck on which his art was being transported. Neither in his personal life nor in his cinema (except for Pyaasa), does one see any evidence of Guru Dutt being either a communist or a socialist. He lived his life in luxury, he was generous with people in his world, and he wasted thousands of rupees on anything that caught his fancy. He was not part of any Leftist group either, nor did he attend their meets to show solidarity with their cause. If anything, he resembled hedonists who lived for themselves while splurging their wealth on flatterers and sycophants.

Guru Dutt was obsessed, much like Raj Kapoor was, with his art. When Raj Kapoor's son, Rishi Kapoor spoke about his father, he was really also talking about another creative genius, Guru Dutt. Let's read this excerpt from Ritu Nanda's biography of her father, 'Raj Kapoor, the One and Only Showman':

"He (Raj Kapoor) was an absolute one-track mind, his whole life revolved around his films. That is all he could think or talk of. With drinks, without drinks, before food, after food, morning, afternoon, noon or night, at home or in the studios, his conversation was only about films. Even if you talked about outer space or Donald Duck, he would bring the conversation back to films."

It is not surprising then to find this true of Guru Dutt too. Because of his commitment to art, the artist in Guru Dutt was a perfectionist. If one can offer a similarity here, one would say that, much like deep-sea explorers, Guru Dutt was a 'deep-cinema' explorer. He explored and examined his art tirelessly, which is why we find that he would persistently shoot and reshoot scenes, sometimes even re-shooting them a hundred times, until they met with his expectations. In an interview available on YouTube, VK Murthy emphasised this finickiness of Guru Dutt with an example. He said that Guru Dutt was extremely particular that the first shot of a scene ought to start right. One day they were all set to shoot a scene near the swimming pool for a scene for Mr. & Mrs. '55. Guru Dutt kept looking at it through the viewfinder to get an idea as to how the shot must begin. Somehow, he was unable to get what he wanted. He asked the cast and crew to pack up for the day. The next day he began by looking through the viewfinder and the very first angle he saw he was okay with it. The song Thandi hawa kaali ghata then got the director's approval. Although he was a man in a hurry, he would not spare any time or cost to get it just right. Again, in Pyaasa, Waheeda Rehman had to climb down a flight of stairs 34 times to get the big man's okay! While he empathised with her for doing this so many times, he never lost sight of the fact that his mistress Art, was someone he could not betray. Yes, he was inherently pessimistic and he wanted a more value-based society, and yes, he would portray that too, but it was important for him to say things correctly or not say them at all.

His films in Phases 2 & 3 never lost sight of this. He was not like KA Abbas and Raj Kapoor who were driven by the social injustice they saw around them; for him, the story about the disadvantaged was good, but how it was expressed and sculpted was the real driving force. For Guru Dutt, film-making was always personal, it was never social; what mattered were his inner yearnings and conflicts and how well he projected them. That's all that mattered. If one looks at his cinema closely, one discovers that he employed cinema to universalise the personal. What was true in his life had to be communicated in the most artistic manner possible.

All his later stories focussed on the protagonist and his conflict, his romantic hero/heroine in an epic struggle against overwhelming odds. Thus, his protagonists were morose, unhappy or pointing to the meaninglessness of existence. Guru Dutt used social ills to portray his personal angst. The unfairness of life was the trigger, but what really absorbed him were his inner angels and demons. Who or what triggered these angels and demons was less important than the angels and demons themselves. What he was keen to present and portray was what happened to a man when he is ravaged by demons, and what remains of him after his personality has been mauled.

If anything, these later films were a study of the human mind, its complexities, its priorities, its limitations, and the power of the external world over an individual who is pulled and pushed by his fears, desires, and a yearning to be understood. He seeks meaning and significance in an uncaring universe. When his protagonist had the dark night of the soul, whether he could he survive it or succumb to it, that was what interested him. This was his *raison d'etre* as an artist. A quiet person unwilling to confide in others, Guru Dutt was interested in sharing his mind through cinema, by way of a story that allowed him a platform for his communication.

In Phase 1, his films were joyous, hopeful and impish. There was wit, banter, and charm. There was a lightness of being. Then came Phase 2, which consisted only of his magnum opus Pyaasa, the film that was like a bridge between his Phases 1 and 3.

In Phases 2 and 3 Dutt chose to make poignant films which tended towards the subject of the meaninglessness of life. His protagonists were victimised by overwhelming forces. Their epic struggles, whether with society (Pyaasa) or with their inner demons (Kaagaz Ke Phool) mattered. The politics was incidental, but the personal was significant. Anything could be the trigger or the cause, because the art was in showing the effect on the protagonist. These stories were essentially about the agony and ecstasy of being human, about Man's nature and how he overcame or succumbed to challenges. Like the novels of DH Lawrence, his films were more psychological than social. The playwright Bernard Shaw used the platform of humour for his plays so that he could do what he always wanted, which was to spread his Fabian message. Guru Dutt did exactly the opposite, he employed socialism to express his inner self. One manipulated art, and the other manipulated inequity. Both, of course, were master communicators in their fields.

Guru Dutt wanted to communicate that some men failed and were the architects of their failures when confronted by a hostile environment. It is important to point out that his message was not that all men failed, only that some did. This is because in his films some were shown succeeding despite the hostile environment they were in. For example, in Pyaasa, Johnny Walker was shown as poor yet he was jovial and upbeat. Similarly, in Pyaasa again, Gulabo was a prostitute and yet she did not become despondent; she retained her courage and optimism. These two were facing the same environment that Vijay was facing, the same nasty set of people, yet their responses were different. Unlike Vijay who was an idealist, they were realists. In Kaagaz Ke Phool, we saw Shanti re-invent herself as a teacher working cheerfully in a village school. Later she returned to the film industry and worked there, to succeed with the same set of people that Sinha had turned away from. In Sahib Bibi Aur Ghulam, Chhoti Bahu had trouble accepting her loneliness but her elder sister-in-law had reconciled herself to hers.

Dutt's stories dig deep into Man's choices, and his psychological weaknesses that get triggered when political or social structures challenge him. He is the architect of his successes and failures, so it is he alone who elevates and destroys his aspirations and dreams. Thus, for Guru Dutt, what really matters is how he fights, how he struggles, how he conquers or how he is vanquished.

When art becomes so personal, it can be seen as narcissistic self-indulgence. However, one must accept that most artists who are geniuses need narcissism to be engaged in such a deep exercise. A strong self-belief is invaluable for the effort, because it motivates them to create a unique work of art. Guru Dutt was no exception.

The writer Nasreen Munni Kabir tells us that Pandit Narendra Sharma, the Hindi poet and lyricist, was also a big fan of Guru Dutt's. He had met Guru Dutt in Almora and had found him "soft, delicate, unobtrusive—there was nothing loud about him—yet the roots of his talents lay somewhere very deep inside him and he could perceive things keenly. I remember when he came to me with his horoscope and Geeta's...I was obliged to tell him that theirs would not be a happy marriage...He married the woman he loved, whatever the consequences. Astrological forecasts must be considered a part of worldly sanity, but artists are insane. Sanity isn't much of an asset for artists...What was remarkable in his films was that he drew from his inner experience which veered around two points: how persons are exploited and how talent can be unjustly exploited by others. He discussed with me one of the very early drafts of Kaagaz Ke Phool, and there it was, this same exploitation…Guru Dutt's presence was like candlelight: subdued light, but nevertheless light. He managed to have a team that was very loyal to him".

Indeed, his team of Abrar Alvi, Johnny Walker, and Rehman stood by him and he had done a lot to deserve this loyalty too (detailed chapters of these team-members follow). Additionally, there were a couple of other important crew members who stood by him as well.

These were, amongst so many others, Niranjan, Shyam Kapoor, Mala Sinha, and S Guruswamy.

Niranjan was the Assistant Director to Guru Dutt. He worked with Guru Dutt right from his first production Baaz, continuing with him in Aar Paar, Mr. & Mrs. '55, and Pyaasa. Niranjan had a big say in a lot of decisions in Guru Dutt's life. Once Abrar Alvi had reassured an agitated Geeta Dutt (who was concerned about Guru Dutt's relationship with Waheeda Rehman) that both Niranjan and he would not allow Guru to abandon Geeta and her kids for Waheeda.

Then there was Shyam Kapoor in the inner friends' circle of Guru Dutt. Shyam was Guru Dutt's Assistant Director in four films: Mr. & Mrs. '55, Pyaasa, Kaagaz Ke Phool, and Baharen Phir Bhi Aayengi. In Aar Paar, he had a cameo acting role when Shakila lip-synched Babujee dheere chalna. In C.I.D., he portrayed the role of a street musician along with Sheila Vaz during the enchanting song Leke pehla pehla pyaar. In Pyaasa, he played the role of Guru Dutt's untrustworthy friend Shyam.

Then there was Mala Sinha who, thanks to Geeta Dutt's recommendation, got her career-changing break as Meena in Pyaasa. She also worked with Guru Dutt in a few films produced in Madras, such as Bahurani and Suhagan. In the end, they were shooting together for Baharen Phir Bhi Aayengi before Guru Dutt passed away. Mala Sinha admired Guru Dutt a lot. She said, "He would look into everything. For example, he would choose the lighting for the scene, saying to Murthy, Krishna, this is the mood of this scene, aisa mood hai; for example, isko half-light, half-shade karo, as in Jaane kya tu ne kahi. He was a genius, an all-rounder, he knew his job, kisi par woh depend nahin karte the. Basically, he had a lot of insaaniyat, sadbhaav, and he loved everyone on his staff. At lunchtime, before he sat down to eat, he would call the Production Manager and find out if everyone had got their lunch, if the workers had eaten, if the makeup man got it, and if everyone in the unit had eaten. Kaun karta hai aisa? Guru Duttjee, meri takleef ke time, when I was raided, the tax people sealed everything. I had no money, I was in difficulty. Others kept away from me fearing that if they helped me, the IT people would come and raid them too. My father and I were worried. But the next day, Guru Duttjee came to my home around 11 a.m., with his pockets full of cash for us! He told my father that he realised we had difficulties and had come to help us." Guru Dutt's generosity and empathy won their hearts that day.

Finally, there was S Guruswamy who was promoted to become a director of the newly created Guru Dutt Films. Guru and he had an excellent rapport between them. He also used to be the Production Controller of the company. About Guru Dutt, Guruswamy narrated an incident in Screen magazine, revealing the filmmaker's innate kindness and empathy. Guruswamy said that 'Guru Dutt had a certain nobility about him.' Once, it so happened that an artiste who had been helped by the company several times began to give them trouble. Guruswamy had pulled the man up and told him that he should not do this, reminding him of how many times he had been helped out of his troubles by Guru Dutt and the company. Guru Dutt over-heard this, and later, in private, told Guruswamy "Never mention about helping someone, it hurts human pride."

That was the nobility in Guru Dutt who was gone too soon…

Suddenly One Night…

One day Guru Dutt said to VK Murthy, "Life mein, yaar, kya hai? Do hi toh cheezen hai—kaamyaabi aur failure. Dekho na, mujhe director banna tha, director ban gaya; actor banna tha, actor ban gaya; picture achhe banaane the, achhe banaaye. Paisa hai, sab kuchh hai, par kuchh bhi nahin raha."

What can one do if someone is unhappy even when he has everything?

His sudden death heightens Guru Dutt's mystique. Whether he committed suicide or whether it was an accidental death due to an overdose of pills combined with alcohol, remains a mystery.

As a child, he saw his parents constantly fight with each other. He became a disturbed young man because we learn from his mother that very early in his life, Dev Anand had prevented him from seriously contemplating suicide. Later, during the making of Pyaasa, he attempted suicide for the first time. He had written a suicide note, leaving everyone in no doubt that his action was intentional and not accidental. He attempted suicide the second time in November 1961 during the making of Sahib Bibi Aur Ghulam. VK Murthy said that he had been with him at the hospital on both occasions.

On October 10, 1964, Guru Dutt was found dead in his bed in his rented apartment at Peddar Road in Mumbai. It is said that he had mixed alcohol and sleeping pills. Some believe that this was his third suicide attempt. However, since his door had been locked from inside, there had been nobody to bring him to life. He had died several hours before his bedroom door was broken open.

The pressure on him to turn out a serious work of art and be a director of reckoning was formidable. Additionally, Geeta and he were parents to two sons and a daughter. He had got accustomed to several pegs of whisky and he would combine his drinks with quite a few sleeping pills. Since his closest friend and drinking buddy Abrar Alvi and he could hold their drinks well, they drank regularly and could polish off a whisky bottle between them. It was bad enough that he was a workaholic, but now he was also an alcoholic taking drugs which were dangerous in high doses.

Yet, he was very disciplined when it came to work. One learns from VK Murthy that Guru Dutt would never touch a drop when he was at work. His work gave him a high. But he had an overactive brain that would not let him sleep, so he would either be over-thinking or brooding excessively. He was such a serious insomniac that writer Bimal Mitra, who stayed with him from time to time, would be amazed at how little sleep Guru got before he got ready to go to work. His mind would not stop racing ahead no matter how hard he tried.

Abrar Alvi, when interviewed, said that Guru would tell Abrar that he was worried his thoughts were too difficult for him to handle, and that he thought that he was going mad. Even a few hours before he passed away, he told Abrar the same thing.

His brother Atma Ram said that Guru Dutt was as undisciplined in his personal life as he was disciplined in his professional life. At work, he was a strict disciplinarian, but away from work, he was lost. He said, "Relationships didn't matter to Guru Dutt, only his films did."

When interviewed, Guru Dutt's sister Lalitha Lajmi reaffirmed that when depressed, Guru Dutt would call her to his home at odd hours. However, when she reached there, he would refuse to say a word. "I felt he wanted to say something. But he never did. Never." She regretted that at that time, psychological issues were not handled well, "In those days, no one really talked about such things. We called a psychiatrist but he charged Rs 500 per visit. My brother Atma laughed that he was 'just talking' with Guru and that he was so expensive. We never called him again."

Perhaps he felt he had done things he could not easily speak about; sometimes talking about very personal issues makes them real in the world and then one has to deal with the consequences of having confided in another human being. On the other hand, he probably felt that nobody could understand the kind of pressure he applied on himself to be a producer, director, actor, husband, lover, father, friend, and businessman all at one time. He had to look at the creative angle of his films but he had to look at the salability of his cinema as well. He knew that nobody was forcing him to do all this, he was doing it out of choice. He knew about the chaos he caused in his family with his irregular hours, his frequent absences from home, his frustration with films not turning out the way he wanted them to, his hanging out with unsavoury elements, his drinks, his chain-smoking, his sleeping pills, in short, his incomprehensible mess. He knew he was a storm in Geeta Dutt's life but he simply did not want to change for her or anyone else.

Lalita Lajmi observed that working in films changes people permanently, especially since the kind of films Guru Dutt was making were innovative and highly creative. The long hours at work and the pressures on a director, a producer and an actor were immense. As a result, he became more and more aloof. Their family picnics became memories since he had no time or attention for anything except his films.

In a BBC audio interview available on YouTube, Lalitha Lajmi spoke about her brother's death. She said that when she had met Guru Dutt ten days before he passed away, she had found him very depressed. He had asked her to join him for dinner, but she had declined saying she had already finished her dinner. She later regretted her refusal, saying that she should have accepted and had a meal with him that day. She had gone to invite her brother to her home for a live sitar recital by Ustad Abdul Halim Jaffer Khan on the evening of October 10, but he had refused, saying that she knew he didn't like parties, so he would prefer to meet her one on one. That was their last meeting. Coincidentally, he died on the very day of her get-together. She recalled that when she entered his room on October 10, "The lights were on, the fan was on, there was an unfinished novel by his bedside, his mouth was open, his one leg was down, his hand was raised as if he wanted to say something... as if he wanted to get up..."

In another online interview, Lalitha Lajmi told Sushmita Bhattrai of Seniorstoday, "Guru began living in an apartment in Peddar Road and kept himself busy with work. On one of those days he had come to my house in Colaba to borrow some crockery; he said he was hosting a small get-together and left asking me to come home for lunch. Those days he was working on Baharen Phir Bhi Aayengi. The screenwriter of the film Abrar Alvi later on told me that Guru had asked him, "What will happen if one mixes sleeping pills with alcohol?" Alvi casually replied, "It could lead to death." It was supposed to be a casual conversation as Guru was always curious about things and would never stop questioning. Everything seemed fine – at least on the outside, things had actually begun to look better. Little did anyone know, however, that there was a tornado inside Guru's head that eventually pushed him off the ledge. He couldn't complete his last film; his will to die prevailed over his capability as a brilliant filmmaker. I found him resting on his bed. He looked at peace. I believe he didn't take his life; rather, life walked out on him and there was nothing anybody could do but accept it as it is."

In an online interview with India Abroad in October 2004, on the 40th death anniversary of his father, Guru Dutt's son, Arun Dutt, said that he views his father's death as an accident. "My father had sleeping disorders and popped sleeping pills like any other person. That day he was drunk and had taken an overdose of pills, which culminated in his death. It was a lethal combination of excessive liquor and sleeping pills."

Arun also wrote an article in India Abroad that carried his piece written in the first person. He said, "When I was eight, I was at school watching a cartoon film on my principal's birthday. We were enjoying the film when suddenly one of my uncles came and took me away. I was very angry with him. I just didn't want to leave. I told him that I would complain about him to my father. When we reached home there was silence in the house. My father was lying down. I thought, at first, that he was sleeping. I never thought he was dead. I had never seen a dead person so I guessed he was asleep. I was too young to realise or understand the loss. But as time passed, I realised he would not come back. Forty years after his death, I realise the importance of October 10, 1964. He passed away early in the morning, around 1 a.m. But the news came post-sunrise after the door was broken down to find his dead body. A lot of theories have been put forth on why he committed suicide. But I think it was an accident. He had scheduled appointments the next day with [actress] Mala Sinha for Baharen Phir Bhi Aayengi, and Rajsaab [Raj Kapoor] to discuss making colour films." Arun Dutt stressed again that he did not believe his father committed suicide because when he had attempted suicide twice before he had left a suicide note. This time since there was no suicide note, it seemed that he had probably had too much to drink and had accidentally overdosed himself.

Guru Dutt's younger brother Devi Dutt also did not believe that Guru Dutt had killed himself, adding that Dutt was suffering from a sleeping disorder and that it must have been an accidental overdose of sleeping pills after drinking. In an interaction with

Filmfare, Devi Dutt said, "After Sahib Bibi Aur Ghulam, Guru Dutt and Bhabhi had patched up. It was decided that the entire family would stay together at 48, Pali Hill once it was redeveloped. On October 9, 1964, he was at his studio with Tanuja, Rehman and director Shahid Lateef for his production Baharen Phir Bhi Aayegi. But Mala Sinha had got stuck in Madras. So the shooting got postponed. Bhabhi had gone to the children's school for PTA and was supposed to send Tarun and Arun across in the evening. We left for home in the car. He asked me to buy kites and maanjha from Bandra as he wanted to fly kites with the children over the weekend. Then we stopped at Charagh Din at Colaba. He bought clothes for the boys and also some for me…Then we stopped at Kanjibhai broker's house at Marine Lines to collect whisky bottles. Guru Dutt asked him to get his money back from investors as he wanted to import coloured stock for Kaneez. When we reached home, he went into the kitchen and began preparing omelettes. He said he'd cook more often when we all lived together. He said that we brothers would occupy the 9th and 10th floors, from where we'd watch the sunset every evening. Just then walked in our Chartered Accountant, Gole Saab. He informed Guru Dutt of the 'final notices' from the IT department for the taxes pending since the past two years. They got into a heated argument. Gole Saab warned that the IT department could raid the studio, office and home anytime. Guru Dutt asked me to go home…On the way out I met Abrar Alvi. I asked him to convey Bhabhi's message to Guru Dutt—that she wouldn't be sending the kids as it was late. That was my last evening with Guru Dutt. The next day, he was no more. I still maintain he did not commit suicide. It must have been due to the sleeping pills after heavy drinking with Abrar," Devi concluded.

Some people, especially Abrar Alvi, who was the last to see Guru Dutt on that day, figured it was a suicide. Abrar and Dutt had on many occasions discussed ways of committing suicide and both had tried it and failed. Abrar and Guru Dutt sat late that night discussing a movie. According to Alvi, Guru Dutt was very morbid in his thinking and conversation. He was distressed by his personal life—his wife, Geeta Dutt, who had distanced herself from him. "He had a sleeping disorder that made him take sleeping pills, and he had been drinking since 5 p.m. that evening."

In her book, Ten Years With Guru Dutt, Sathya Saran writes, "Abrar Alvi felt 'he must have pulled one of his stunts', taken a tablet to worry us, to trouble all of us…Guru Dutt lay on his bed in his kurta pyjama; on the bedside was a glass with a little pink liquid still left in it. Of course, I knew he had killed himself: we had discussed it so many times. "It's Sonaril" I told them, which he used to get through his driver from a chemist in Khar. "We used to talk about it: the ways to kill oneself. I had even tried it once, and he had at least twice before. We had realised a man cannot kill himself by swallowing sleeping pills…Guru had worked it out. He told me, "You must take it like a mother gives medicine to her child…crush the tablets and dissolve them in water."

Did Guru Dutt give up his life because the world's applause stopped? Or did he realise that his creative juices had dried up? Did he care too little for his life and too much for his art? His two or possibly three suicide attempts show us that he was determined to die and that it was only a matter of time before he succeeded. After the failure of Kaagaz Ke Phool, nothing made sense to him; apparently, even his belief in God could not rescue him from the darkness in his mind. Waheeda Rehman said that he was attracted to death and he longed for it. One wonders if it was that longing that triggered his excessive intake of alcohol and sleeping pills.

Shyama, his co-star in Aar Paar, spoke on Guru Dutt in an interview with Filmfare: "He was a very good director. He would not okay the shot till it was perfect. He would be well prepared. He knew exactly where to place the camera and would get impatient if things didn't happen the way he wanted. He was strict, a man of principles and also very sensitive. He'd enact all the expressions for me when I was doing Aar Paar. He was good at that because he was also a dancer. He had come home for my birthday party, just a week before he died. I guess he died due to an overdose of alcohol. I don't think he committed suicide. I worked with him in Bahurani and not once did he mention being depressed. But he had an unhappy family life. Separation from your wife and kids can be killing."

OP Nayyar was friends with Guru Dutt. In an interview with writer Mandar Bichhu, the composer offered us an insight into Guru Dutt's state of mind, "Talking of Guru Dutt, I always feel a pang of guilt. He used to confide his personal problems to me. His wife Geeta and his flame Waheeda, both had deserted him in the end and he was pretty disturbed. At around 2 a.m., the same night that he committed suicide, my wife told me, "Raj Kapoor has phoned for you. He is saying that Guru Dutt is totally inebriated and is crying inconsolably, repeatedly calling for Nayyar Saab!" I was too tired and sleepy to go. I just told my wife to give some excuse. The next morning at 10 a.m., I had an appointment with Guru Dutt at his residence. I reached there and Abrar Alvi, his dialogue writer, told me, "Guru has gone." Incredulously, I asked, "Where?" He said, "Guru Dutt is dead! His dead body is inside!" True to my straight-talking nature, I just blasted those two women for ruining Guru's life: Geeta—right there in front of Guru's dead body in the drawing room, and Waheeda, at the time of the funeral!"

It is hard for ordinary people like us to understand the mind of a genius like Guru Dutt. Yet one tries to make sense of his death because one admires him so much. During his most creative phases he attempted suicide twice. How does one reconcile these two opposite pulls, one, to live at the peak of creativity, and the other, to drown and be nothing? He would be upbeat and then he would be downcast; he would be flying off the handle and yet be persuasive and kind. Perhaps psychiatrists would be able to assess this, but one really wonders why his most creative phase drove him to consider self-destruction as a solution. One cannot also overlook the fact that to be part of a love triangle can sometimes be overwhelming for anyone who is deeply sensitive, and perhaps Guru Dutt was similarly conflicted. He realised that he loved his wife the most but he was also involved with a young actress. These pulls and pushes of his life became overpowering and he became sleepless. That's when alcohol became useful.

Deep and sensitive people often find life overwhelming and resort to escape, whether it is through alcohol, drugs, promiscuity, workaholism, substance abuse, relationship addiction, or gambling; some finally even escape life through suicide.

In a way, he was the Icarus of Hindi cinema who had flown so close to the sun, his destruction was inevitable. Guru Dutt's wings first caught fire during the making of Pyaasa, then the fire almost consumed him during Sahib Bibi Aur Ghulam, and, finally, it destroyed him during the making of Baharen Phir Bhi Aayengi.

When he died, Guru Dutt was involved in two other projects, apart from Baharen Phir Bhi Aayengi. One was Picnic, starring actress Sadhana, and the second was director K Asif's epic, Love and God. Picnic remained incomplete and Love and God was released two decades later with Sanjeev Kumar replacing Dutt in the lead role.

According to writer Darius Cooper, "He committed suicide but the cinematic work he has left behind makes him, for this writer, part of the first great troika of Indian cinema along with filmmakers Satyajit Ray and Ritwik Ghatak."

While none of us can be certain about his mysterious death, many of us are sure that a director of the calibre and stature of Guru Dutt has yet to be seen in the Hindi film industry.

The poet who gave us Dekhi zamaane ki yaari, Kaifi Azmi, was shocked when Guru Dutt passed away. He wrote a ghazal for Guru Dutt which said it all:

Rehne ko sada dahr mein aata nahin koi

Tum jaise gaye, aise bhi jaata nahin koi

Ek baar to khud maut bhi ghabra gayi hogi

Yoon maut ko seene se lagaata nahin koi

Darta hoon kaheen khushk na ho jaaye samandar

Raakh apni kabhi aap bahaata nahin koi

Maana ke ujaalon ne tumhein daagh diye the

Be-raat dhale shamma bujhaata nahin koi

Saaqi se gila tha tumhein, maikhaane se shikwa

Ab zeher se bhi pyaas bujhaata nahin koi

Har subah hila deta tha zanjeer zamaana

Kyun aaj deewaane ko jagaata nahin koi

Arthi to uttha lete hain sab ashk baha ke

Naaz-e-dil-e-betaab utthaata nahin koi…

The Guru Dutt Timeline

1900

Guru Dutt's father, Shivshanker Rao Padukone, was born in a Chitrapur Saraswat Brahmin family. Shivshanker was a pampered child since he was the last of 13 children and also because his mother died when he was only 13 years old.

1907

Guru Dutt's maternal grandparents lost three of their six children to the Spanish Flu.

1908

Vasanthi Baindur, her parents' seventh child, was born in Burma (which was part of British India till 1937). She had three elder brothers, Vittalrao, Ramnath and Raghuvir, who had survived the Spanish Flu.

1917

Vasanthi's father abandoned the family, forcing his eldest son, Vittalrao, to quit his education and take up a job. He became the breadwinner of his family which consisted of his mother, his sister Vasanthi, and two brothers, Ramnath and Raghuvir. Since his father had left debts for them to settle, Vittalrao was under severe financial stress. Additionally, he was concerned about the expenses they would incur as and when Vasanthi got married. Plus, there was pressure on him to get Vasanthi married at the earliest. He was hired at Rs 35 per month as a telegraphist in the Central Telegraph Office in Madras. Because his earnings were not enough for the family, Vittalrao was anxious. A childless couple among his relatives adopted his younger brother, Ramnath, easing some of his financial load.

1920

On December 21, 1920, Vasanthi married Shivshankar Rao Padukone who was then studying for his B.A. in Mangalore. At the time of her marriage, she was only 12 years old, while he was 20.

1923

Vasanthi went to join her husband in Panambur, near Mangalore when she turned 15. By this time he had become the headmaster of a 100-student Gram Panchayat school.

1924

Shivshankar would often get malaria, so a palmist, who was consulted for his health, read Vasanthi's palm and told her that she would get a son within a year and he would be world famous. That first child was Guru Dutt (earlier he was named Vasantkumar, as mentioned in a bit). Vasanthi was happy in Panambur, but her moody and headstrong husband quit his job to look for better opportunities in Bangalore. Vasanthi failed to persuade him to remain in Panambur. When he left for Bangalore, she visited her cousin BB Benegal in Mangalore. Benegal admired Tagore and would borrow books from a library for Vasanthi to read. Later that year, when her husband got a job in a bank in Bangalore, he sent for his wife to join him there. In October, they shifted to Chamrajpet in Bangalore where Vasanthi and her widowed mother together set up their home. Vasanthi conceived immediately. She had excessive morning sickness, so she stopped attending the missionary school she had joined to learn embroidery. She spent her nine months of pregnancy reading Marathi books on saints Ramakrishna Paramahansa and Swami Vivekananda so that her unborn child would be instilled with spiritual values and be a very brilliant child.

1925

On Thursday, July 9, 1925, at noon, with rain, thunder and lightning outside the nursing home, Vasanthi gave birth to her firstborn, Guru Dutt. He was under 6 pounds in weight. He was the only boy born on that day in the nursing home. Soon he was found to be a playful child who smiled easily. His mother said that he was a cute fair-skinned child with large eyes and curly black hair. Her elder brother Vittalrao suggested two names for the infant. Gurudutt was the first choice because he was born on the birthday of the Vaishnava saint Madhavacharya and also because he was born on a Guruvaar, but they opted for the other name which was Vasantkumar.

1927

Vasanthi wrote her recollections of Guru Dutt in a book, Nanna Maga Guru Dutt (My son, Guru Dutt) where she shared that Guru Dutt as an infant was weak and could not take the Bangalore cold and kept catching the flu virus. Yet, he was given to smiling at anyone who came near him. However, he was also stubborn and short-tempered. At this time, Vasanthi was deeply influenced by Mahatma Gandhi and would attend meets where she offered prayers and sang Kannada bhajans.

Since Guru's favourite colour was red, his mother put on a red outfit for him on his second birthday. While running back home after a visit to the neighbour's home, the little boy fell near a well, hurting his forehead badly. He developed a high fever and was seriously ill for over two weeks. The worried Vasanthi was told there was an evil spirit over him, so a Mantravadi was called to remove the spirit. The holy man told them that his name was unlucky for him and that they needed to change his name from the unlucky Vasantkumar. The second name which Vittalrao had offered was adopted and his name was changed to Gurudutt. Meanwhile, Vasanthi's cousin, who was a doctor, agreed to heal the boy after some persuasion because Shivshankar had fought with him. When the boy finally recovered, the first word he uttered was, 'Amma'. After his recovery, every evening when the diyas were lit for the idols in their Puja room, he would shut his eyes and, in his baby voice, sing the bhajan, 'Raghupati Raghav Rajaram.' While growing up, he witnessed constant fights and conflicts between his parents, and, seeing his father's black moods, Guru would turn silent. It was as if he was internalising his insecurity and pain.

1928

Guru Dutt's father resigned and took his family to Mangalore again, where he became the Manager of Sadanand Printing Press. During this time, Vasanthi would write short stories for local magazines. They lived with her nephew in Mangalore. Guru Dutt, then three, became friendly with bus drivers and cleaners nearby, and they would take him for bus rides. He enjoyed watching the repairs of buses, where he would hand over tools to them. He enjoyed listening to his mother when she told him stories from the Panchatantra. He was also very fond of his prayers. He would have his meals only after he recited several stotras. After some time, they moved to their own home which was located near a jail from where they would hear the painful cries of jailed prisoners when they were tortured. Guru Dutt would run to his mother and ask her why they were hurting those inmates. He would be disturbed by those cries.

Once again, Shivshankar quit his job.

They went to live with her brother in Ahmedabad, whose mentally ill adopted father would sometimes shout and turn violent. He would beat his father till he returned to his quiet self. Guru Dutt found the cries, the violence and the pain too much, and this scarred his psyche. He could not sleep and would cry silently. They had come to Ahmedabad for a change but things were worse here.

When Vasanthi was in the eighth month of her second pregnancy, her brother asked them to leave, because he already had too many responsibilities. All three of them (Vasanthi, her mother and Guru Dutt) moved to Calcutta to her brother's home in December when Guru Dutt was four years old. She wrote that when she spanked him for being stubborn, he would not cry loudly; she would only see tears roll down his cheeks. He was admitted to an English medium school run by Jesuits called the David Hare School.

Guru Dutt loved music and dance and he especially loved SD Burman's folk music. Later, Shivshankar joined his family in Calcutta, where he became a journalist. He loved poetry and literature and he even wrote poetry which was, unfortunately, never published by any tabloid. Guru Dutt imbibed his father's love for literature and poetry.

1928

In December, Guru Dutt's brother, Shashidhar, was born in Calcutta. Guru Dutt was very attached to his little infant brother and played a lot with him.

1929

In July, Shashidhar suddenly died when he was seven months old. Guru Dutt was traumatised. He became more introverted and silent.

1930

Atma Ram, Guru Dutt's brother, was born. Their father, Shivshanker, got a job in Burmah Shell. Guru Dutt quickly learnt to speak Bengali. During this period, Jatras used to be performed near their home, Guru Dutt loved watching and listening to them. Sometimes he would watch them the whole night, fascinated with the idea of seeing men perform as women. Then Guru would imitate them in front of Atma Ram. He would mime their gestures and powder his face, wearing a cloth around him like a dhoti, and then he would sing and act.

1930

Guru Dutt was very religious and, every day, he would visit the Kali temple in Calcutta. But when they performed the goat sacrifice, he didn't want to see it and he would return home. He had become an introvert, with introverted hobbies. A bookworm right from age four, he would collect books and read them. He also loved flying kites and playing with tops and marbles. His mother said that he was a very intelligent child whose curiosity knew no limits. He would constantly ask questions and if one was answered, another one was immediately ready. But, according to his mother, what was truly remarkable about him was his incredible memory. He never forgot. His mother remarked, 'Prashna poochna uska swabhav tha, kabhi kabhi uske prashno ka uttar dete dete main paagal ho jaati thi. Kisi ki baat nahin maanta tha, apne dil mein agar theek laga to hi woh maanta tha, impulsive tha. Man mein aaya to karega hi zaroor!"

1930

Geeta Roy was born on November 23, 1930, in Faridpur, now in Bangladesh. She was born five years after Guru Dutt.

1932

Guru Dutt's sister Lalita was born in Calcutta.

1938

Guru Dutt's brother Devidas (later called Devi Dutt) was born in February. He was the family's fifth child, after Guru, Shashidhar (who passed away), Atma Ram and Lalita.

1939

Atma Ram fell ill and then recovered. In the same year, Guru Dutt bought a parrot and cage and taught him to speak. He would patiently teach it a new word every day and then make it repeat that word the next day. On weekends their grandmother would take them in a tram to visit the home of their uncle, BB Benegal. The children loved those outings because they would spend their time watching films. Benegal was a film publicist and his house had all sorts of arty things, like paintings and posters. The children found these outings and paraphernalia fascinating.

1940

On one of the days when Guru Dutt attended a Saraswat cultural get-together, he wore a dhoti and did a surprise performance of a snake charmer. The audience loved it, and his uncle Benegal, very impressed by his talent, recorded his movements with an 8 mm camera.

1940

Guru Dutt would attend Uday Shankar's dance performances when the latter visited Calcutta. One day after he watched dance maestro Uday Shankar's performance, he told his mother how desperately he wanted to train under the maestro at his Academy in Almora. He would also watch films, classical dances and Bengali plays. His mother wrote that a girl from his class called Amarjit would visit their home but her parents stopped her from visiting him after some time. Guru Dutt was fifteen then. His mother wrote in her autobiography, "He drank and he smoked bidis, he was a problem child. If anybody provoked him he would immediately flare up; he had a short temper but then he would soon repent if he made any mistake."

1941

When he was 16, Guru Dutt passed his matriculation exam in Calcutta, his mother also passed her matriculation exam in the same year. His younger brother, Devi Dutt said, "My mother was one of the few girls in the Saraswat Brahmin Community to pass her matriculation exam for which she was awarded a Parker pen by the community. My father was upset because of not being invited. So when my mother and my brothers Guru Dutt and Atma Ram returned home with the prize, my father grabbed it to throw it out of the window. But Guru Dutt stopped him. As a young child, I watched this scene. It was 1941. Through the years, Guru Dutt, who was 13 years older than I, became a father figure to us—brothers Atmaji, Vijay and sister Lalitha."

1941

Vijay, Guru's youngest brother was born. Guru Dutt gave him that name, because Hitler had then captured Italy. Many Indians, led by Subhas Chandra Bose, wanted to fight the British and make them quit India, so they sided with Hitler, the enemy of the British, because he would help checkmate the ruling British Raj in India. Hitler had also agreed to help Subhash Chandra Bose to raise an army to fight the British. That army was to be called, 'The Free India Legion.' Guru Dutt, incidentally, used the name Vijay for his role as the protagonist in his most famous movie Pyaasa.

1942-1944

Guru Dutt received a 5-year scholarship with the Uday Shankar India Cultural Centre in Almora with a stipend of Rs 75. His uncle Benegal stepped in and helped with the initial expenses for his training in Almora. When he went to Almora, Guru Dutt was so poor that didn't even have a proper jacket to keep him warm, but since he was so loveable, others helped him with warm clothes. Meanwhile his family moved to Bombay and they began living in a small flat in Matunga. Their hardships continued. Guru's father Shivshankar took up a clerical job, his mother taught in a school, his grandmother looked after the children and young Lalitha ran errands.

In Almora, Uday Shankar was quick to spot Guru's talent and predicted that the young man would join films and attain great heights. Guru shared a room with Sardar Malik who was also learning dance there, and who would also make it as a music composer. Guru Dutt had always been interested in dances. He used to spend a lot of time with his mother's cousin Balakrishna B. Benegal who used to paint cinema posters. Incidentally, Guru Dutt's grandmother and filmmaker Shyam Benegal's grandmother were sisters. Shyam Benegal is the son of the younger brother of Balakrishna Benegal.

Students at the Almora Centre were put through a strict regime. They had to do yoga, create dance themes, stitch their costumes, learn to use makeup, etc. The whole idea was to make them self-reliant, to give them a good foundation. Since Guru Dutt was very likeable, everyone, including Uday Shankar, took to him. He dutifully wrote to his mother every week and cooked his food, he loved cooking. At the Centre, Guru Dutt met Zohra Sehgal who would perform in Uday Shankar's 1948 film Kalpana.

One day Guru sent word to his mother that he was coming with Uday Shankar's troupe to Bombay for a performance at the Royal Opera House. His mother and Lalita were looking forward to seeing Guru after a long time. They saw the famous Tandav Nritya performed by the maestro and a beautiful solo performance by Guru titled, 'The Swan'. After the performance, his mother went backstage with Lalitha to meet Uday Shankar and her son Guru Dutt. The maestro told his mother that her son was very talented. After some time, the Almora Academy had to shut down (because it was run by a British Grant which was not easy anymore since World War II was on). Many young dancers came to Bombay looking for a job.

1944-1947

However, Guru Dutt was removed from the Centre because of a scandal. Devi Dutt, in an interview with Filmfare, recalled, "Another memory is that of the afternoon in 1944 when a long-haired man stood at our door. He was Guru Dutt but he was unrecognisable. He had been sent back from Uday Shankar's School of Dancing and Choreography in Almora because he had got involved with Vijaya, a leading lady of the company". Vasanthi then telegraphed their uncle Benegal for help, requesting him to come down to Bombay as he knew some directors and producers. When Benegal arrived in Bombay, he got Guru a job. Guru signed a three-year contract with Baburao Pai of Prabhat Film Co. Ltd., Pune, as an Assistant Choreographer. The Prabhat Film Co was started in 1929 by V Shantaram and a few other partners. It functioned in Kolhapur till 1933. In 1939, it moved to Pune where 45 Hindi and Marathi films were made in its studio.

Guru Dutt worked in a minor role as Lord Krishna in the film Chand (1944), where he was also an assistant director.

He became an Assistant Director to Vishram Bedekar in the film Lakharani (1945) in which he also had a small acting role.

The film Hum Ek Hain was produced by Prabhat Film Co Ltd. It was directed by PL Santoshi, and it starred Durga Khote as the mother, with Dev Anand, Rehana, Ram Singh and Rehman in it. The film also had Cuckoo, who Guru Dutt later signed on for his movie, Mr. & Mrs. '55. In the film's credits, Guru Dutt is mentioned against the words, "Dance Competition", and this is because he directed the dances of the film. This was another way of saying he was the film's choreographer.

At Prabhat, Guru Dutt got involved with a junior dancer called Vidya who was working under him. He ran away with her to Bombay, brought her to his parent's home and introduced her to his mother as his future wife. But this girl was already engaged to someone who threatened police action. Interestingly, she was also involved with a lawyer from Pune. The lawyer sent her a legal notice. It is said that the lawyer's wife wanted Guru Dutt and Vidya to get married so that the girl would leave her husband alone!

Guru Dutt shifted back to Bombay, much to the relief of the girl's boyfriend who had threatened him. Nobody knows what happened to the lawyer's marriage. In this sad, unhappy period of 10 months of unemployment, he wrote several short stories for the Illustrated Weekly of India, a magazine belonging to The Times of India group, but, most importantly, he also wrote the novel Kashmakash which was to become the story of the 1957 movie Pyaasa. Since he used to express himself best in English, his stories were written in English. It was around this period that Guru Dutt wanted to commit suicide and Dev Anand prevented him from doing so. Many years later, Guru Dutt's mother referred to this in a public function, where she said, "This Guru Dutt you all know is not the son I gave birth to but one whose life Dev Anand saved." Around this time, it is said that he was engaged to Suvarna from Hyderabad. That engagement did not last long.

1947

He was Assistant to Director Anadinath N Banerji in the film Mohan. Dev Anand and Hemavati were the lead stars in the movie. Guru was then employed as a freelance assistant with Baburao Pai who had left Prabhat and started his own company called Famous Pictures and Studios.

1949

Guru Dutt worked as an Assistant Director with Amiya Chakravarty in the movie Girls School.

Geeta Bali, Sajjan and Shashikala were the lead stars in the film.

1950

In Sangram, a Bombay Talkies production, he became Assistant Director to Gyan Mukherjee, who became his guru and mentor. The film's lead stars were Ashok Kumar and Nalini Jaywant. The plot of the crime drama consisted of a policeman who had a crooked son, which gives us a glimpse into the beginnings of the cinema noir tradition in the Hindi film industry. With music by C. Ramachandra, the movie was a box office success. The film's theme of romance, mystery and crime all together inspired several Dev Anand and Guru Dutt films.

Later Guru Dutt had placed a large blowup of Gyan Mukherjee behind his office desk. Mukherjee died suddenly on November 13, 1956. The film Pyaasa is dedicated to him, and some believe the story of Kaagaz Ke Phool is influenced by Gyan Mukherjee's success and failure in the Hindi film industry.

1951

Dev Anand asked Dutt to direct his film Baazi which became a hit. (See the chapters on Dev Anand and Baazi for details)

1952

Jaal. Guru Dutt again directed a Dev Anand starrer which received reasonable success. (See the chapter on Jaal).

1953

Baaz. The movie flopped. This was Guru Dutt's first co-produced film, partnering with Geeta Bali's sister, Haridarshan Kaur. Guru Dutt was the lead actor and director of the film too. (See the chapter on Baaz for details)

1953

Guru Dutt married Geeta Dutt on May 26, 1953. According to Lalita Lajmi, those were their happy days. "They bought a house in Pali Hill and were so much in love. A happy couple, working together, hosting dinner parties. They had two beautiful sons. Their first-born child Tarun, was born on the same day as Guru, 9th July (1954) and later Arun, the second-born on the 10th of July (1956) so Geeta always celebrated the birthday of all the three together."

1954

Aar Paar was released and was a box office success. Guru Dutt was the film's producer, director and lead actor, co-starring with Shyama and Shakila. (See the chapter on Aar Paar for details)

1954

Guru and Geeta's first child, Tarun, was born on July 9, 1954.

1955

Mr. & Mrs. '55. Another successful film from Guru Dutt. Guru Dutt co-starred in this film with Madhubala. He was the film's producer and director too. (See the chapter on Mr. & Mrs. '55 for details)

Guru Dutt met the 17-year-old Waheeda Rehman in Hyderabad. She signed a three year contract with Guru Dutt Films but because she was under 18, her mother signed it on her behalf.

1956

C.I.D. Released on April 6, 1956. This was a blockbuster film, directed by Raj Khosla and produced by Guru Dutt. It starred Dev Anand and Shakila in the lead roles. Waheeda Rehman was introduced as a supporting actress in this film. (See the chapter on C.I.D. for details)

1956

Guru and Geeta's second child, Arun, was born on July 10, 1956.

1956

Sailaab. Released on July 17, 1956. The movie flopped. The lead actors were Geeta Dutt and Abhi Bhattacharya. (See the chapter on Sailaab for details).

1956

During the making of the film Pyaasa, Guru Dutt attempted suicide for the first time.

1957

Pyaasa released on 22.2.1957. This was a massive hit film, and Guru Dutt is most identified with this feature. In the same year, Naya Daur was released and Dilip Kumar, who had refused the role of Vijay in Pyaasa, won the Filmfare Award for Best Actor for Naya Daur. Mother India got the Filmfare Award for Best Film and Mehboob Khan was chosen as the Best Director. The Best Music Director Award went to OP Nayyar for his musical album of Naya Daur. Pyaasa didn't make it in any category. There was not even an award for V K Murthy as Best Director of Photography. Nargis, who had been keen to play Gulabo in Pyaasa, got the Best Actress award for Mother India. Pyaasa starred Mala Sinha and Guru Dutt in the lead with Waheeda Rehman as the supporting actress. (See the chapter on Pyaasa for details).

1957

The film Gouri was announced after Pyaasa's success but it was shelved after a few scenes had been shot. It was to star Geeta Dutt and Guru Dutt in the lead roles. (See the chapter on Gouri for details).

1957

Waheeda Rehman's mother passed away.

1958

12 O'Clock. A film by Pramod Chakravorty who was married to Laxmi, Geeta Dutt's sister. Guru Dutt and Waheeda Rehman co-starred in it. The film was a box office success. (See the chapter on 12 O' Clock for details).

1959

Kaagaz Ke Phool released. Guru Dutt's last film as a film director because when the film flopped, it broke Guru Dutt's heart. The film starred Guru Dutt and Waheeda Rehman in the lead. (See the chapter on Kaagaz Ke Phool for details).

1960

Chaudhvin Ka Chand was released on 15.7.1960. This was the biggest hit film made by Guru Dutt Films. Mohammed Rafi got his first Filmfare Award as the Best Male Playback Singer, and so did Shakeel as the Best Lyricist of the Year. In the same year Mughal-e-Azam was released, and it, too, became a super-hit. It swept most of the Filmfare awards that year. In the previous year, V Shantaram's Navrang was released and became a mega-hit film. Chaudhvin Ka Chand starred Guru Dutt and Waheeda Rehman in the lead. (See the chapter on Chaudhvin Ka Chand for details).

1960

Guru Dutt's father passed away. Guru Dutt told Bimal Mitra in 1961/62 that after his father's death, lots of troubles (jhanjhat-jhamele) had come into his life. He seemed to be superstitious about it. He told Bimal Mitra that he had attempted suicide too. He said, "Kaafi takleef jheli! Kaafi kasht bhoga! Lekin kitni-kitni takleef jhelni padi, aap ko kya bataaooon!" He added that it was not because of financial problems that he had attempted suicide. He had gone to Calcutta for the shoots of Sahib Bibi Aur Ghulam, and that's when things had become unbearable.

1962

Sahib Bibi Aur Ghulam released. It met with medium success. The film starred Guru Dutt and Meena Kumari in the lead, with Waheeda Rehman as supporting actress. (See the chapter on Sahib Bibi Aur Ghulam for details).

1962

Sautela Bhai. Guru Dutt co-starred with Pranoti Ghosh in this film directed by Mahesh Kaul.

1962

The Dutts went on a holiday to Kashmir.

1962

Guru Dutt and Geeta Dutt's only daughter Nina was born on August 19, 1962.

1963

Bharosa. Guru Dutt acted in the film directed by K. Shankar, in which Asha Parekh was his co-star.

1963

Bahurani. Guru Dutt co-starred with Mala Sinha in this film directed by T. Prakash Rao.

1964

Sanjh Aur Savera. Meena Kumari and Guru Dutt acted in this film directed by Hrishikesh Mukherjee.

1964

Guru Dutt died on Oct 10, 1964, when he was only 39 years old. It was either an overdose of sleeping pills or a suicide.

1964

Suhagan released. Guru Dutt acted in the film directed by K. S. Gopalakrishnan, the movie was released after Guru Dutt had passed away. His co-star was Mala Sinha.

1965

Guru Dutt did not see the release of his friend Dev Anand's cinematic masterpiece Guide which was released in February 1965, four months after he passed away. Waheeda Rehman got the Filmfare Best Actress award for her performance in this film in which she was shown rising from the ashes after attempting suicide thrice (reminiscent of Guru Dutt's three suicide bids).

1966

Baharen Phir Bhi Aayengi released. The film was directed by Shahid Lateef and it starred Dharmendra, Mala Sinha and Tanuja. (See the chapter on Baharen Phir Bhi Aayengi for details).

1972

Geeta Dutt died due to liver problems on July 20, 1972. She was only 42 years old.

1989

Guru Dutt's eldest son Tarun committed suicide in a room strewn with family photographs. He was only 35 years old.

1994

Atma Ram died when he was 63 years old. He was an active trade unionist before he moved to London where he scripted documentaries for James Beveridge. He produced several films including Shikar (1968), Chanda Aur Bijli (1969) and the Dev Anand starrer Ye Gulistan Hamara (1972).

2014

Guru Dutt's second son, Arun Dutt died on July 26, 2014 when he was 58 years old. He died due to several health complications. He was married to Kavita and they have two daughters, Gouri and Karuna.

2023

Lalita Lajmi, Guru Dutt's sister, passed away on February 13, 2023. She was 90 years old. Her daughter, Kalpana Lajmi died on September 23, 2018.

Currently, Nina, Guru Dutt's only surviving child and daughter, lives in Bombay with her husband Naushad Memon, who is the nephew of the late actors Mehmood and Minoo Mumtaz. They have two children, a daughter and a son.

Guru Dutt's Filmography

As a Producer

1. Baaz (1953). Produced by HG Films (i.e. Haridarshan Kaur and Guru Dutt)

2. Aar Paar (1954). Produced by Guru Dutt Films Pvt. Ltd.

3. Mr. & Mrs. '55 (1955). Produced by Guru Dutt Films Pvt. Ltd.

4. C.I.D. (1956). Produced by Guru Dutt Films Pvt. Ltd.

5. Pyaasa (1957). Produced by Guru Dutt Films Pvt. Ltd.

6. Kaagaz Ke Phool (1959). Produced by Guru Dutt Films Pvt. Ltd.

7. Chaudhvin Ka Chand (1960). Produced by Guru Dutt Films Pvt. Ltd.

8.   Sahib Bibi Aur Ghulam (1962). Produced by Guru Dutt Films Pvt. Ltd.

9.   Baharen Phir Bhi Ayengi (1966). Produced by Guru Dutt (released posthumously)

As a Director

1.   Baazi (1951). Produced by Navketan Films

2.   Jaal (1952). Produced by Filmarts

3.   Baaz (1953). Produced by HG Films

4.   Aar Paar (1954). Produced by Guru Dutt Films Pvt. Ltd.

5.   Mr. & Mrs. '55 (1955). Produced by Guru Dutt Films Pvt. Ltd.

6.   Sailaab (1956). Produced by Mukul Roy

7.   Pyaasa (1957). Produced by Guru Dutt Films Pvt. Ltd.

8.   Kaagaz Ke Phool (1959). Produced by Guru Dutt Films Pvt. Ltd.

9.   Chaudhvin Ka Chand (1960). (Songs directed by Guru Dutt). Produced by Guru Dutt Films Pvt. Ltd.

10. Sahib Bibi Aur Ghulam (Songs directed by Guru Dutt). Produced by Guru Dutt Films Pvt. Ltd.

As an Actor

Names of films in which Guru Dutt starred, with the year of release, followed by the name of the film's director, and the lead co-stars:

1. Baaz — 1953, Guru Dutt; Geeta Bali
2. Aar Paar — 1954, Guru Dutt; Shyama
3. Mr. & Mrs. '55 — 1955, Guru Dutt; Madhubala
4. Pyaasa — 1957, Guru Dutt; Mala Sinha, Waheeda Rehman
5. 12 O'Clock — 1958, Pramod Chakravorty; Waheeda Rehman
6. Kaagaz Ke Phool — 1959, Guru Dutt; Waheeda Rehman
7. Chaudhvin Ka Chand — 1960, M Sadiq; Waheeda Rehman
8. Sahib Bibi Aur Ghulam — 1962, Abrar Alvi; Meena Kumari, Waheeda Rehman.
9. Sautela Bhai — 1962, Mahesh Kaul; Pranoti Ghosh
10. Bahurani — 1963, T Prakash Rao; Mala Sinha
11. Bharosa — 1963, K Shankar; Asha Parekh
12. Sanjh Aur Savera — 1964, Hrishikesh Mukherjee; Meena Kumari
13. Suhagan — 1964, KS Gopalakrishnan; Mala Sinha

His Other Projects

Lakhrani (or Lakharani) (1945). Prabhat Film Co. Guru Dutt was the Assistant Director to Vishram Bedekar. He also had a small acting role in the film whose lead actors were Durga Khote and Sapru.

Hum Ek Hain (1946). Prabhat Film Co. Guru Dutt was the Dance Competition Director and Assistant Director under Director PL Santoshi; again, he had a small appearance as an actor. The lead actors were Dev Anand and Rehana.

Mohan (1947). Famous Pictures. Guru Dutt was Asst. Director under Director Anadinath N Banerji. The main actors were Dev Anand and Hemavati.

Girls School (1949). Lokmanya Productions, Guru Dutt was First Asst. Director under Director Amiya Chakravarty. The lead cast was Geeta Bali and Sajjan.

Sangram (1950). Bombay Talkies, he was Asst. Director under Director Gyan Mukherjee. The lead actors were Ashok Kumar and Nalini Jaywant.

Professor was a film planned with Kishore Kumar and Waheeda Rehman as lead actors, but it never got filmed.

Gouri (shot around 1956/1957) was an incomplete production in which Guru Dutt was the actor, the producer and the director, while his wife Geeta Dutt was the main actress. The music was by SD Burman; this was to be a bilingual film, in English and Bengali. Chetan Anand's wife, Uma Anand, was to play a role in the English version of the film. The film was shelved. (See the chapter on Gouri for details).

Raaz. During the making of Kaagaz Ke Phool, Guru Dutt began work on Raaz, which was adapted from Wilkie Collins' *The Woman in White*. The film starred Sunil Dutt as an army doctor and Waheeda Rehman in the double role of twins. Guru Dutt eventually replaced Sunil Dutt as the lead actor. Some scenes were shot in Simla (according to other sources the scenes were shot in

Kufri in Kashmir) and two songs were recorded by composer RD Burman. This would have been RD Burman's maiden film if it had been completed. Abrar Alvi, in his interview with Sathya Saran spoke about Guru Dutt regarding Gouri and Raaz, "Guru Dutt was ruthless. I have never known a more uncompromising director. He spared no one, not even his wife, whom he had cast in a film called Gouri, only to scrap it when it did not measure up to his expectations, not even himself when he found his acting inadequate in Raaz, of which he had shot 12 reels!"

But after shooting so diligently, Guru Dutt dropped Raaz. Two songs were recorded for that film by composer RD Burman. One track featured three dancing girls and was sung by Geeta Dutt, Asha Bhosle and Shamshad Begum. But after shooting and editing five or six reels, Guru Dutt shelved the film, as we saw earlier. The story was later made by his friend Raj Khosla as Woh Kaun Thi, with music by Madan Mohan. The film became extremely successful.

Also, there was a contract between Guru and Waheeda. She waited for it to end after which she immediately signed the film Mujhe Jeene Do with Sunil Dutt, who was doing the lead role in that film. This upset Guru a lot. With Guru's approval, she had already acted with Sunil Dutt in Ek Phool Char Kante (1960), so their chemistry was already in place.

Kaneez (1962) was an incomplete production. Guru Dutt was to be the film's director. The film fraternity received a shock when he announced Kaneez, which had to do with Alibaba and the forty thieves. He wanted to show how even Alibaba could have contemporary significance. The characters were to be interesting humans in modern life. This was slated to be Guru Dutt's first colour film but the film also failed to make it to the finish-line and was shelved after initial filming. Kaneez was to star Simi Garewal, who complained to the Cine Artists Association and ensured that she was paid her remaining dues.

Love And God (1963-1964). A few scenes were shot with Guru Dutt as the hero but they had to be re-shot after his death, with Sanjeev Kumar substituting for him. It was produced and directed by K Asif. However, tragedy struck the project again when Sanjeev Kumar and K Asif both passed away before the film was completed. Later, producer KC Bokadia completed it by using substitutes, and the film was finally released in 1986. It was a flop because it ended up as a hotchpotch movie.

Picnic (1964) too was an incomplete production with Sadhana and Guru Dutt in the lead. This film was later shelved because of Guru Dutt's death. One of its N Datta songs, Kitna rangeen hai ye chaand sitaaron ka samma, sung by Rafi and Asha, is available on YouTube.

There was a Bengali film called Ek Tuku Chhoan for which Guru Dutt filmed just one scene. The film was based on Gulshan Nanda's novel Neel Kamal. This film, too, was eventually shelved.

Sh Sh Sh was a comedy directed by Atma Ram. It was canned four days after its shooting started. It was to star Johnny Walker and Dhumal. Later it was successful as the Marathi play Maruchi Maushi.

Moti Ki Mausi, starring Tanuja and Salim Khan. Sadly, the film was never completed, one of the reasons being that its director Niranjan died suddenly.

Neel Kamal. In 1962, Guru Dutt signed Nanda and Biswajit for this film which was to be directed by M Sadiq. But then he had second thoughts; he felt the audiences would reject a ghost story. Later the story with the same title was released with Raj Kumar and Waheeda Rehman and it was successful.

SECTION ONE

Guru Dutt's Film Albums

1. Baazi

2. Jaal

3. Baaz

4. Aar Paar

5. Mr. & Mrs. '55

6. Sailaab

7. C. I. D.

8. Pyaasa

9. 12 O'Clock

10. Gouri

11. Kaagaz Ke Phool

12. Chaudhvin Ka Chand

13. Sahib Bibi Aur Ghulam

14. Baharen Phir Bhi Aayengi

15. Guru Dutt in films produced in Madras

1

Baazi

Date of release: June 15, 1951

Banner: Navketan

Producer: Dev Anand

Director: Guru Dutt (Assistants Raj Khosla and CM Nagotra)

Story: Guru Dutt and Balraj Sahni

Screenplay and Dialogues: Balraj Sahni

Director of Photography: V Ratra (Assistant VK Murthy)

Choreographer: Zohra Sehgal

Editor: YG Chawhan

Cast: Dev Anand, Geeta Bali, Kalpana Kartik, Roopa Varman, K N Singh, Johnny Walker, Rashid Khan, Krishan Dhawan and others

Music Director: SD Burman

Music Assistant: Suhrid Kar

Lyricist: Sahir Ludhianvi

Singers: Geeta Roy, Shamshad Begum, Kishore Kumar and the chorus

Songs: Total 8 songs, all solos. Geeta Roy (Dutt)-6, Kishore Kumar-1, Shamshad Begum-1, the chorus- 2

1. Aaj ki raat piya—Geeta (Kalpana Kartik)

2. Dekh ke akeli mohe barkha sataaye—Geeta and chorus (Geeta Bali)

3. Laakh zamaane waale—Geeta (Kalpana Kartik)

4. Mere labon pe dekho—Kishore (Dev Anand)

5. Sharmaaye kaahe ghabraaye kaahe—Shamshad (Geeta Bali)

6. Suno gajar kya gaaye—Geeta and chorus (Geeta Bali and dancers)

7. Tadbeer se bigdi hui—Geeta (Geeta Bali)

8. Ye kaun aaya ke—Geeta Roy (Kalpana Kartik)

Like Alfred Hitchcock who used to be seen in his films for a few seconds, Guru Dutt makes his cameo appearance in the opening scene of the movie where he is shown seated by a roadside hydrant, with his back to the camera. He is seen smoking when an expensive car pulls up. We see his profile as he turns his face, and he seems puzzled to see a costly car stopping by in such a shady area. Suited and booted, the character actor Rashid Khan steps out of the back seat, carrying a walking stick. He advances purposefully towards Dutt, pauses to light a cigarette, then goes past him to descend a staircase. The camera turns around to watch the man go to the basement. No word has been said yet. That is how Dutt introduces suspense, from the very first scene! Again, in Jaal, Guru Dutt would make a cameo appearance as a fisherman, in a blink-and-miss kind of role. Deeply influenced by Western cinema, this ambitious young man wanted to leave his signature on his films until he began to act in them as the protagonist.

Released on June 15, 1951, the Navketan film Baazi premiered at Swastik Cinema on Lamington Road in South Mumbai. Baazi, in Urdu, means a gamble. At this time Guru Dutt was only 27 years old. The film was a success at the box office, it even celebrated its silver jubilee. Two of the main reasons for its success were the filming of the songs and the songs themselves.

Betting Big!

The film established many people's careers and lives. Although this was not Sahir's first film, it was in this film that his work was first acclaimed. Nor was this Johnny Walker's first film since he had been doing bit parts as an extra earlier too. It was during the breaks of the film Hulchul (released, like Baazi, in 1951, but much earlier) that Balraj Sahni had noticed how Johnny Walker, then an extra, would entertain the crew with his drunken act. Sahni introduced him to Guru Dutt and the rest is history. Johnny Walker said, "Baazi was the first film in which people noticed me. Before that whenever I'd take a friend to the cinema to see a film in which I had acted, I'd appear and then disappear before we knew what happened." Similarly, Raj Khosla, who had always wanted to be a playback singer, was encouraged by Dev Anand to become an assistant director to Guru Dutt, after which there was no looking back for Khosla. In an interview Raj Khosla recalled, "Dev said to me, 'Guru Dutt is going to direct my next picture, why don't you become his assistant?' So I met Guru Dutt!" Of course, Baazi was Guru Dutt's first directorial effort too, and one knows how the success of this film changed his life.

The plot of Baazi centres on a risky gamble made by the protagonist played by Dev Anand. Behind the scenes, the film was a real-life gamble since two newcomers were placing bets on each other's success. The risk taker that Dev Anand was, he handed over the director's reins to Guru Dutt, who was still a fresher. Both of them were about to make a name for themselves.

Baazi also brought two beautiful and talented women into the lives of these two handsome bachelors. Geeta Roy who was already a singing sensation, was recording the song Tadbeer se bigdi hui taqdeer bana le when Guru Dutt walked in, saw and heard her for the first time, and instantly fell in love with her. Meanwhile, Kalpana Kartik was introduced in this film. Dev Anand, nursing his tears after his breakup with Suraiya, turned to Kalpana on the rebound.

The two couples later got married. So many life-changing bets were taken during the film whose subject was coincidentally, gambling! Baazi was the turning point in their lives, both professionally and personally. All four fell in love, got married and had children.

Baazi set the trend for other similar Bombay noir crime thrillers. Some claim that the film was a copy of a Hollywood film called Gilda, which starred Rita Hayworth as the irresistible seductive woman, with Glenn Ford playing the part of the man who reciprocated her love. When I watched the film on YouTube, I was struck more by the differences between the two films than by their similarities. Yet, as one moves forward through Guru Dutt's cinema, one observes that both Bengali and Hollywood cinema played a significant role in providing Guru Dutt with the impetus and inspiration he desired.

The cinematography by V Ratra was adequately supported and assisted by VK Murthy. There were plenty of fascinating shots;

some scenes, as with cinema noir, were intentionally in half-light and half-darkness. Most films of the time did not have close-ups, but this film had plenty.

Guru Dutt was quite nuanced in his presentations, and he employed symbols too. For example, a staircase would represent the descent of Man's morality when he filmed villains descending a flight of stairs.

Guru Dutt was ahead of his time in quite a few ways. For one thing, in this film, he gave Geeta Bali top billing, above Dev Anand. Then, as a film director, he would have different endings for his films, and later decide which one to finally okay for the film. Originally, Dev Anand shared in his Filmfare interview, this film had two endings. One end had Dev Anand go to the gallows, and the other—the one that Guru Dutt finally chose—had the inspector slyly conning the villain into admitting his crime and making it easy for the hero.

Coming to this film, the plot is unusual: for one, here the nautch girl is the heroine, and the good girl is the supporting actress. While the nautch girl dies, the good girl pairs up with the crooked gambler who has changed and gone legit. The vamp dies in the end, protecting the hero, a convenient narrative ploy which has been used time and again to get the shady lady out of the lives of decent, socially acceptable members of society. After all, the director needed to pay attention to the audience and its tastes, because it meant box office returns!

The SD Burman Songs!

The songs of this romantic thriller became extremely popular, with Geeta Roy winning hearts with six solos, which included three songs sung onscreen by Kalpana Kartik (Dr Rajani). They included Laakh zamaane waale, the romantic solo sung for an absent Dev Anand; Ye kaun aaya ke mere dil ki duniya mein bahaar aayi, sung in a situation which was later repeated in a few films, where the heroine sings for one man but another man believes she is singing for him. In this case, she was singing for Madan (Dev Anand) while it was Ramesh (Krishan Dhawan) who was deluded. Such a situation became a hit with audiences, inspiring other directors to use it for their later films. For example, fourteen years later in 1965, in BR Chopra's Waqt, the song Kaun aaya ke nigaahon mein chamak jaag uthi, is sung by Sadhana for Sunil Dutt while Raj Kumar believes she is singing for him. Again this situation inspired Guru Dutt for his last film where he created a similar song Aap ke haseen rukh pe where Mala Sinha believes Dharmendra is wooing her but he is singing for her sister Tanuja! Coincidentally, in most of these songs, the triangular grand piano occupies centre stage as a symbol of the love triangle.

Aaj ki raat piya is a Geeta Roy seduction solo sung by Kalpana Kartik to a perplexed Dev Anand. Then there is Dekh ke akeli mohe barkha sataaye, with Geeta Roy lip-synching for Nina (Geeta Bali) in a club.

The most popular song of the film belonged to Geeta Roy, which, despite being a ghazal, has been used as a club song. The solo, Tadbeer se bigdi hui taqdeer bana le, was also the film's mahurat shot. It's a seduction song sung onscreen by Geeta Bali in a club for Dev Anand, while she is playing a guitar. Dev Anand is shown attempting to go up the stairs (like the piano, the staircase was often a symbol in Guru Dutt's films) but her song and beauty entices him down, both literally and figuratively. Dev Anand, in a chat with author Akshay Manwani, narrated how, when he was in Jodhpur and Baazi was in the cinema halls, the distributors of the film told Dev Anand that many Air Force pilots stationed there would come in time to the cinema-hall only to watch this song. Dev Anand recalled, "They would come only for this song, yeh popularity hoti hai!"

Biographer Nasreen Munni Kabir, in her biography of the genius, applauds Guru Dutt when she states that this song "…is another fine example of Guru Dutt's instinct for using songs that not only hold attention for their own poetic and artistic merit but also to advance the story. The words of the song act as a catalyst for Madan. The struggle with his conscience is over and by the end of the scene, Madan has decided to throw the dice, gamble with his life and join the Star Club…Madan is very much a fifties screen hero, a loner unprotected by class or family, who is willing to bend moral codes to survive…the old view of right and wrong becomes blurred as Madan's values are determined by an instinct for survival rather than by a belief in traditional norms."

One of the non-Geeta solos is Dil ye kya cheez hai aur dil ki tamanna kya hai (Mere labon pe) where Kishore Kumar sings a flirtatious song for Dev. The other song is a Shamshad Begum solo, Sharmaaye kaahe ghabraaye kaahe, sung by a seductively dressed Geeta Bali, who is attempting to ensnare Dev Anand in a club. Interestingly, while both Kalpana Kartik and Geeta Bali lip-synch in Geeta Roy's voice, Geeta Bali gets to sing a Shamshad Begum song too. A point worth noting here is that Geeta Bali lip-synched four songs, and Kalpana Kartik three, but Dev Anand lip-synched only one song.

The Cinematographer VK Murthy

The song Suno gajar kya gaaye, a Geeta Roy solo with a chorus, is most important when one studies Guru Dutt's success. The dancers are in Arabian attire when the song starts with a giant bell in the background. It was in this scene that Guru Dutt noticed VK Murthy who was then the assistant of V. Ratra. Murthy, unlike Ratra, was a slim man. It is he who suggested to Dutt that the shot could be filmed through the mirror, moving to the scene where the women are dancing, to first show the dancers through the mirror and later glide away from the mirror, to show Dev Anand, with his back to the camera, slowly moving forward to take a seat near the performers. In a video interview with Govind Nihalani, Murthy confided that they wanted to avoid showing Dev from the front because at that time he appeared slightly overweight; thus, it was important to shift the camera's focus away from the front of his body. Since V Ratra was a heavy-built man, he could not manage to wriggle into the position required to film the shot the way Murthy wanted, so the skinny Murthy shot the scene himself. Once the scene was done, an impressed Guru Dutt offered him the job of the Director of Photography for his next film. It is a breathtakingly innovative shot, on par with Hollywood's best cinema. Geeta Bali is performing a snake dance, and her dancing companions also have snake-styled headgear. In the film, Geeta Bali loves Dev Anand so she is cleverly warning him, through the song, of the danger he could be in. This is one of those warning or chetavni (warning) songs that became identified with both Dev Anand and Guru Dutt. (There is a separate chapter on such songs later in this book). She reminds him that time is of the essence and he should indulge himself, husn bhi faani aur ishq bhi faani hai, hans ke bita le do ghadi ki jawaani hai, samay guzarta jaaye. The dance is high in drama with villains preparing to draw out their guns and shoot. The excitement and suspense of the scene, in a very big way, contributed to the film's success at the box office. And the success, in no small measure, belonged to Guru Dutt.

The SD Burman biographer, HQ Chowdhury, perfectly described the musical team of Baazi when he observed, "The Baazi songs were scintillating and perfect to match India's first 'Film Noir'. Sahir wrote the ghazal Tadbeer se bigdi hui taqdeer bana le, which Dada (SD Burman) converted into a night-club song. An aghast Sahir protested. But that did not convince the stubborn Dada to change the tune; he never liked interference in his work…" Chowdhury further added, "Geeta now came out of her melancholic world to float freely in the world of Hindi film music. Dada thus converted his wailing Geeta into a lively, sensuous singer. A new chapter was opened for Geeta Roy, a new style of composition and singing."

Incidentally, for SD Burman, the year 1951 was a windfall year. He had six films with many hit songs. Chowdhury offers us an interesting bit of info, "The year saw Dada with his first car. Dada's first car was a black Austin A 40." All eight of them, Dev Anand, Guru Dutt, SD Burman, Sahir Ludhianvi, Geeta Bali, Kalpana Kartik, VK Murthy, and Johnny Walker, were riding on the wave of the success that this film brought them.

Dev Anand summed up Baazi perfectly when he wrote in his autobiography, "A hit film is like the Almighty's blessings to all those associated with it. Overnight, Guru Dutt started riding a big horse. My position further stabilised and Dada created a niche for himself in film music spelling magic amongst moviegoers."

Meanwhile, what did the critics make of it? Here is the irrepressible Baburao Patel, in the August 1951 issue of Filmindia in his critique of Baazi: "Baazi has quite a few beautiful bits in songs and dances, several excellent passages in the dialogue and a beautiful performance by that inimitable artiste Geeta Bali. And if you can forget the unholy mess the director and those two new girls

(Roopa Varman and Kalpana Kartik) make, Baazi may be seen for its beautiful bits."

Be that as it may, the audience loved the film and its direction, and gave the makers the much-coveted box office returns. Patel could not deter the audience which, quite simply, couldn't get enough of this movie!

2

Jaal

Released in Bombay on October 3, 1952.

Producer: TR Fatehchand

Director: Guru Dutt (Assistant Directors: Raj Khosla & Atma Ram)

Story: Guru Dutt (influenced by the Italian film Bitter Rice)

Screenplay: Guru Dutt

Dialogues: MA Lateef

Director of Photography: VK Murthy (Assistants: Nariman Irani, Mohan and Tata Rusi)

Choreography: Professor KS More

Editor: JS Diwadkar

Cast: Geeta Bali, Dev Anand, Purnima, KN Singh, Kammo, MA Lateef, Raj Khosla, Krishna Kumari, Ram Singh, Rasheed, Johnny Walker (credited as Badruddin) and others.

Music Director: SD Burman (Assistant: N Datta)

Lyricist: Sahir Ludhianvi

Singers: Lata Mangeshkar, Geeta Dutt, Hemant Kumar, Kishore Kumar and chorus

Songs: Total 8 songs: Lata Mangeshkar-4, Geeta Dutt-3, Hemant Kumar- 2, Kishore Kumar-1 and the chorus-3 songs.

1. Chori chori meri gali aana hai bura—Lata & chorus (Geeta Bali)

2. De bhi chuke hum—Kishore & Geeta (Dev Anand & Geeta Bali)

3. Hans le ga le dhoom macha le—Lata & chorus (Geeta Bali)

4. Pighla hai sona duur gagan par—Lata (Geeta Bali)

5. Soch samajh kar dil ko lagaana—Geeta (Kammo)

6. Ye raat, ye chaandni phir kahaan—Hemant (Dev Anand)

7. Ye raat, ye chaandni (Chaandni raaten, pyaar ki baaten)—Hemant & Lata (Dev Anand & Geeta Bali)

8. Zor laga ke haiyya—Geeta & Chorus (Geeta Bali)

Dev Anand and Guru Dutt would often go and watch films together. One day they went to see the 1948 Italian film Bitter Rice at the Excelsior cinema in Bombay. Wrote Dev Anand in his autobiography: "We both fell in love with it. Guru Dutt took out his cigarette, lit it and said, 'I am basing my next film on this.' 'I am with you'. I was also inspired. The villain Vittorio Gasman, a roguish character, had all the shades of villainy in him. I did not mind doing that type of role for a change."

The theme of the film was that the rigid structures of society twisted the human spirit and made a criminal out of a person. This appealed to the two idealistic friends, who, through a film wanted to send the message that no one was born bad, that one's circumstances made one a criminal. Guru Dutt got busy writing the story and screenplay for the film.

The film opens with Mirza Ghalib's lofty idealism reflecting the mindset of the young Guru Dutt at the time:

Na suno gar bura kahe koi, na kaho gar bura kare koi

Rok lo gar galat chale koi, baksh do gar khataa kare koi

They were able to convince a recent Sindhi migrant TR Fatehchand to produce the film for them. The film was shot in Malwan, a fisherman's village near Ratnagiri, on the Maharashtra-

Goa coast. In 1952, when this film was being shot, Goa was still under Portuguese control. It was almost a decade later, in 1961, that Goa joined India. Jaal's story, in sum, is about a ruthless smuggler and philanderer called Tony Fernandes (Dev Anand) who, along with his partner Lisa (Purnima) is hiding from the police in this village. Here Tony meets the innocent Maria (Geeta Bali) and pretends to fall in love with her while she actually falls in love with him. After several twists and turns in the plot, Maria reforms him through her innate goodness, and he ends up becoming a decent, god-loving man.

Through the screenplay, one learns of Guru Dutt's ethical mindset at that time. For example, there is an interesting scene in which Maria is about to enter a church. When Tony asks Maria where she is going, she replies, "Andar, tum nahin chaloge?" Tony sniggers, "Wahaan? Wahaan to sirf kamzor hi jaate hain!" Maria, who was reflecting Guru Dutt's philosophy then, offers a brilliant riposte: "Kamzor to woh hain jo andar jaane se darte hain!" Tony laughs at her remark. The film attempts to show that beneath Tony's bravado and contempt is his guilt and awareness that he has transgressed God's commandments, that he is not entering the church for fear of God's retribution. Later, he goes a step further by becoming more daring. He enters the church and utters a bare-faced lie when he commits himself to her, "Aye maalik, main ikraar karta hoon, saath nibhaoonga!" Still, the simple-hearted and completely besotted Maria continues to see the goodness in him, so she waits, and her wait is rewarded. He reforms and Jaal ends on a happy note!

Another fascinating Guru Dutt dialogue in the film is between Maria and Simon, a fisherman in love with her. Maria: "Ek baat poochoon, Simon? Tumne mohabbat ki hai na?" Simon laughs:

"Mohabbat ki nahin jaati hai, Maria, mohabbat ho jaati hai!" Maria: "Kaise?" Simon: "Main to sirf itna jaanta hoon ke ye woh aag hai jo lagaaye nahin lage, aur bhujaaye nahin bhujti. Mere dil mein bhi yehi aag lagi hui hai, aur woh tumhaari lagaayi hui hai!"

But, unfortunately for Simon, she is already in love with the ruthless Tony who, as we saw, lies even in church to dupe her into trusting him. Tony has such a mesmerising effect on her that he as if hypnotizes her into meeting him at night through the euphonious Hemant Kumar love song Ye raat, ye chaandni phir kahaan, sun ja dil ki dastaan.

Dev Anand shared an interesting anecdote in his autobiography. During the shooting of this film, KN Singh got Dev Anand quite high on Feni, the Goan alcoholic drink. By the time the shot was ready, Dev Anand was drunk. Guru Dutt informed them that there was no time for a rehearsal since the tide was rising and they had to quickly show Dev Anand and Geeta Bali going towards the sea. Guru Dutt told Dev Anand, "It's all arranged, just hold Geeta's hand and run into the water; as soon as you reach ankle-deep water, look towards me, near the camera. I shall cut the shot then." When the camera was switched on, Dev pulled Geeta along, running into the sea. Guru Dutt shouted for them to stop, but Dev kept running further and further into the sea, nearly drowning both of them. They were rescued by a strong sea wave that threw them back to the shore at the feet of Guru Dutt, who ordered a pack up, seeing that Dev Anand and Geeta Bali were still giggling!

VK Murthy

Guru Dutt's artistic oeuvre, combined with VK Murthy's cinematography is on display when one of the most spectacular scenes in the film is viewed. The scene is on a Ferris wheel in which

Lisa tries to warn Maria about Tony's dishonest intentions and crooked nature. This scene is brilliantly directed, causing high drama and suspense. As the wheel gathers momentum, Maria is bewildered, but Tony's seductive Hemant Kumar song Ye raat ye chaandni plays on in her heart and she emotionally succumbs to Tony, completely ignoring her friend's warnings. Another beautifully directed scene from the Murthy-Guru Dutt duo is when Maria is shown getting entrapped in an outsized fishing net, symbolising how completely she is trapped by Tony's smooth talk and charming facade. The scene creates high drama with its beautiful visualisation, and it becomes a fascinating moment in the film. In his later film Guide, Dev Anand used the fishing net as a symbol again, this time to trap Raju (Dev Anand) at the end of the song Mose chal kiye jaaye.

The Songs

Of course, we have the inevitable chetavni or warning song, which we find in so many Navketan and Guru Dutt films. The song, sung in a bar where an unnamed dancer (played by Kammo) warns Maria about Tony, has a unique fan base of its own. When she lip-synchs Geeta Dutt's Soch samajh kar dil ko lagaana, we fear for Maria's safety, because Tony is preparing to ensnare her. He is aware that his efforts to seduce Maria are being thwarted by the crooner of the song, so he looks disturbed. The best part about the song is the excellent capture of Maria's conflict by an astute VK Murthy. The camera angles, the shift from the dancing singer to Tony, from Tony to Maria, and back to the dancing singer—with all three betraying distinctly different feelings—heighten the tension and drama of the scene. This was Guru Dutt, who almost always employed songs to enhance the audience's experience of the film while he employed songs to further the plot.

Pighla hai sona, which is a Lata Mangeshkar solo sung onscreen by a pretty Geeta Bali, is an intoxicating, sensuous melody. The other fascinating number from Lata Mangeshkar is Chori chori meri gali aana hai bura. The enchanting rhythm, the fun backing vocals, and the interesting lyrics make this Lata song a heady cocktail. The Goan ambience is so authentic that one can imagine that the song must have had the audience dancing in the aisles!

De bhi chuke hum dil nazraana dil ka, by Kishore Kumar and Geeta Dutt, is a light romantic *nok-jhok* or *chhed-chaad* song, the first of many to show up in Guru Dutt's films. These are songs that belong to the stable of "He tries to woo her but she won't hear of it". These were often found sung by Johnny Walker in Guru Dutt's films. But this time it is Dev Anand and Kalpana Kartik doing the honours.

Yet, the *piece de resistance* in the Jaal bouquet of the Sahir-SD Burman combo is the pair of tandem songs. For the first time in a Guru Dutt-directed film, we find a Hemant Kumar solo later followed by a duet, and both, even today, resonate with us. Ye raat, ye chaandni phir kahaan with Hemant Kumar singing for Dev Anand is a solo, while Hemant's Ye raat, ye chaandni phir kahaan, counterpointed with Lata's Chaandni raatein pyaar ki baatein is equally charming. The Hemant Kumar seduction solo and its poetic romance which tempts Geeta to forget her inhibitions and join him on that beautiful night, is, perhaps, a greater classic. At the start of the film, the instrumental version of this Hemant Kumar song has also been used as the background score during the titles.

Yet, somehow, one must admit that the movie is not a polished product. The camera is far from still when it needs to be. Surprisingly, it is shaky even during the film's titles, moving without reason. Plus, the script is awkward. It lacks authenticity in parts. For example, one rarely comes across Indian Catholics speaking chaste Urdu. But, to compensate for the film's less-than-perfect camera work and gauche script, the music excels. S D Burman moves mountains with each song, but while the music entraps us, so do most of the beautiful camera angles and shots captured by VK Murthy.

In Dev Anand's autobiography, one reads about the spunky Geeta Bali and how once when Dev was driving speedily with her, their convertible met with a serious accident, with both of them becoming unconscious and hospitalised in Pune. Dev Anand was in hospital for a month and some journals had even declared him dead! Geeta Bali got a cut on her forehead but she too survived the mishap. In her subsequent films the cut on her forehead was often visible. Incidentally, the doctor who treated them there was none other than Dr. Shreeram Lagoo who later joined the film industry as a character actor.

Finally, here are a couple of snatches of the film's reviews. Filmfare heaped reasonable praise on the film in its November 1952 edition: "Slick direction, competent narration, naive quality about narration…Guru Dutt has done, on the whole, a fairly good job in wielding the megaphone."

Known for his barbs, Baburao Patel of FilmIndia, could not but offer Guru Dutt his grudging respect: "This picture establishes him as a director who knows much of his job and is no longer the amateur of Baazi. Guru Dutt entertains in Jaal with his smooth direction, and, in future, if he only adds more purpose and some power to his presentation, he could be included among our intelligent directors."

3

Baaz

Released in 1953

Banner: HG Films

Producers: Haridarshan Kaur & Guru Dutt

Director: Guru Dutt (Assisted by Raj Khosla, Atma Ram & Niranjan)

Story & Screenplay: Guru Dutt

Dialogues: LC Bismil & Sarshar Sailani

Director of Photography: VK Murthy (Assistants: Moses, Prabhakar & Rusi)

Choreographer: Vinod Chopra

Editor: YG Chawhan

Cast: Guru Dutt, Geeta Bali, Kuldip Kaur, KN Singh, Sulochana Devi, Johnny Walker, Purnima, Tun Tun, Yashodhara Katju, Jaswant & others.

Music Director: OP Nayyar (Assistants: GS Kohli & Sebastian)

Lyricist: Majrooh Sultanpuri

Singers: Geeta Roy Dutt, Mohammed Rafi, Talat Mahmood & the chorus

Songs: Total 9 songs, all solos. Geeta Dutt: 7. Mohammed Rafi: 1. Talat Mahmood:1. Chorus in 2 songs

1. Ae dil ae deewaane—Geeta (Geeta Bali)

2. Chham chham chham (Jaago jaago savera)—Geeta (Geeta Bali)

3. Ghata mein chhupke (Jo dil ki baat hoti hai)—Rafi (Guru Dutt)

4.   Har zabaan ruki ruki-1 (Ae watan ke naujawan)—Geeta & Chorus (Geeta Bali)

5.   Har zabaan ruki ruki-2 (Ae watan ke naujawan)—Geeta & Chorus (Geeta Bali)

6.   Maanjhi albele—Geeta (Yashodhara Katju)

7.   Mujhe dekho hasrat ki tasveer hoon main—Talat (Guru Dutt)

8.   Taare chaandni—Geeta (Kuldip Kaur)

9.   Zara saamne aa—Geeta (Geeta Bali)

After directing Baazi for Navketan Films and Jaal for Filmarts, Guru Dutt took a confident step forward. He co-produced this film with Haridarshan Kaur, Geeta Bali's sister, and directed it too. Thus, it is with the film named after a falcon (Baaz) that Guru Dutt also took flight. In the film, the lead pair Geeta Bali and Guru Dutt were romantically involved.

While Baaz had a memorable musical score by newbie OP Nayyar who was still trying to get his foothold in Hindi cinema, the brilliant lyrics were written by Majrooh Sultanpuri.

Guru Dutt Wore Many Hats!

Guru Dutt wore many hats in Baaz: he made his acting debut as lead actor in this film which he not only co-produced and directed, as observed before, he even wrote the film's story and screenplay! As a director, he was assisted by the budding talents, Raj Khosla, Niranjan and his own younger brother Atma Ram. OP Nayyar, on his part, was assisted by the brilliant musical team of GS Kohli and Sebastian.

An interesting bit of trivia here is about an actor named Jaswant with whom Haridarshan fell in love and who she married. Jaswant's original name was Syed Irshad Hussain and he was in Pakistan when the Partition happened. But he was quite unhappy there, so he crossed over to India, where he adopted Jaswant as his screen name. Jaswant had left behind a wife and two children in Pakistan when he migrated to India. With Haridarshan, his second wife, he had two children too. One of them is the actress Yogeeta Bali who also had two marriages, the first with Kishore Kumar and the second with Mithun Chakraborty. Meanwhile, Jaswant suffered financial losses in the film industry, after which he began regretting his migration to India. So he migrated back to Pakistan to reunite with his first wife and children, this time abandoning his second wife and two kids.

Baaz flopped, because, unlike the previous films Baazi and Jaal, the story was not about a common man who went wrong and redeemed himself. It was about piracy, Goans, and rebellion against the Portuguese (who owned Goa at the time), and so on. The audience's empathy and identification with such characters was missing, and, worse, the film was poorly directed. Guru Dutt's amateurish presentation was visible in several scenes.

However, while the film was a failure at the box office, it was a vital one in many ways, since it paved the way for some work-life relationships that lasted till the end of Guru Dutt's life. During the making of this film, some friendships were forged, some alliances made, and some love stories that lasted too. Jaswant's cousin Abrar Alvi also became acquainted with Guru Dutt at this time and was with him right from Baaz till virtually the last day of Guru Dutt's life.

According to Abrar Alvi, he owed his working relationship with Guru Dutt to Raj Khosla. One day, while working on a scene with Guru Dutt, Raj Khosla was writing the script. Since the Mangalorean Guru Dutt wanted an Urdu expert to consult with, Raj Khosla asked Abrar's view on the scene for the dialogue. Abrar Alvi offered his opinion. Guru Dutt, who was listening quietly to his rationale, took him aside later and told him that he had decided to consider him for the job of a screenwriter for his next film, Aar Paar. After a few tests were passed, Abrar was hired. Their friendship and work together was stormy but deep, while they fought often, their respect for each other remained steady. Abrar became Guru Dutt's closest friend. Apart from Ratan, Dutt's house help, Abrar Alvi was the last man to see Guru Dutt alive.

Back to the film! This was the first film in which Guru Dutt worked with composer OP Nayyar and this was also his first film with lyricist Majrooh Sultanpuri and singer Mohammed Rafi. Earlier, as director, he had worked with SD Burman and Sahir Ludhianvi in Navketan's Baazi and Jaal. Incidentally, it was Geeta Dutt who encouraged Guru Dutt to sign on OP Nayyar for the film. She had worked with OP Nayyar in Aasmaan (1952). Also, it was in this film that Talat sang his first song for OP Nayyar and the only song he ever sang in a Guru Dutt production. The song, Mujhe dekho hasrat ki tasveer hoon main is a classic, a favourite with stage artists in live shows. Talat also sang one more song for Guru Dutt, but that song, Tumhi to meri pooja ho, was in Suhagan (1964), a Madras production.

Baaz also marked the auspicious start of a long association between OP Nayyar and Majrooh Sultanpuri. This composer and lyricist team went on to create 127 songs together, for 20 film albums! Who did they owe this to, but to Guru Dutt and Geeta Dutt?

Incidentally, another first was the Rafi song Ghata mein chhupke (Jo dil ki baat hoti hai). This was a qawwali and the first of many songs that Rafi sang for both composer OP Nayyar and producer-director Guru Dutt. Rafi was Guru Dutt's voice in almost all his films. Geeta Dutt, on her part, had three extremely beautiful songs here, Zara saamne aa, Taare chaandni, with the most memorable being the sad song Ae dil, ae deewaane.

While Guru and Geeta tied the knot in 1953, Haridarshan, of course, had her own love story with Jaswant during these shoots. Baaz also paved the way for some long associations with Guru Dutt. He often created roles for Johnny Walker and continually employed Mohammed Rafi as his voice in his films. Even if the script had no room for Johnny Walker, Guru Dutt would weave in a role for him.

VK Murthy's cinematography, however, could not rescue the indifferent project that Baaz was. The film was rejected by the audiences, despite a few extraordinary scenes from the feisty Geeta Bali. Guru Dutt, as an actor, was nothing to write home about.

4

Aar Paar

Released in 1954

Banner: Guru Dutt Productions (for partners Guru Dutt, Atma Ram and S Guruswamy)

Producer: Guru Dutt (Financed by KK Kapoor)

Director: Guru Dutt (Assistants: Raj Khosla, Atma Ram and Niranjan)

Story: Nabendu Ghosh

Screenplay: Nabendu Ghosh

Dialogues: Abrar Alvi

Director of Photography: VK Murthy (Assistants MD Moses, K Prabhakar and B Rusi)

Dance Director: Surya Kumar

Editor: YG Chawhan

Production Executive: Guruswamy

Cast: Shyama, Guru Dutt, Jagdish Sethi, Shakila, Johnny Walker, Bir Sakuja, Rajinder, Agha, Jagdeep, Kum Kum, Noor, Ameer Banu, etc., with Rasheed and MA Lateef as guest artists.

Music Director: OP Nayyar (Assistants Sebastian and GS Kohli)

Lyricist: Majrooh Sultanpuri

Singers: Geeta Dutt, Mohammed Rafi, Shamshad Begum and Suman Kalyanpur

Total songs: 8: Geeta Dutt-7, Mohammed Rafi-3, Shamshad Begum-1, Suman Kalyanpur -1.

1. Arrey na na na tauba tauba—Geeta and Rafi (Johnny Walker and Noor)

2. Babujee dheere chalna—Geeta (Shakila)

3. Hoon abhi main jawaan—Geeta (Shakila)

4. Ja ja ja ja bewafa—Geeta (Shyama)

5. Kabhi aar kabhi paar—Shamshad (Kum Kum)

6. Mohabbat kar lo, jee bhar lo—Geeta, Rafi and Suman (Guru Dutt and others)

7. Sun, sun, sun sun zaalima—Geeta and Rafi (Guru Dutt and Shyama)

8. Ye lo main haari piya—Geeta (Shyama)

A Blockbuster Hit

The first film produced by Guru Dutt Productions, Aar Paar, received its censor certificate on July 4, 1954. Five days later, the film was released in Novelty Cinema, Bombay. Films were almost always released on Fridays and this was no exception. But Friday, July 9, 1954 was special. It was the birthday of the 29-year-old Guru Dutt. Going by the audience's euphoric reaction to the film, one can only imagine the kind of double celebration they must have had. Incidentally, their son Tarun was also born on the same day! The Dutt household must have been euphoric!

Nobody could have described it better than the genius OP Nayyar who exclaimed that this film was 'a super duper hit!' Incidentally, Aar Paar was the first film of 'Guru Dutt Productions' to have three partners, Guru Dutt, his brother Atma Ram and the film's Production Controller/Executive Guruswamy. Later, Guru Dutt Productions was renamed Guru Dutt Films. And, still later, it was re-named Guru Dutt Films Pvt. Ltd.

Aar Paar was yet another cinema noir film from the Guru Dutt stable, after Baazi and Jaal; it was racy and exciting and made its mark on the box office thanks substantially to the intoxicating, foot-tapping music of OP Nayyar. This was Nayyar's 'lucky strike' film since it was his first hit film after three consecutive flops: Aasmaan, Chham Chhama Chham, and Baaz. This was also the second time OP Nayyar and Guru Dutt were working together; earlier they had worked together in Baaz. How they happened to work together in Aar Paar is a fascinating story which is detailed later in the chapter on the OP Nayyar & Majrooh Sultanpuri team in this book.

The OP Nayyar Magic!

Each one of the eight songs was sheer magic. People were found debating with one another on which was the best song of the film. They continue doing this even today! They were, and are, of course, spoilt for choice. OP Nayyar, the wizard with his magical baton, had come into his own. He had arrived with such a bang in this film that it led to a mad scramble by other film producers to sign him on for their films which had already been assigned to other composers! These producers began to dump the old for the new, and this led to some amount of anger from the affected music fraternity, which included Lata Mangeshkar. OP Nayyar first refused to accede to their demand that he should return the advance he had received because breaking his contract with the producers seemed unethical to him. Later, Nayyar asked these angry men and women that if he, hypothetically, acceded to their request, would they reimburse him the money he returned to the producers? None of them was willing to reach into his or her pocket, and Nayyar, always a good reader of human nature, went smiling all the way to the bank! They did not know that this newcomer was the tough OP Nayyar who would never succumb to any bullying, even if it came from the stalwarts of the music and film world. For example, he has the distinction of being the only composer to have never once utilised Lata Mangeshkar's voice in any of his film albums, instead, he groomed Asha Bhosle to make a place for herself as a top notch singer.

As we know, while success helps us make friends, it, simultaneously, dishes out a few enemies and the new kid on the block, OP Nayyar, was no exception to this. He made his early share of enemies, thanks first to his displacing many maestros (and also singers), and then to the phenomenal success of the Aar Paar album!

Meanwhile, in a small town called Jaora in Madhya Pradesh, a half-sleepy teenager heard the title song, Kabhi aar kabhi paar, and was dazzled! This was Arshad Sultan, the man who was to later become a very dear friend of OP Nayyar's. He later wrote, "As if touched by a live wire, the song sent a sensational wave throughout my body. All of a sudden my drowsiness vanished." He later wrote a couple of books on Hindi cinema's music and sheltered OP Nayyar at his home in Bombay in the latter's bad days.

The effect of OP Nayyar's magical music extended to youngsters and old people alike. Everyone felt invigorated and enthusiastic with the joyous melodies that, out of nowhere, a little-known composer had suddenly brought into their lives. (More details on the fascinating team of OP Nayyar, Majrooh Sultanpuri and Guru Dutt follow in the special chapter on their team.)

Casting for the Film

Back to the film which was a romantic crime fiction thriller, which some claim is inspired by the Hollywood film Drive A Crooked Road.

Initially, when Geeta Bali refused the lead role, the newly-wed Geeta Dutt rescued her husband from his dilemma by approaching Shyama for the role. Shyama not only accepted the lead role happily, she was willing to work hard for the film. She loved working with Guru Dutt and found him to be a romantic and an all-rounder. "He used to tell us how to act, how to laugh, how to dance, how to pull faces. As an actor he was confident, but unless he was satisfied, he would shoot take after take. He was a good dancer, I remember in the song Sun, sun, sun zaalima, he got the camera whirling around us. There was nothing on that set, just a car in a garage!"

In another interview with Filmfare, she remarked, "He was a very good director. He would not okay the shot till it was perfect. He would be well prepared. He knew exactly where to place the camera and would get impatient if things didn't happen the way he wanted. He was strict, a man of principles and also very sensitive.

He'd enact all the expressions for me when I was doing Aar Paar. He was good at that because he was also a dancer."

Shakila, too, was equally delighted to work with him not once but twice (the second time in C. I. D.). As the cabaret dancer cum vamp in Aar Paar, Shakila observed, "The first day I worked with Guru Dutt for Aar Paar involved a song sequence. I went to the sets, a room with cardboard boxes lying everywhere, it looked like nothing. Everyone asked Guru Dutt how he could film there. But he did. The song was, Hoon abhi main jawaan, ae dil, and how fantastically he picturised it!" For Guru Dutt, a song was not a distraction or a form of enjoyable escape from the narrative, no way. For him, a song was equally important because he ensured that it had, as writer Nasreen Munni Kabir aptly observed, "As much dramatic weight as the dialogue." The song would be integrated smoothly into the narrative, thus ensuring that, instead of it slowing down the film and or being its superfluous appendage, it helped move the plot forward. Lyricists became second scriptwriters!

Kum Kum was Guru Dutt's discovery. Beginning with Aar Paar, she appeared in a few films of Guru Dutt. She was perfectly suited to the Shamshad Begum teasing title song of the film, Kabhi aar, kabhi paar.

Cars!

Guru Dutt who had a penchant for using new images signifying material progress, began Aar Paar with a car journey; he even used a car as a site for romance. He went further to use the car for a cynical song like Mohabbat kar lo jee bhar lo! His interest in cars needs a minute's retro journey.

Cars were difficult to buy. After booking a Fiat, one had to wait in line for seven years to get its delivery! Thus, there was a considerable amount of 'on money' (black market) running where the booking slip would be sold to someone who was cash-rich and impatient and had the money to pay such large amounts. These slips were transferable and so rich people were the first to brandish their cars and zip through Bombay's empty streets with a superior smile on their faces. Cars fascinated Indians because they signified modern India on the move, and became status symbols. Filming a romance between a gorgeous woman and a handsome boyfriend behind the wheel, then combining this with the heady music of OP Nayyar, with Shyama wooing Guru Dutt with *Ye lo main haari piya, hui teri jeet re*, the whole experience was intoxicating for the audience!

I am sure very few songs were filmed till then in which a car became the location of a full-fledged song-laden romance! Guru Dutt intensified the thrills of the situation with a moving car. Shyama wooed a surly Guru Dutt until he succumbed to her charms and, to the delight of the audience, he finally took one arm off the steering wheel and put it around Shyama. *Roothna manaana* was enjoyable. Everyone was happy to see Kaalu Birju (Guru Dutt) melting to Nikki's (Shyama's) charms. The instrumentation of the song is as incredible as are the VK Murthy shots, which, combined with clever back projection, focus on the two lovers as they zip through Bombay's streets. The enthusiastic and innovative VK Murthy turned his camera's attention from the face of an angry Guru Dutt to the winsome charms of a beautifully sensuous Shyama, to alternate with the bus, car and tram-occupied streets of Bombay. Seriously, what more could one ask?! It was, in the Bombay lingo, "Paisa wasool!" But so enamoured was Guru Dutt with the car that he went one step further and employed the car again in another song, this time for a cynical vocal trio, Mohabbat kar lo, jee bhar lo!

In an interview with Mumbai Mirror, Lalita Lajmi said that the character of Nikki, played by Shyama, was shaped on Guru Dutt's first crush. When they were living in Calcutta, there was a garage owner's daughter, a Punjabi girl who had knocked the socks off 14-year-old Guru Dutt. She would drop by to visit Guru Dutt and his family, and, when leaving, coyly drop her hanky! Wonder if Nikki's original ever saw the film!

With Aar Paar came the huge breakthrough that Guru Dutt sought. All his ducks were nicely in a row, and he had a great team consisting of the musical wizard OP Nayyar in combo with lyricist Majrooh Sultanpuri, Mohammed Rafi and Geeta Dutt as his main singers supported by Shamshad Begum. He also had the polyglot Abrar Alvi to offer him several dialects and peculiar street-spoken dialogues, and then there was VK Murthy to film his narrative in creative close-ups. Shyama and Shakila's close-ups elevated them to the level of international Hollywood beauties of the time. He cast himself as the hero opposite Shyama with brilliant support from Johnny Walker and Shakila.

The inventive language used both by Majrooh in the lyrics and by Abrar in the script made for a crisp and enjoyable story. Before

Aar Paar, most films used language that was theatrical or somewhat formal, but with this film, Majrooh and Abrar both created the lyrics and the dialogue that were more colloquial. This was the language that was heard on the streets of Bombay. This shift was risky, but Guru Dutt wanted the audience to identify with the characters. He wanted the language to be a bridge and not a wall between them. The effort was for the film to represent, in an exciting manner, the common man and his challenges and aspirations.

Guru Dutt also preferred that songs have no preludes, and jump straight away into lyrics in the singer's voice. In that way he ensured there was no wastage of time, keeping the film racy and exciting, so the songs often went straight from dialogue to song, with no instrumental music to bridge the transition.

OP Nayyar, in several interviews and also to me personally, mentioned that Guru Dutt was fascinated by Western pop songs and wanted him to emulate them to ensure the film's music became a hit. Babujee dheere chalna was, thus, inspired quite generously by the Doris Day classic, Perhaps Perhaps Perhaps, but what is equally interesting is that the Doris Day song was itself a copy. The original 1947 Cuban song was Quizas, quizas, quizas, sung by Bobby Capo with Osvaldo Farres as its songwriter.

Aar Paar was a winner. OP Nayyar became a household name. Later, he narrated an anecdote about his days of making music for Guru Dutt. When Nayyar composed Babuji dheere chalna, the actor-producer-director liked the mukhda but wanted drastic changes in the antara. "I told him to change the situation and I'd change the tune," Nayyar said. "But he was adamant. So after a week, I took the very same tune to him and told him that I'd made changes. He heard it and said it was perfect. Guru Dutt could be stupid at times…One day, while shooting for Mr. and Mrs. '55, he called and asked me whether I liked the picturization of a song. I told him I didn't like the camera angles. He asked, 'What do you know about the camera anyway?' And I asked him, 'What do you know about music?' After that day, he stopped interfering with my music."

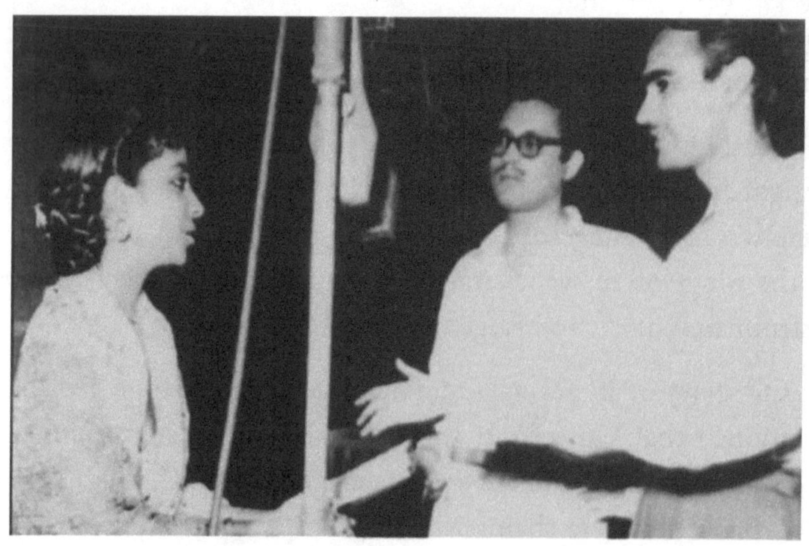

Interestingly, although Suman Kalyanpur sang along with Rafi and Geeta in the impish Mohabbat kar lo jee bhar lo, neither is she credited with it in the film's crew, nor does she recall singing for the film. A mystery indeed.

In its July 1954 issue, Baburao Patel's gutsy magazine Filmindia reviewed the film with an interesting observation: "Guru Dutt makes a mild, maidenly impression. And yet he shows plenty of pep and activities at places, the high pitched moustache substantially contributes to fixing up the sex of the hero."

5

Mr. & Mrs. '55

Released on Friday, April 29, 1955, at
Swastik Cinema, Mumbai.

Banner: Guru Dutt Films Pvt. Ltd.

Producer: Guru Dutt

Director: Guru Dutt (Assistant Directors: Atma Ram, Niranjan and Shyam)

Dialogues: Abrar Alvi (story and screenplay later claimed by Abrar Alvi)

Cinematographer: VK Murthy

Editor: YG Chawhan

Choreographer: Surya Kumar

Art Director: DR Jadhav

Cast: Guru Dutt, Madhubala, Lalita Pawar, Johnny Walker, Yasmin, Kum Kum, Radhika (Kum Kum's sister), Uma Devi, Rooplaxmi, Moni Chatterjee, Rasheed, Cuckoo, Agha, and others with Al Nasir and Bir Sakhuja as guest artistes.

Music Director: OP Nayyar (Assistants: Sebastian and GS Kohli)

Lyricist: Majrooh Sultanpuri, all songs, except song No. 7 (listed below) is by the composer's wife, Saroj Mohini Nayyar

Singers: Geeta Dutt, Mohammed Rafi, Shamshad Begum and chorus

Songs: Total—9: Geeta Dutt—6, Mohammed Rafi—5, Shamshad Begum—1, and chorus—2

1. Ab to jee hone laga—Shamshad (Rooplaxmi)

2. Aeji dil par hua aisa jaadu—Rafi (Guru Dutt). The instrumental version of this song forms the background music of the film's titles.

3. Chal diye banda-nawaaz—Geeta and Rafi (Guru Dutt and Madhubala)

4. Jaane kahaan mera jigar gaya jee —Geeta and Rafi (Johnny Walker and Yasmin)

5. Meri duniya lut rahi thi—Rafi & Chorus (unknown actor)

6. Neele aasmaani—Geeta (Cuckoo)

7. Preetam aan milo—Geeta (lyrics by Saroj Mohini Nayyar) (Background song for Madhubala)

8. Thandi hawa, kaali ghata—Geeta and chorus (Madhubala and friends)

9.   Udhar tum haseen ho, idhar dil jawaan hai—Geeta and Rafi
     (Guru Dutt and Madhubala)

When Abrar Alvi was in college, he had written a play called 'Modern Marriage.' This was a social comedy, a romantic fiction story which was used by Guru Dutt in the film Mr. & Mrs. '55. But for reasons best known to Guru Dutt, Abrar Alvi is not credited for the film's story or screenplay, though he is credited for the dialogues.

This satirical account of angry and emancipated women who hate men was brilliantly supported by a delicious script. For example, in an exchange between Lalita Pawar and Guru Dutt, she asks him, "Communist ho?" He replies wittily, "Jee nahin, cartoonist hoon!" Incidentally, the character of Guru Dutt was patterned on RK Laxman, the famous Times of India cartoonist. In fact, Laxman's cartoons are found all over the film. The audience loved the witty lines written by Abrar Alvi. One could hear the absolute delight and clapping from the audience when Guru Dutt quipped, "Aap ke wakeel saab shareef nahin hain?"

Author Darius Cooper aptly observed that Guru Dutt's comedies were made during the euphoric period in India that lasted between 1951 and 1957. Both Aar Paar (1954) and Mr. & Mrs. '55 (1955) reflected the joy and thrill of being set free (British colonial rule had ended in 1947) and people felt they could achieve a lot if they aspired for it with hard work. For once, they could write their own destiny.

In the story, a tyrannical misandrist, the man-hating woman Sita Devi (Lalita Pawar), tries to inject the same hatred in her niece Anita (Madhubala), hammering the young girl with notions about men being untrustworthy. But this aunt needs her niece to have a fake, temporary marriage for some mercenary reasons. A bridegroom named Preetam (Guru Dutt) is obtained. The twist happens when

Anita falls in love with Preetam, with the aunt putting up a stiff resistance. The woman locks up her niece to prevent her from joining her hired husband. She wants to have complete control over Anita so that she can control the latter's wealth and inheritance after her marriage.

Feminists were not the only ones who had trouble accepting this film's conservative narrative. The trouble with this successful film was that it reflected the orthodox, patriarchal mindset of Indians at the time. In the 1950s, a woman's place was in the home. Once she became a wife, her needs came last, after those of her husband and his family. That was the ethos in which the story was filmed, with one eye on the box office. The film did not want to challenge gender stereotypes and make waves. It wanted only to make money and keep audiences entertained.

Keeping such a social background in mind, consider this scene in which the liberated Anita is in conversation with Preetam's sister-in-law, while the latter is busy with her household duties. A scandalised Anita asks the lady why she has had three children in four years when so many responsibilities rob a woman of her freedom. The sister-in-law's reply to Anita is exactly what a typical 50s or 60s woman would have given: "Ghar ke kaam kaaj mein hi toh grihasti ka sukh hai. Kaisi azadi? Jo aurat apne bal bachchon ko bojh samjhe aur unse azaadi chaahe, woh bhala maa kaise kehla sakti hai?" In sum, for a woman, her children and domestic chores should be her only source of happiness. Of what significance is that freedom when a mother considers her children as a burden?

Anita then moves on to the next question, a difficult one, the answer to which can make any modern woman of today squirm, because it permits a man to abuse their women if needed. Anita: "Kya aap ke pati peet-te bhi hain kabhi aap ko?" Preetam's sister-in-law replies with a relaxed and calm face, "Tan man se pyaar wohi karte hain." Essentially, her subtext is saying "It's okay for him to hit me from time to time because he is the same person who loves me with his entire being". Guru Dutt was reflecting the way men saw women in those days. Wife-beating was fine as long as the husband loved his wife!

Shocking though Guru Dutt's rationalising may seem to us today, he was only projecting the mindset of Indian society when he accepted Abrar Alvi's story and script. Alvi had written the story many years before he met Guru Dutt. Meanwhile, the film shows how this last statement has a profound effect on Anita. She is overcome with remorse and abandons her feminist notions. The scene is followed by a romantic song from Preetam, the waltz *Udhar tum haseen ho idhar dil jawaan hai*. The heroine has a change of heart and now permits herself to fall for the poetic lover. After all, the film seemed to say, men will be men, and if they love you, all's fair in love. On the other end of the spectrum, in the same film, we see a satirical portrayal of a demonised feminist enacted by none other than Lalita Pawar. She controls Anita with her negative views on both men and marriage. The message of the film is this: doormats are good, feminists are bad. Admittedly, this was a bit over the top, yet, one must remember that this is a '50s film, plus it was a satirical comedy which was not meant to be taken seriously.

As far as Preetam's love for Anita is concerned, he is shown as a slightly possessive lover. In this film, Preetam doesn't want his buddy Johnny to even smell the hanky that belongs to Anita! Guru Dutt often used clothing in a symbolic sense; here the hanky becomes the woman he loves and he can't have any other man touching or sniffing her! These were the small subtleties that showed up in Guru Dutt's cinema. He didn't want to show jealousy and possessiveness overtly, preferring to make it subtle for the discerning viewer. Another repeated set which was a symbol in many of Guru Dutt's films was the bench. The bench was an important piece of furniture in Pyaasa too, for example. Here, too, we see Preetam sitting on a bench. It often represented his nomadic state, with the bench being a kind of refuge for him from the material world which could not offer him the support he wanted.

The fascinating role of Johnny Walker here as the true friend of Guru Dutt is another one of Guru Dutt's coups. A film that has one pair of lovers is good, a film with two pairs is even better! As the steadfast but crazy buddy of Preetam, Johnny lights up the screen with VK Murthy giving him close-ups from time to time, with him looking straight at the camera as if he was talking not only to his friend but even to us! An example of this 'fictional rupture' thanks to Murthy's impish camera is when Johnny is about to pay for Preetam, and when opening his wallet, he says, "Moonh udhar!" (Turn your face away!). This effort to have Johnny look at the camera and talk to us is like breaking through the cinematic medium to reach out and talk to us. Time and again Murthy makes him 'talk' to us, thus dissolving the distance between us while also making him not just Preetam's buddy, but ours as well. Johnny is more like us, with our peculiarities, whether in speech or facial expressions, than the hero of the film. When a character looks at the camera to speak to us, it is known as, 'breaking the fourth wall' and Dutt let Murthy use this technique in many films. For Guru Dutt, Johnny Walker was his lucky mascot, and he would often lighten the mood on the sets as well with his innate sense of comedy and fun.

OP Nayyar's music was delightful, to say the least, and Madhubala and Guru Dutt appeared to be made for each other, eye candy twice over. Geeta Dutt's version of CH Atma's song Preetam aan milo was added later in the film, if one were to accept the observations of Harmandir Singh Hamraaz published in his log Hindi Film Geet Kosh No.3 (1951 to 1960).

Johnny Walker was in his elements with Jaane kahaan mera jigar gaya jee, sung to perfection by Rafi and Geeta Dutt, a teasing chhed-chhaad song to live for! Madhubala with an umbrella by the swimming pool with Thandi hawa kaali ghata was a sight for sore eyes although one never got to see her in a swimsuit! But the song that was truly a masterpiece in the film was Udhar tum haseen ho, idhar dil jawaan hai, a romantic waltz that oozes romance from its every pore!

A week after the release of this film, Guru Dutt flew to Calcutta and wrote to his wife Geeta, "I am feeling very lonely here. Try to come as soon as you can. The picture is doing good business here and the reports are good." From the success of this film, one can see that the satire of 'women who were too emancipated for their own good', was well received. The patriarchal mindset was firmly in place in the '50s and this film was not going to challenge the status quo, it was too concerned with the box office to attempt something that daring.

6

Sailaab

Released on July 17, 1956

Banner: MR Films

Producer: Mukul Roy

Director: Guru Dutt & Ravindra Dave

Story: Nabendu Ghosh

Dialogues: Sarshar

Editor: Biren Nag

Cast: Geeta Bali, Abhi Bhattacharya, Bipin Gupta, Ram Singh, Smriti Biswas, Helen, Sulochana Devi, Moni Chatterjee, Rashid, Uma Devi, Agha, etc., with Johnny Walker as a guest artist.

Composer/ Music Director: Mukul Roy (Assistant Kanu Ghosh)

Lyricists: Majrooh Sultanpuri, Hasrat Jaipuri, Shailendra and Madhukar Rajasthani.

Singers: Geeta Dutt, Lakshmi Roy, Hemant Kumar and chorus.

This film was released but there is no trace of it anywhere.

This Guru Dutt directed film had nine songs. The music director of all songs was Geeta Dutt's brother Mukul Roy, who was also the film's producer. Song No. 2 listed below was sung by Lakshmi Roy who was Geeta Dutt's sister.

There are 4 lyricists in the film: Majrooh Sultanpuri (4 songs), Hasrat Jaipuri (2 songs), Shailendra (2 songs) and Madhukar Rajasthani (1 song).

Total songs: 9. Geeta Dutt: 7 solos, Lakshmi Roy: 1 solo. Hemant Kumar: 1 solo. Chorus: 2 songs

1. Aa gayi aa gayi aa gayi re raat raag-bhari aa gayi—Geeta (lyricist Shailendra)

2. Baaje dil ke taar, kare ye pukaar, nas nas mein pyaar bhar re—Lakshmi Roy (lyricist Hasrat Jaipuri)

3. Chaand ke aansoo shabnam ban ke, kisi ke pyaar—Geeta (lyricist Madhukar Rajasthani)

4. Hai ye duniya kaun si, ae dil, mujhe kya ho gaya—Hemant (lyricist Majrooh Sultanpuri)

5. Hai ye duniya kaun si—Geeta (lyricist Majrooh Sultanpuri) (tandem with song No.4)

6. Jiyara baat nahin maane kisi ki—Geeta (lyricist Hasrat Jaipuri)

7. Om Hari om Hari om Hari om—Geeta and chorus (lyricist Majrooh Sultanpuri)

8. Tan pe rang, sakhi, man mein rang, sakhi—Geeta and chorus (lyricist Majrooh Sultanpuri)

9. Ye rut ye raat jawaan, bekal dil ke armaan—Geeta (lyricist Shailendra)

All except two songs of this film (Ye rut ye raat jawaan and Hai ye duniya kaun si) were recorded between February and April 1954, although the film was released later in 1956. As per the log of Harmandir Singh Humraaz, Hai ye duniya kaun si was added to the movie after it was released.

Very little is known about this 135-minute-long film. The film was originally assigned for direction to Ravindra Dave, who directed the first four reels of the film before he abandoned the project midway. On a rescue mission, Guru Dutt was asked to bail out the film, so he directed the rest of it. He was helping out Geeta Dutt's brother Mukul Roy, who, as observed earlier, was not only the film's producer but also the film's composer.

The film centres on a rich man, Gautam (Abhi Bhattacharya) who takes a flight to visit his father in his tea plantation in Assam. Due to stormy weather, the plane makes an emergency landing and Gautam is badly hurt. He loses his memory and meets a girl named Kanchan (Geeta Bali). He falls in love with her despite opposition from her village community which has no tradition of marriage. His father finds him and takes him back to Calcutta. When his mother dies, his memory returns. As soon as he remembers his (pre-accident) past, he forgets what happened in the village, so he has no recollection of Kanchan at all. When she finds him in Calcutta, he does not recognise her. She is shocked and returns to her village to renounce the world and embrace religion. However, as luck would have it, he gets his memory back in time and he is reunited with Kanchan.

The story has an obvious connection with Kalidasa's Shakuntala. Despite this, it failed to impress the audience. Sadly, it is said that when the film flopped, Geeta Dutt had to declare personal bankruptcy. The film was trashed by critics and the public alike with Baburao Patel calling it 'a perfect instrument of torture.'

When this film was released in 1956, Guru Dutt was working feverishly on two films. One was his production, C.I.D., to be directed by Raj Khosla, which would be released on November 2, 1956, followed by Pyaasa, released three months later, on February 22, 1957. Sadly, since no prints of Sailaab are available, it is a huge loss for the fans of Guru and Geeta Dutt. Sailaab means flood; perhaps the prints were metaphorically washed away in a flood.

7

C. I. D.

Released in 1956

Banner: Guru Dutt Films Pvt. Ltd.

Producer: Guru Dutt

Director: Raj Khosla (Assistant Director: Pramod Chakravorty, Bhappi Sonie and Padmanabh)

Screenplay and Dialogues: Inder Raj Anand

Director of Photography: VK Murthy (and the late Anwar Pabani)

Editor: YG Chawhan

Choreographer: Zohra Sehgal

Costume Designer: Bhanu Athaiya

Cast: Dev Anand, Shakila, Johnny Walker, Waheeda Rehman, KN Singh, Bir Sakuja, Minoo Mumtaz, Kum Kum, Tun Tun, Mehmood, Jagdish Raj, Sheela Vaz, Bela Bose and others

Music Director: OP Nayyar (Assistants: GS Kohli and Sebastian)

Sound Recordist: Mukul Bose

Production Executive: Guruswamy

Lyricists: Majrooh Sultanpuri (all songs were Majrooh's except Song No. 1, mentioned below, which was by Jan Nissar Akhtar)

Singers: Mohammed Rafi, Asha Bhosle, Geeta Dutt, Shamshad Begum and the chorus

Songs: Total 8: Geeta Dutt-3, Mohammed Rafi-5, Shamshad Begum-4, chorus-1.

1. Aankhon hi aankhon mein ishaara ho gaya—Rafi and Geeta (Dev Anand and Shakila)

2. Ae dil hai mushkil—Rafi and Geeta (Johnny Walker and Kum Kum)

3. Boojh mera kya nao re—Shamshad and chorus (Minoo Mumtaz and others)

4. Jaata kahaan hai deewaane—Geeta (deleted song)

5. Kahin pe nigaahen kahin pe nishaana—Shamshad (Waheeda Rehman)

6. O leke pehla pehla pyaar-1—Rafi and Shamshad (Sheela Vaz and Shyam Kapoor)

7. O leke pehla pehla pyaar-2—Rafi, Shamshad and Asha (Sheela Vaz, Shyam Kapoor and Shakila)

8. O leke pehla pehla pyaar-3—Rafi and Asha (Sadly, this song cannot be traced.)

The black and white film C.I.D. with a runtime of 2 hours and 26 minutes was again a super hit. Of all Guru Dutt's noir films, this one had the most intoxicating mix of brilliantly talented artists. Produced by the perfectionist Guru Dutt, the film starred Dev Anand and Shakila in lead roles. As mentioned in the chapter on Dev Anand, the two friends had a pact that they would work with each other in their films. Dev Anand had already fulfilled his end of the bargain when he signed on Guru Dutt to direct his film Baazi; Guru Dutt returned the favour by casting the actor as the hero in this film. Guru Dutt was busy with his pet project Pyaasa at this time, so with C.I.D. coming along, he had two films on his hands. Guru Dutt handed over C.I.D.'s directorial reins to his friend Raj Khosla who had proved his excellence to Guru Dutt when they had worked together in Baazi, Jaal, Baaz, and Aar Paar.

In a televised interview available on YouTube, director Raj Khosla spoke at length about almost entirely being inspired by Guru Dutt. He also spoke about Guru Dutt's ability to quickly spot talent. One day, Raj Khosla had asked an uninitiated Abrar Alvi his opinion on a scene they were working on. Guru Dutt, Raj Khosla said, was aware that since he was from Bangalore he wasn't as familiar with Hindi as North Indians were. Abrar Alvi offered his opinion to Raj Khosla on the scene while Guru Dutt listened in. Initially impressed, Dutt next put Abrar Alvi through a series of writing tests that went on for several days. At the end of it, he asked Abrar Alvi to be the screenwriter for his next film, Aar Paar. As for Raj Khosla, he had come to the Hindi film industry with hopes of becoming a singer but it was Guru Dutt who moulded him into an assistant film director. Thus, many in this film's cast, including Abrar Alvi, Raj Khosla, VK Murthy, Waheeda Rehman, Johnny Walker, Kum Kum, Minoo Mumtaz, and others got their breaks in Guru Dutt's films and owed their successful careers to him.

Raj Khosla learnt a lot from Guru Dutt, but, like the latter, he was cynical of the people who worked in the industry. He once remarked, "I love filmmaking but I hate the film industry. It is a losing game; there are no winners here." Quite like him, Guru Dutt too found himself an alien, an outsider in a magical make-believe universe. Neither of them really 'belonged' since they were truly creative.

Working with the genius Guru Dutt, Raj Khosla brought out a stunning film, with never a dull moment. C.I.D.'s songs were not cigarette songs, instead, they were charming extensions of the plot and, sometimes, they even intensified the suspense of the film. The song Kahin pe nigaahen, kahin pe nishaana is a great example of this.

OP Nayyar, another risky bet that Guru Dutt had placed, had already given him a windfall in Aar Paar and Mr. & Mrs. '55. The light romantic crime fiction that C.I.D. was, OP Nayyar was his immediate choice. Each song of this film, too, became a blockbuster hit.

For example, Kum Kum and Johnny Walker lip-synched what is now known as the Bombay anthem: the song Ae dil hai mushkil jeena yahaan, was sung by Geeta Dutt and Mohammed Rafi. The teasing first part of the song which was a non-Bombayite's critique of the metro, was met with the hard-nosed karmic outlook of Bombayites who give good for good and bad for bad. The complaints of Rafi are met by the wisdom of Geeta. Majrooh's lyrics laid bare to us the two faces of the enigmatic city of Bombay. No song has quite captured the essence of the commercial capital of India quite like this one has, and it went on to become the film's most popular song. The comedy generated by Johnny Walker, the visual splendour of Bombay's sea face, whether of Worli or Marine Drive, the horse and carriage with its ghoda-gaadi beat, the brilliant lyrics of Majrooh Sultanpuri, it's a deadly few minutes in cinema's history! Nobody cared that the melody owed something to the original Oh My Darling Clementine, which Nayyar had taken and made into something far beyond what it was! The music alchemist was instructed by Guru Dutt to listen to Western pop albums, to pick up the beats and use them for his films. Nayyar heard them, he sometimes listened and at other times he simply took the baton and ran to the finish line, much to Guru Dutt's delight!

In Mr. and Mrs. '55, Kum Kum played the role of a traditional happy housewife who transformed a modern liberated woman into a gharelu naari! In C.I.D., Kum Kum was peppy and pretty, and the love interest of Johnny Walker.

Dev Anand as Inspector Shekhar, was stunning. Shakila as Rekha was everyone's dream girl, she was a classic beauty and acted perfectly! The newcomer Waheeda Rehman as Kamini made everyone sit up and take notice! She was the woman who looked out for Inspector Shekhar while she belonged to the gang of criminals. Some felt she stole the show, perhaps because VK Murthy and Raj Khosla succeeded in giving her the giant build-up that Guru Dutt demanded of them. The drama generated in the fascinating OP Nayyar/Majrooh/Shamshad song Kahin pe nigahen, was heightened by the purposeful, mean face of the evil Dharamdas (Bir Sakuja), who his moll (Waheeda) was enticing away from the hidden Inspector Shekhar, while she was egging the latter to escape. The audience wanted Shekhar to make good his escape, and he did so, but not before the villain saw him slip away. The sheer drama of the scene, the music, the acting, the suspense, it was paisa vasool! This brilliant sequence is a perfect example of inspired filming from the entire Guru Dutt team.

Then we have the fascinating Boojh mera kya naav re! The song begins with a soft piano play followed by the delicate notes of the sarangi and one is suddenly swept away by the percussion and wind instruments including the flute. Then the vocals begin with the bewitching voice of Shamshad accompanied by the impish castanets, and all along we see the romance bloom between Dev Anand and Shakila while Minoo Mumtaz and the other village belles tease them with their, "We can see it, you are falling in love!" This is one of the most alluring melodies from Nayyar. It has an enticing prelude with incredible interludes. In my opinion, this is the *crème de la crème* of the Nayyar-Shamshad-Majrooh combo! Hats off to Guru Dutt for being so selective about the music for this film, that it made the film a huge runaway success at the box office! The audience applause was thunderous when Shamshad mouthed these Majrooh lines:

Dilwaalon ke beech mein meri akhiyaan hain badnaam
Hoon ek paheli phir bhi koi pooche mera naam
Boojh mera kya naav re...

It was sheer magic!

While, in retrospect, many claim Waheeda stole the show because she went on to become a major actress, even minor stars like Johnny Walker, Bir Sakuja, Kum Kum and Minoo Mumtaz held their own when Dev Anand and Shakila were topping the popularity charts. As far as direction went, Raj Khosla could not be faulted for letting Guru Dutt down in any way. Guru Dutt had delegated the job to the most brilliant man on his team. He always knew who could surpass his or her brief. Waheeda Rehman, as the good woman in a bad gang, was outstanding, even though she and Raj Khosla crossed swords on the issue of her attire in her solo Kahin pe nigaahen kahin pe nishaana.

The famous journalist Baburao Patel with his acerbic pen wrote his review of the film with these dismissive words, "C.I.D. is not merely an unpleasant crime tale. It is a stupid crime tale. It is thin as air and as unconvincing as a Russian prisoner's confession."

All one can do is laugh at such a review! And that's exactly what Guru Dutt did. He laughed all the way to the bank!

8

Pyaasa

Released on 22nd February 1957, at Minerva Cinema
in Bombay.

Banner: Guru Dutt Films Pvt. Ltd.

Producer: Guru Dutt

Director: Guru Dutt (Assistant Directors: Niranjan and Shyam)

Story and Screenplay: Guru Dutt's novel, "Kashmakash"

Dialogues: Abrar Alvi

Director of Photography/ Cinematographer: VK Murthy (Assistants: Moses and Prabhakar)

Editor: YG Chawhan

Production Manager: GL Kashmiri

Production in charge: S Guruswamy

Choreographer: Surya Kumar

Costume Designer: Bhanumati (Assistant Designer: Ramlal)

Art Direction: Biren Naag

Cast: Guru Dutt, Mala Sinha, Waheeda Rehman, Rehman, Johnny Walker, Kum Kum, Leela Mishra, Shyam Kapoor, Tun Tun, Radheshyam, Ashita, Tulsi Chakravorty, Mehmood, and others

Composer/ Music Director: SD Burman (Assistant: Suhrid Kar)

Lyricist: Sahir Ludhianvi (plus a recitation of Jaleel Manikpuri's couplet)

Singers: Mohammed Rafi, Geeta Dutt, Hemant Kumar, Johnny Walker & chorus. Also a poem recited by Guru Dutt.

Songs: Total 9: Geeta Dutt-5, Mohammed Rafi-5, Hemant Kumar-1, Johnny Walker-1, the chorus-1.

1. Aaj sajan mohe ang laga-lo—Geeta (Ashita)

2. Ho lakh musibat raste mein—Rafi and Geeta with chorus (Guru Dutt, Mala Sinha and others)

3. Hum aap ki aankhon mein—Rafi and Geeta (Guru Dutt and Mala Sinha)

4. Jaane kya tu-ne kahi—Geeta (Waheeda Rehman)

5. Jaane woh kaise log the jinke—Hemant (Guru Dutt)

6. Rut phire par din hamaare—Geeta (Waheeda Rehman) (Deleted song)

7. Sar jo tera chakraaye—Rafi and Johnny Walker (Johnny Walker)

8. Ye kooche ye neelaam-ghar (Jinhen naaz hai)—Rafi (Guru Dutt)

9. Ye mehlon, ye takhton (Ye duniya agar)—Rafi (Guru Dutt)

"The success of Pyaasa is the best reward of my career. The theme was heavy, and I was not sure the audience would like it."

– Guru Dutt

When Guru Dutt said this, he probably had no idea that one day this film would be regarded as one of the top hundred films of the world. Like a story that haunts us repeatedly, Pyaasa returns to our minds whenever we feel defeated by the world.

Pyaasa and its Origin

Before Guru Dutt married Geeta Roy and much before Waheeda Rehman was anywhere on the horizon, Guru Dutt was unemployed and going through a rough patch between 1946 and 1947. As a 22-year-old voracious reader, he spent his time reading and writing. It was in this uncertain period, living with his parents in their tiny home in Matunga in Bombay, that he wrote the story 'Kashmakash' which he later re-titled Pyaas, before retitling it again as the film Pyaasa. Guru Dutt's son Arun Dutt said that Kashmakash was written in English because his father thought in English.

Pyaasa is easily the favourite of connoisseurs who study the auteur Guru Dutt. While a handful regard Kaagaz Ke Phool as his most outstanding work, the debate is almost always won by those who hold Pyaasa as superior to it. Some critics link the two films and believe that Kaagaz Ke Phool is like a loose sequel, that it is the same story at heart, but more serious and truthful. Some also hold that Kaagaz Ke Phool represents Guru Dutt's personal life, which at the time was falling apart. Of course, both films depicted the theme of the artist and his angst in a pragmatic, socially hypocritical universe. Guru Dutt was concerned with satisfying the audiences through the plot in Pyaasa, making changes to the narrative if his film's distributors insisted. But after the success of Pyaasa, i.e., for Kaagaz Ke Phool, he didn't want to bend his knee to the box office. He hoped that, for once, instead of his understanding the audience and giving it what it wanted, the audience would understand the artist and reward him for it.

Still, it must be granted that were it not for Pyaasa and its box office success, there would have been no Kaagaz Ke Phool. Being so deeply connected, the study of one often leads us to the other. Perhaps Guru Dutt intended for us to connect the dots. He was a man of few words as many from his family and friends have said. These include Abrar Alvi, Waheeda Rehman, Raj Khosla, Lalita Lajmi, VK Murthy and others. But he was constantly expressing himself through his cinema. He wanted to be understood through cinema which was not only his medium, it was his voice.

But let's return to Pyaasa.

The story, in sum, was about a struggling poet, Vijay, being rejected for his poverty by his sweetheart Meena. In one stroke, when she rejected him, she rejected both: his impoverished state and his art. She reflected the values of the commercial world: she devalued his art because the world devalued it; in her mind, the worth of a man was evaluated in the marketplace. His efforts, his talent, and his genius, when rejected by the world and devalued by society, were meaningless. It was through Meena that Guru Dutt brought home to us how deeply the social fabric influences our choices. Materialism in the external world often leads us to make cold, pragmatic choices. The cynical lyrics of Sahir Ludhianvi, combined with the crusty, often sarcastic barbs of dialogue writer Abrar Alvi, were both potent devices employed by Dutt to do two things: one, to expose the hypocrisy of the pragmatic world and, two, to intensify the isolation of a idealist like Vijay.

One is reminded of Ayn Rand's The Fountainhead, whose protagonist, the architect Howard Roark stood tall and alone, refusing to compromise with mediocrities like the Peter Keatings and Ellsworth Tooheys in his world. There are many similarities between the two protagonists, Guru Dutt's Vijay and Ayn Rand's Howard Roark. In 1943, in its first year of print, this Ayn Rand novel sold 7500 copies. One suspects that Roark may have influenced the inspired-by-books Guru Dutt. His Pyaasa hero Vijay, too, faced rejection from his sweetheart Meena, who rejected him despite his genius. Howard and Vijay were non-conformists, and their respective women, Dominique Francon and Meena loved them till the end and yet married wealthy conformists Peter Keating and Ghosh respectively. Ghosh, the wealthy proprietor of Modern Publishing House, had shades of both successful mediocrities: he resembled the ordinary Keating but he was also a lot like the slimy journalist Toohey. Pyaasa's Ghosh and The Fountainhead's Toohey were bent upon destroying these two creative idealists because their existence threatened their importance, seated as they were on top of the structure of mediocrity.

Vijay's conflict extends to us in the audience: we feel his alienation is not just his but ours too. We empathise with him because most of us have experienced this personally; we find ourselves thwarted from fulfilling our dreams for pragmatic concerns of roti, kapda aur makaan, etc. To intensify his kashmakash, Vijay is intentionally placed in a regressive and materialistic environment to mirror, by sharp contrast, how allergic his deep-rooted idealism is to it. His purity, idealism and morality become an albatross around his neck refusing to let him compromise for his success. But morality is often a burden for us as well; entrenched in idealism we fail; thus, this failure belongs not just to Vijay but to us all.

Guru Dutt also deepened the contrast between the haves and the have-nots, between those who had compromised and those who hadn't. The film achieves its objective: the viewer goes into the cinema hall as himself and, when it ends, he emerges as Vijay. The transformation of the audience within a few hours is the astonishing coup accomplished by Guru Dutt's Pyaasa.

The Impact of the Love Triangle in Pyaasa

A love triangle consisting of a married woman, a much older, wealthy husband, and a rejected young lover was the central plot in Guru Dutt's Pyaasa. Because of its iconic success, this became a formula used by later filmmakers. Six years later, in 1963, BR Chopra used it in Gumrah, a film released during Guru Dutt's lifetime. Then again, in 1965, a year after Guru Dutt passed away, audiences filled cinema halls to see his friend Dev Anand's Guide, where a married woman, Rosie (Waheeda Rehman) again married to an aged but wealthy man, Marco (Kishore Sahu), has an extra-marital affair with a glib and handsome bachelor Raju (Dev Anand). Guide went past Pyaasa when it, through a brilliant script and narrative, succeeded in making the extramarital affair of the protagonist, Rosie, acceptable.

Interestingly, while Gumrah's rejected bachelor, Rajendra (Sunil Dutt), simply gets shut out when the door is slammed in his face by his lady love, Meena (Mala Sinha again as Meena!), it is the bachelor Raju of Guide who martyrs himself for a higher cause. One senses that Vijay Anand might have been influenced by a line from Pyaasa. In one scene, Vijay tells Meena, 'Zindagi ki asli khushi doosron ko khush rakh ke haasil ki jaati hai.' Raju the Guide dies, obliging the villagers so that humanity may live. While Raju rises from pragmatism to spirituality, Meena of Pyaasa descends to materialism. Guru Dutt's Vijay, in search of a less hostile and narrow-minded world, turns away from the crass commercialisation that corrodes Man's soul and which makes him, like Marlowe's Dr. Faustus, sell his soul for something he desperately desires. It is not only Meena who strikes the Faustian bargain; so do Vijay's brothers, the publisher, and even his friends who let him down and betray him. When it is almost the entire society that lets an artist down, how can talent survive? Dutt is asking us to examine ourselves: do we also support such rank commercialisation?

Guru Dutt Leads the Pack

A thematic study of Guru Dutt's Pyaasa and Kaagaz Ke Phool becomes vital. The effort here is to find out what makes Pyaasa great, whether it was the theme or the presentation or a combination of both. Was it ahead of the pack, a trailblazer in a conservative society? What were films like before and after Pyaasa was released?

One tries to understand the reason why this theme engrossed Guru Dutt so much. Why was he interested in finding out if a world can exist where an artist is rewarded for his talent, instead of being trampled underfoot like the symbolic bee in the first scene of Pyaasa? Bimal Roy's Devdas had presented alcohol as a way out of the difficult situation, it permitted the protagonist to drink his way to death, because he could not, under any circumstances, be allowed to break up a marriage, however much he and Paro loved each other. Gulabo resembles Chandramukhi from Devdas in that she, too, loves him while he loves someone else; Pyaasa's Vijay resembles Devdas in that he, too, becomes disheartened and depressed. But while Devdas had to die, Vijay continued to live by simply walking away from the society which had a corroded soul.

If Guru Dutt had watched Gumrah (at least because Pyaasa's Mala Sinha and Sahir were also in Gumrah), what did he make of it? Did he think that it was inspired by Pyaasa, or was it meant as a rejection of it? Interestingly, in Gumrah, the artist's unconditional love was rejected to uphold the institution of marriage, while in Pyaasa, it was the artist who rejected just such a loveless world. Through these two films, we can get an insight into the minds of the two men: BR Chopra who chose tradition over true love, and Guru

Dutt who held that the individual must not yield and conform to society's hypocritical and materialistic constraints. Pyaasa was shifting the paradigm, turning things topsy-turvy; it was showing the housewife as a gold-digger and the prostitute as a noble soul. Gumrah, on its part, supported the opposite position. Chopra was delivering the message that the straightjacket, however suffocating and uncomfortable it might be, had to be accepted because the family or social structure must not be disturbed. Thus, in Chopra's cinematic universe, anyone who sacrificed his/her joy to fit into the world's straitjacket was worthy of admiration, and his/ her sacrifice was to be lauded. Clearly, Guru Dutt prized the inner world over the outer world while to B R Chopra social acceptance was most important.

The Meena in Pyaasa and the Meena in Gumrah were quite similar. Apart from the fact that Mala Sinha enacted both roles, both Meenas upheld the institution of marriage, both relished their status and wealth, and both were willing to have a clandestine extramarital affair. BR Chopra was re-employing the character of Pyaasa's Meena as Gumrah's Meena, because, in the end, she, too, would uphold the status quo. Yet, while Guru Dutt's Meena is condemned for being a coward and a gold-digger, Chopra's Meena who chooses family over love, would be shown not as a coward but as the epitome of virtue. As a woman, Chopra's Meena must martyr herself for the greater good. Her dead sister's and brother-in-law's problem (the motherless children) becomes her problem, she must adopt his problem and, consequently, be faithful to him for the cause of society. Chopra's Meena must sacrifice her personal needs for the needs of the family and society at large, even if her husband is being vicious enough to terrify her through blackmail and scary stalking. That she sacrificed her personal wishes for his children did not stop him from stooping low. But Chopra showed us that the husband could do no wrong, and even if he did something vicious to keep his wife in check, it was to be applauded.

In his next film, Kaagaz Ke Phool, Guru Dutt proves, through the rise and fall of Suresh Sinha, that such self-abnegation is destructive. When Suresh turns away from love for the 'greater good' (in this case, his daughter's needs, which echo society's needs), it leads to sorrow and death. This choice suffocates the artist within him and, consequently, the life force that gave meaning to his life, withers and dies. In Pyaasa, Vijay ends on a note of hope because his will to live is protected by the unconditional love of Gulabo who abandons the world for him. Noble and heroic, both Vijay and Gulabo are non-conformist rebels in pursuit of a life of purity, in search of a world where the artist and his art get the respect that is their due.

Pyaasa's audience loved the film and went to revisit it time and again.

Surprisingly, Chopra's fans, too, approved of the husband in Gumrah going so far as to frighten the life out of Meena through blackmail. The audience accepted that the end justifies the means because the husband could adopt fair or foul means to keep his wife in check. However, the hero of Pyaasa would not compromise in his life or with his art; he was repulsed by amorality and immorality. In his life, ends cannot justify means. Most importantly, in Dutt's world, the greater good is served through honesty. Integrity being paramount, compromise was out of the question.

When the protagonist had to choose between a character's freedom to flourish or to support society's structures, Chopra, through Gumrah, chose society. The individual was shown surrendering his passion and desire to conform to society. The Chopra brothers reinforced these traditional taboos and themes in some of their films. Taking the cue from BR Chopra, his younger brother Yash Chopra offered the same answer in Kabhi Kabhie (1976), as Amitabh, the ex-lover of Raakhee, accepted the harsh reality and bowed to it. Again, in Silsila (1981), Rekha, with whom Amitabh was seen sharing an intimate soul connection as well as a fulfilled sexual relationship, had to be dumped in favour of the completely grim-faced Jaya, merely because the latter was pregnant with Amitabh's child. The Chopras often used children (born or unborn) to resolve the difficulty their protagonists found themselves in. The Chopras' insistence on such compromises would naturally lead to not one but four unhappy spouses, but then everyone in the audience knew this was not a serious film but escapist cinema, so rationalism didn't bother the film's audience or its creators.

Scripts were written with such glaring flaws that they became ludicrous. Some film banners even had a whole team of story writers at their disposal and still got it wrong! They conformed in the end and took the easy way out of the mess. To ensure box office returns, the matrimonial boat had to remain afloat, but to attract the crowds they needed to show some salacious scenes; thus, they built up characters in one way, but, in the end, they did something completely out of character. So what if the two of them were incompatible, so what if there was simmering rage on both sides, but hey, there was a crazy twist, the protagonist jumped ship, swam back to the shore and made it back to his mediocre life. Such films simply wanted the moolah, and reinforcing traditions was one certain way of ensuring the moolah came in.

Silsila titillated the audience with seductive scenes of Amitabh romancing a sensuous Rekha in Denmark's tulip gardens, or walking in the cold in Delhi's Lodhi Gardens, sharing love and laughter, while a grumpy, priggish Jaya Bachchan waited in the wings. It was delightfully voyeuristic because of the off-screen romance of

Amitabh and Rekha; after the seduction was done, Amitabh and the audience went back to their boring and staid wives and lives. After all, who had ever heard of an extramarital affair turning into a marriage? So the facile way out of the messy romance was to declare, out of the blue, the pregnancy of the unhappy wife, with whom not a single intimate scene had been shown! Titillating and then conforming was a successful box office formula; everyone was happy, and everyone's marriage was safe!

The difference was stark. Credibility was the difference between Pyaasa and Gumrah just as it was between Guide and Kabhi Kabhie. Such films highlighted the difference between Guru Dutt and Vijay Anand on the one hand and most of the other filmmakers on the other. Guru Dutt had matured, he was going past his successful fun flicks. However, several others were not leaders who shaped the world, they were only followers who found out what sold, and they sold it. Film-making was an expensive business requiring finance, thus, many films were adopting lucrative, and if one may add, ludicrous business models.

To be a game-changer, one sometimes has to live on the edge, Guru Dutt certainly was a game-changer, which is why today he is recognised as one of the topmost directors of the world. He risked it by daring to turn the tables around. For example, in Pyaasa, Meena, ruled by her head, marries a rich man because he can give her all the comforts she desires, while Vijay, ruled by his heart, offers her poverty and discomfort. But it is this standing up for himself, despite the daunting challenges, that makes Vijay heroic; a compromising Meena could be heroic in a Chopra film like Gumrah, but she would certainly not be lauded in a Dutt film like Pyaasa.

The Single Man as the Inconvenient Lover

Let's examine the theme of the single man as the loser, which was a sine qua non in the '50s, '60s, and '70s. Single men who threatened the sacrosanct institution of marriage were almost always villains, and they, more than women, were portrayed as a real threat to society. The single woman, i.e., the vamp, could not go to menacing levels to break up a marriage, but the single man would stop at nothing; he could even resort to criminal methods to achieve his objective.

Even today, the audience is uncomfortable when a married woman leaves her husband for her lover. Consisting substantially of arranged marriages, Indian society firmly holds that once they are married, the spouses must work it out, period. One must understand that while the Indian audience is conservative, it is also more pragmatic and head-centric than the audience in the West. By and large, Indian society rejects the idea that incompatibility or being in love with someone else are valid grounds for divorce. But imagine this: 68 years ago, with Pyaasa, the story writer in Guru Dutt was pushing the envelope way ahead of his time. He wanted to show us how we were cheating our souls when we succumbed to the collective needs of society.

The inconvenient lover of Yeh Raaste Hain Pyaar Ke (1963), played by Rehman, is shot dead by the angry husband Anil Sahni, played by Sunil Dutt, but Pyaasa's lover chooses to move towards another world with someone who loves his art and loves him for himself. In a few years, Vijay Anand pushed the envelope in Guide and showed us that it was okay to have an extra-marital affair as long as one was true to one's inner being. Guide's Raju helped a Devdasi dancer by becoming the facilitator of her success; yet, when things soured between them, her wealth did not tempt him to stay on. He opted out to preserve his dignity. It is Meena in Pyaasa who is shown as having made the wrong choice when she stays on in a marriage that lacks the intimacy, understanding, and joy she needs. Her marriage is as stale as is that of Rosie in Guide. When the other man Raju from Guide walks away from the past he shared with Rosie, he is aware of the uncertainties that await him, yet he has a spring in his step because his inherent charm, kindness, and compassion go with him wherever he goes. It is Meena, by contrast, who abandons her decency, ditches a poor man, and after having achieved her security, hankers to add him to her marital existence, hinting at an extra-marital affair, which the idealist Vijay spurns. Meena's greed and selfishness define her personality. On his part, true to his nature, Raju in Guide finds a home with poor villagers, gives them the support they need, and they both pay their karmic debts to each other. Meena in Pyaasa earns no good karma, and thus, Vijay rejects her for her selfishness. Vijay tells her that she has to lie in the bed she has made and that she alone has to pay the price of her compromise. She has not heeded her heart's call to choose his unconditional love, instead, after cold calculation, she chose to marry a hard and hateful man. Her lack of fulfilment is the price she needs to pay for the road she has taken. She cannot escape this through a clandestine romance with him. In short, she is in the ditch because she has chosen to step into it, and Vijay was not willing to get into the ditch to give her company.

In Pyaasa, the irony of the situation is enhanced when Vijay is in the living room of Meena, his ex-girlfriend, singing a cynical love song with book-lined walls behind him. He is in their home, where her wealthy husband, Ghosh, is seen as an erudite and socially successful man. And yet, despite all the books in his living room, Ghosh is portrayed as a boorish, jealous and uncaring husband. The irony lies in the fact that he, despite his reading and apparent learning, subscribes to the same materialistic values as the Mammons do. It is as if, through the story, Guru Dutt is telling us that materialism is everywhere and that over-dependence on wealth corrodes even the souls of otherwise decent people such as Meena. The message is that nobility lies not in one's reading but in being faithful to one's deeply cherished values of integrity and decency. Similarly, while Meena is shown reading Life magazine at her home, ironically, she has not read or understood how to live a life of honesty. Meena falls into the clutches of greed, just as most of society does. Thus, she epitomises the very society that Vijay loathes. Culture, Guru Dutt is showing us, is not about the number of books or magazines you have read; it is about the direction you choose to take when you are put to the test. At the end of the day, one's education is irrelevant, it is all about the choices one makes.

Nobility and selflessness go hand in hand, and it is in Gulabo that Vijay finds that nobility of soul when she opts for his poetry and supports him despite his disinterest in her. Although a prostitute, Gulabo becomes a symbol of all those who will stand by a loser because they believe in him and not in his externals. Education, the film warns, does not guarantee decency or culture. Guru Dutt was well read but, due to his family's financial condition, he could not be supported beyond school. Perhaps his voracious reading had made him conclude that book learning is powerless when it occupies a devious brain.

Guru Dutt's Challenges on Celluloid

Was it possible that Vijay's rejection of Meena was rooted in self-pity, a narcissistic rejection of someone who had hurt his ego? Some analysts might ask if Guru Dutt's persistent self-pity was rooted in his first love—an unrequited one—which became a pattern in his life, becoming a self-fulfilling prophecy. One does observe that such self-pitying vanity was expressed by him even in his role for outside productions, as in Bharosa, in which he sang, 'Is bhari duniya mein koi bhi hamaara na hua'. It appears as if this was a role and script he was naturally identified with because they reflected his predilections. As a tragic hero fighting the odds and as a victim of destructive circumstances, Guru Dutt resembled Dilip Kumar. Like the thespian, the roles of a morose pessimist were offered to him. In the same way, Mala Sinha, too, was like a second Meena Kumari, since she was often cast as the tragic unwed mother whose lover had forsaken her, and who, all alone, had to confront the orthodoxy of society. The themes of Guru Dutt's later films thus dealt with society's savage response to those who broke its rules. This is the common thread in the epic Dutt trilogy of Pyaasa, Kaagaz Ke Phool and Sahib Bibi Aur Ghulam.

The Significance of Pyaasa

After a string of successful rom-coms like Aar Paar, Mr. and Mrs. '55, and C.I.D., Guru Dutt changed tracks and abruptly departed from this genre to get into the serious and real world with Pyaasa. He had been keen on filming Pyaasa for six years before he shot it, but every time he spoke about it to his friend Abrar Alvi, the latter would ask him to wait a little longer. But this story was Guru Dutt's magnificent obsession. He desperately wanted to share it with the world, perhaps because it represented his rejection and his struggles.

He had little success in getting support for this story; it wasn't the best kind of story to finance, with the subject being the difficulties and challenges faced by a talented painter who, to begin with, was an anti-hero and a loser. In the novel, the protagonist Vijay is a disillusioned painter, but on celluloid, Guru Dutt changed his profession to a poet, and there is good reason for doing so. In those days, music in films impressed financiers, who knew that people would buy tickets to watch good songs. Earlier, KL Saigal in Shah Jahan (1946), and Bharat Bhushan in Mirza Ghalib (1954), had played poets and wowed audiences with their songs. Consequently, it made more sense for the protagonist to be a poet who could sing his experiences, both good and bad, all within the framework of Guru Dutt's story.

Guru Dutt aimed to portray on celluloid how real talent is repeatedly sacrificed at the altar of pragmatism. The artist, however talented he might be, finds himself a victim of shrewd and ruthless mercenaries who invade, paradoxically, hallowed spaces like publishing houses, where the written word is expected to instil depth and values in readers. Publishers can often be coarse and hard, buying their way out of situations and supping with the devil if it can make their company's bottom-line look good. This has destroyed many artists, who live and die in a state of poverty, helpless to change their destinies because not only are they poor, they are fighting powerful and ruthless materialistic structures.

Pyaasa begins with the hapless, homeless, and unappreciated poet Vijay, who is overwhelmed by the material world. It ends with him unmasking the hypocrisy of shallow people. After his *j'accuse* moment, he condemns them by walking away from their pretence of morality. Initially, he is rejected despite his talent; later, after they believe he is dead, he is applauded. But he knows he is not appreciated for himself, he is lauded for commercial reasons. The film not only condemns the philistines of society; it goes further to show us the poet's emotional scars and how cynicism has taken root in him thanks to such exploitative commercialisation. But while the film examines a young poet's victimisation and descent into depression, it also unearths a couple of diamonds in the dust. Gulabo is one of them. Prostitutes are seen as the dregs of society, but Gulabo is shown as a woman who, despite all her challenges, preserves her pristine heart and carries within her the invaluable qualities of kindness and compassion. She is showcased as a cultured person who has a real understanding of art, and because of that, falls in love with the genuine artist.

Guru Dutt's excellent direction, his impeccable performance as the protagonist, and VK Murthy's powerful cinematography collaborate to create a poem of despair, a work of art that reaches deep into the soul of the audience, which, when the film ends, has mostly changed for the better. Since the audience is the society that Vijay has put in the dock, it assumes a sense of responsibility and is forced to introspect about this artist's failure. It feels a sense of shame combined with some measure of guilt. Not to forget that it is, of course, us, those who sit in the audience, who are the hypocrites he has exposed. We are the double-faced audience that applauds a film about an artist's struggles, while in real life we do exactly what the villain or the heroine did: neglect or hurt the genuine artist, thus destroying his will to live. And yet, as soon as he is dead, we acclaim him and peg a high price on his art.

Guru Dutt, the prophet of doom, understood human nature only too well. In 1972, fifteen years after the release of Pyaasa, I went to watch Pakeezah a week after it was released at Lotus Cinema in Worli, Bombay. The cinema hall was nearly empty, with black market touts desperate to offload their tickets at any price they could get. But there were very few buyers. There were probably about thirty people in the upper stalls of the single-screen cinema hall, and, somehow, we forced ourselves to sit through it till the end. The film was tedious and poorly directed, and its colours were garish. Meena Kumari seemed unfit for the title role, she looked overweight and haggard, besides being painted too much. The film's saving grace was its music. With all that, the film was a big flop, stunning distributors, because they had booked the cinema hall for a couple of weeks. I recall reading a review of the film which came down heavily on Meena Kumari when it wrote that she had 'a uniformly wooden face.' A week or two later, on March 31, Meena Kumari passed away. Now an amazing thing happened. There was a sudden turnaround in the film's popularity. There were no tickets available, and people suddenly discovered that Pakeezah was a fantastic film. There were innumerable obits written about Meena, the film was praised to the skies, and everyone now discovered that it was, indeed, a masterpiece. The resemblance to Guru Dutt's Pyaasa was eerie. Similarly, Vijay was a failed poet but once he was dead, he became a genius! The same audience, the same film, and the same actress, but two different responses! Guru Dutt knew about such things; he saw through society's sham appreciation and fake rejection too. Incidentally, Meena Kumari was also a poetess, and her anthology of poems called I Write, I Recite, published in her lifetime, became successful only after she passed away.

Vijay, like Guru Dutt, is thirsty for a more compassionate world, where the real artist is acclaimed. He hopes to be seen, not as a liability, but as one of society's most valuable assets. As society's conscience-keepers, teachers and writers guide us away from making soulless choices and lead us towards a more cultured existence. During the sequence Ye duniya agar mil bhi jaaye, there are two audiences. One audience is watching Vijay the poet in an auditorium in the film's story, and the other, meaning us, is the audience who is watching the film in a cinema hall. Guru Dutt challenges society in two ways. As Vijay, he demands that the audience in the film must approve of the poet while he lives, and simultaneously, the audience watching his film must appreciate the artist (Guru Dutt included) during his lifetime.

Guru Dutt wanted to prove to us that a purely materialistic worldview leads us to downgrade the man who not only dares to think for himself but who goes a step forward by expressing himself through poetry. By devaluing a poet, society hurls itself into the abyss of mindless hedonism, which leads to its downfall. Yet, tragically, it is the idealist Vijay who is seen by society as a wastrel; even a woman who loved him has discarded him to walk towards his opposite, an unscrupulous rich man.

When filmmaker Kumar Shahani reviewed Henri Micciollo's monograph 'Guru Dutt (1925-1964) L'Avant-Scene Du Cinema', he aptly summed up Guru Dutt in his observation, "His art does not fall easily into the categories that are hallowed by our cultural elite. It is neither revivalist nor realist, in any sense in which the terms are used. Its popular appeal whenever it had any, was because of the Devdas syndrome, which lasted until the early sixties, among our middle classes. The hero, not unlike others of his kind in popular literature and films, inflicted untold suffering upon himself— all in the pursuit of lost purity."

Vijay and the Three Women in his Life

Vijay's thirst accidentally finds an admirer in Gulabo, a prostitute who first loves his poetry and then him. It is Gulabo, enacted superlatively by Waheeda Rehman, who becomes his sole hope in a chaotic and crass world.

Incidentally, Gulabo was a real prostitute who Abrar Alvi had met in a Bombay brothel. She had been taken aback by Abrar's courteous manner because other clients had always spoken to her with vulgarity, abuse, and loathing. Abrar was fascinated by her and they became friends. He visited her regularly until he got busy with his work with Guru Dutt's film Mr. & Mrs. '55. She would keep sending for him, but being very engrossed in the work for the film, he had kept putting it off for days. One day he chanced upon a body being taken to the crematorium. It was Gulabo's. Abrar Alvi was devastated and guilt-ridden. One day he shared the story with Guru Dutt who found it so interesting that he asked him to shape Pyaasa's Gulabo on his late friend.

As an aside, this role worked wonders for Waheeda Rehman's career in films. She was noticed by many, including the genius Satyajit Ray. He gave her a role in the film Abhijan, which was released in 1962, five years after Pyaasa. The Ray film was based on the book of the same name, Abhijan, written by Tarashankar Babu. Waheeda Rehman's character in the novel was named Photki, but for reasons that seem too coincidental to be dismissed lightly, Ray renamed her Gulabi. In his study of Satyajit Ray, Andrew Robinson wrote, "Waheeda Rehman, who plays Gulabi, was the first star of the Bombay cinema to work with Ray. Though her normal fee equalled the entire budget of a Ray film, she willingly agreed to appear for much less in what was comparatively a small part. Her performance is one of considerable charm and subtlety". Obviously, Ray had seen Pyaasa and had been so taken in by Waheeda Rehman's performance in it that he, not only signed her on for his film, he even called her Gulabi! Surprisingly, Ray never talked about Guru Dutt, while Guru Dutt referred to him a few times including in his essay 'Classics and Cash' (reprinted by Nasreen Munni Kabir in her biography of Guru Dutt).

Pyaasa becomes a morality play in cinema; it engages with good and evil and upholds the values of honesty and integrity. A famous auditorium scene (the actual location was the Asiatic library in Bombay) shows the poet when he turns up alive, his form, appearing in the doorway, as if he was crucified like Christ. He is not betrayed by one Judas but by universal, bottomless greed. The world wants to shoot the messenger because he challenges the status quo. Conformists detest the rebel because he threatens to upset the apple cart. He continues to expose society's descent from its lofty ideals, moving down towards a dual existence where hypocrisy rules. Pragmatism is in the dock, and so is an amoral existence; greed, too, is in the dock, and so is marriage and the false foundation it is built on. Only Gulabo is moved to tears in admiration when she hears him sing his beautiful song, Yeh mehlon yeh takhton yeh tajon ki duniya. Others are stunned to learn that the 'dead poet' is an 'alive poet' and they feel duped, their tears and concern have been in vain! The poet is alive; why had they been duped into believing he was dead? He didn't deserve their praise!

Meena represents what he loathes. Vijay's ruthlessly casual answer to Gulabo about Meena succinctly expresses his contempt for the latter: "'Meena, society ki ek shareef aurat jo shauq ke liye pyaar karti hai, aur apne aaraam ke liye pyaar bechti hai.' Essentially, this is the harshest thing he could have said about Meena, a woman he still loves; he condemns her with his bitter verdict, saying that, as a woman, she has sold her body for comforts, and after having 'earned' that wealth, she is now ready to utilise the wealth to 'buy' his love. The tragedy is that he has not only lost her to the vile Ghosh, his rival but, worse, to Mammon. By attempting to buy his love, she exposes her soul's corrosion and her inner ugliness, and he can now see how much she resembles her uncouth husband, who had similarly purchased her with his wealth. She is, despite her tears of concern, just another Ghosh.

Incidentally, the parallel between Meena and his personal life at this point seems inevitable. The married Meena Ghosh is ready to engage in an extramarital affair, wanting to choose love after she has received all the comforts she wants. In a way, this was similar to Guru's personal life. He married a richer, well-established woman, Geeta Roy, and having married her, he, too, wanted to have a relationship with a single woman. In a way, Guru Dutt is accusing himself, through his film, of being equally corrupt, and much of the dialogue of the film is not really about Vijay accusing Meena, but Vijay accusing Guru Dutt for straying from his idealism. Perhaps he was revealing himself through Meena: like her, he, too, was willing to deceive his spouse and have a clandestine affair. He is Meena in his weak moments. One wonders if the film had a cathartic reason: whether, through the film, he wanted to purge himself of his guilt.

But in the end of the film there is hope, Vijay is hopeful because, in the form of Gulabo, the prostitute, he has found a safe space.

Gulabo disregards wealth when she loves him for his thoughts, which he expresses through his poems. It is said that the ultimate compliment for a poet is paid when someone recognises and loves his poetry.

There are quite a few convenient coincidences in the film. The fact that a discerning woman has bought his poems and that they have met each other seems a bit too contrived. One learns that, for the most part, Guru Dutt believed in destiny. The discerning and compassionate prostitute, while being the most unlikely candidate, is shown as the only one who can, through the power of her love and faith, recognise the gold in Vijay. Although she is a streetwalker who works for money, she places materialism on the lower rung of her value system. While she can deaden her emotions when she physically yields to strangers for money, she simultaneously displays an acrobat's elasticity that the idealist in Vijay is incapable of. It is her flexibility that makes her compartmentalise her life so that she can function smoothly. Of course, the realist that she is, she has seen it all, and she has adjusted to it, but Vijay is unwilling to bend his rigid values and be like her. When he walks away from it all, she accedes to his request to join him because she knows she can survive anything, and she can, thus, be his support and help him survive. Her role is like that of Van Gogh's mistress, who bought his paintings in secret, so he could sustain himself. Gulabo, too, wants to help him out. From his essay on the role of cash in the creation of classics, he had mentioned Van Gogh, so, perhaps, he wanted to replicate Van Gogh's mistress through Gulabo.

In that sense, when she played Rosie in Guide, it was, for Waheeda Rehman, a role reversal, because just as Raju in Guide helps Rosie out of her distress, in Pyaasa, it is Gulabo who is the knight in shining armour rescuing Vijay, the damsel in distress.

Guru Dutt, the risk-taker, challenges stereotypes when he reverses the roles, and he does this subtly without emasculating Vijay, the pristine idealist. Vijay was not only an idealist, he has a strong moral compass. We sense that, if it ever came to it, he would just as easily walk away from Gulabo if she challenges his idealism.

The other woman, Meena, meanwhile, lives in a daily hell of her own making, living with a selfish and unscrupulous husband. The sadistic husband Ghosh intentionally hires her ex-lover to humiliate him in her presence so he can subject her to agony. Guru Dutt asks us through the song Jaane wo kaise log the, if Meena had done the right thing by selling her life to such a horrible brute for a few pieces of silver.

The Indian Woman's Dilemma

It's time to take a step back and play the devil's advocate here. For instance, how would Vijay have supported Meena when he was an unemployed poet, with no steady income to support a family? In the 1950s, women had not yet joined the workforce in large numbers. Although Vijay was her heart's desire, he could offer her zero protection and security. She was choosing wealth, but, for a woman in those times, was not choosing survival over deprivation the right thing to do? A parallel is being drawn between Meena and Gulabo, because in a sense, both sell their bodies for money, one in marriage and the other in prostitution. A prostitute is not committed to anyone; she sells her body to several unknown customers. A wife such as Meena, on the other hand, sells her body to one person to whom she is married. It isn't a perfect scenario, but it can still be justified. What turns Vijay's stomach is when she is willing to stray from her marriage by offering herself to him. This makes Vijay contemptuous of her; after all, he contends that if she made a promise, she should go through with it. It appears that, to Vijay, physical commitment is of little consequence; what matters is that she had once promised herself to him in her heart and had broken that promise, and now she has promised herself to Ghosh, and she is ready once again to break her word.

Gulabo makes no promises and breaks no commitments, and in that, there is integrity and honour, which Vijay finds acceptable. Gulabo is betrayed by some customers who cheat her of her earnings, and in that sense, Meena is attempting to be like those customers who cheat, who want to get the pleasure, and who don't want to hold up their end of the bargain. Is she not like the man who throws Gulabo out of the car, refusing to pay for his pleasure? Vijay, who has been through emotional humiliation thanks to Meena's rejection of him, is revolted by her amorality.

The first woman in Vijay's life was his mother. The role of the mother, portrayed by Leela Misra, brings out the utter helplessness of both the mother and son in the face of a society that rejects the unemployed artist, an idealist not in step with reality. It is his mother's unconditional love which sees him through the nights of despair caused by rejection and poverty, it is his mother who keeps him alive, away from self-harm. However, she, too, like Vijay, is helpless and cannot rescue him because he can't provide her with a roof over their heads.

After his mother's death, it is Gulabo who wants to keep him alive and prevents him from losing his sanity or succumbing to despair. His mother's unconditional love for her son is one of the most poignant scenes of the film. Gulabo, with the same unconditional love, becomes a pillar he can lean on. Gulabo's character is undemanding; like his mother, she wants to rescue him.

One wonders why Guru Dutt showed no physical intimacy between Gulabo and Vijay. It is possible that he was making a point about Gulabo's love being one-sided. So, while she has romantic feelings for him, to him, she appears as a friend he can lean on. We, in the audience, hope that in time, he would begin to love her as deeply as he loved Meena.

Society's Spiritual Bankruptcy

The spiritual bankruptcy of the society of the time is portrayed most ruthlessly by Guru Dutt when he exposes the parasites that prey on other people's poverty, failures or deaths. These maggots feed off dead bodies; father and son, who present themselves as pillars of society, visit the same prostitute when nobody's looking. One is reminded of Ibsen's Nora in A Doll's House. The duplicity and hypocrisy all come crashing down the day Nora discovers the truth about her husband's love for her. She walks out on her husband, who, like Ghosh, represents society at its worst. His pretence is unmasked. When Nora slammed the door behind her, it is said, it shook all of Europe. Vijay, too, walks out because he cannot be part of this hypocritical and corrupt society anymore.

In the Sahir poem, the harshest critique of a rotten, decaying society finds expression. Men and women are flawed human beings because of their emotional poverty, intellectual vacuity and spiritual bankruptcy. Through the song Jinhe naaz hai, Sahir and Dutt show us that souls who visit brothels and prostitutes are beyond redemption.

Yahaan peer bhi aa chukey hain, jawaan bhi

Tanomand bete bhi, abba miyaan bhi

Yeh biwi bhi hai aur behen bhi hai, maa bhi

Jinhen naaz hai Hind par, who kahaan hain?

(Holy men and young men have frequented this place.

Lustful sons and their fathers too,

She is a wife, a sister, a mother,

Where are those who take pride in the nation?)

The film exposes society's secret liaison with hedonism while in public it holds conformism dear; it shows us the duplicitous underbelly of a society whose deeds scarcely ever match its ethical words. It pretends to have the moral fibre and integrity that Vijay has, but it is revolted by him since he is a constant reminder to them of their real ugly faces. Pragmatic to the last, Meena never once hints at leaving her comfortable marriage to join Vijay; all she wants is for Vijay to become an add-on to the other comforts of her life. But, unlike Meena, once Vijay decides on something, he is ready to abandon one kind of unfulfilled life so it can make room for a new way of living. He believes in being honest and wholehearted, at all costs. Just before he ends his last meeting with her, he points out to her the reason why he is rejecting her, and why he loathes what she represents:

> "Mujhe kisi insaan se koi shikayat nahin. Mujhe shikayat hai samaaj ke us dhaanche se jo insaan se uski insaaniyat chheen leta hai, matlab ke liye apne bhai ko begaana banaata hai, dost ko dushman banaata hai. Mujhe shikayat hai us tehzeeb se, us sanskriti se jahaan murdon ko pooja jaata hai aur zinda insaan ko pairon tale rounda jaata hai, jahaan kisi ke dukh-dard pe do aansu bahaana buzdili samjha jaata hai, jhuk ke milna ek kamzori samjha jaata hai. Aise maahol mein mujhe kabhi shanti nahi milegi, Meena. Isi liye main duur ja raha hoon, duur."

CASTING WOES

This is what Waheeda Rehman, his co-star in Pyaasa, said a few decades later in Dilip Kumar's autobiography, The Substance and the Shadow: "The other regret is that Dilip Kumar and Guru Dutt did not come together in Pyaasa. It would have become a bigger world classic than it is today." Had Guru Dutt been live, perhaps she would not have said this. Perhaps most of us would disagree with her. In fact, on merit alone, the film rises above Devdas because it is Guru Dutt who is the pyaasa. After all, he brings his life's experiences, and his private angst to the role that is shaped by **his** life and it is not Dilip Kumar's life. Pyaasa was not about Guru Dutt, the actor, but Guru Dutt, the young man who had experienced pain in his life and was projecting the pain of his defeat in the film. It is Guru Dutt's anti-hero personality and his very commonness as an actor that played their part in making the audience empathise with Vijay's hapless condition. We felt rejected when he was rejected, and his humiliation, too, was ours. While there is no denying the fact that Dilip Kumar was an outstanding actor, we must accept that if Dilip Kumar had performed the role of Vijay, the frustrated poet, it would have been seen as a role in which Dilip played a larger-than-life Dilip. It is well known that Dilip preferred the camera be on him as much as possible, even when his co-stars were mouthing their lines. But in Pyaasa, for example, even a supporting actress like Waheeda Rehman, or a comedian like Johnny Walker had close-ups in the film. Rehman's role was exhibited in close-ups to exhibit his menacing villainy—Rehman, as a counterpoint to a cynical and depressed Guru Dutt, was given plenty of footage to show how destructive he was. Also, had Dilip Kumar been Vijay, VK Murthy would not have had the free hand he had when he was filming Pyaasa when he took close-ups of Rehman and others. On the other hand, Guru Dutt was visible when required; as the actor, he was never larger than life; his character, though, was.

Guru Dutt's first choice for the role of Vijay was Dilip Kumar. He was expected to attend the mahurat of the film at Kardar Studio. As luck would have it, BR Chopra's office was in the same compound; Dilip Kumar went to meet Chopra for the script of Naya Daur at his office. The Pyaasa team headed by Guru Dutt was ready for the shoot; it awaited Dilip Kumar's arrival for a very long time before Guru Dutt gave up hope. He finally decided to take on the role himself. Someone was sent out to get a couple of bees for the mahurat shot. The mahurat shot was the first scene of the film where Guru Dutt recited poetry and saw a bee being crushed to death by a trouser-clad man.

Initially, the idea was for the two women's roles to be performed by Madhubala and Nargis. At that time, Abrar Alvi said, Dilip Kumar wanted Madhubala's role as Meena to be made softer and kinder. Dilip Kumar did not want Gulabo's role to be meatier and softer because Madhubala would be playing the lead as Meena. Abrar and Guru did not want to change Meena's character. Guru Dutt was in a fix. Like an angel, his wife Geeta helped him out of the mess. The then-upcoming actress Mala Sinha and playback singer Geeta Dutt were close friends. Geeta Dutt was one of the few people who had helped Mala at the start of her career. They had worked together in many Hindi and Bengali films. Mala Sinha's maiden Nepali film, Maiti Ghar, also had a few songs by Geeta. He accepted Geeta's recommendation and gave Mala the role of Meena. Waheeda was already under contract with Guru Dutt Films so she played Gulabo, the second lead in the film. Thus, Waheeda was working on two films at the same time, as a vamp in C.I.D. and as the prostitute with a golden heart in Pyaasa.

There are other versions as to why Dilip Kumar did not take on the role of Vijay in Pyaasa. In his autobiography, Dilip Kumar shares that he had committed to a film by Gyan Mukherjee, so he didn't even accept the Naya Daur offer from the Chopra stable because, quote, "It was not possible for me to work on two scripts simultaneously because that would lead to overlapping thoughts and ideas, which could affect the content of both films adversely".

Later he added, "I explained to Chopra Sahab that it was for this very reason that I had not welcomed the idea of doing Pyaasa when offered to me by the producer director Guru Dutt, because I was then involved in Devdas, and, though the subject of Pyaasa was very inviting for a serious actor like me, I felt there was a similarity in the shades of the character of Devdas and the hero of Pyaasa. The logic was quite simple: if I had accepted Pyaasa unthinkingly, it would have been released close on the heels of Devdas, and one of them would have been overshadowed by the other. It made bad business sense to me. Guru Dutt eventually played the hero in Pyaasa, which was released in 1957. Gyan Mukherjee's film did not take off due to some financial hassles, and I was ready to consider Naya Daur".

Later, when Madhubala and Dilip Kumar had a falling out, Madhubala was replaced by Vyjayantimala in Naya Daur. Thus, even if Madhubala and Dilip Kumar had worked in Pyaasa, the film would have had many troubles. Whichever story one chooses to believe, and there are so many stories to every film, in the end, one is happy things played out as they did. In my humble view, all one can feel is gratitude for this film which was a Guru Dutt feature from start to finish. The film immortalised Guru Dutt not only as its author and director but also as its protagonist par excellence.

Pyaasa's Legacy

Pyaasa was rated as one of the best 100 films of all time by Time Magazine. In the 2002 Sight & Sound critics' and directors' poll, two of his films, Pyaasa and Kaagaz Ke Phool, were among the top 160 greatest films of all time. The same 2002 Sight & Sound poll ranked Guru Dutt at No. 73 in its list of all-time greatest directors, and the eighth highest-ranking Asian filmmaker in the poll.

Recognised the world over as one of India's greatest films, Pyaasa fascinates because it is, at the same time, populist and niche. As film critic Edgar Cochran observed on a web portal, "Pyaasa masterfully combines what Guru knew was commercially successful and appealing with India's signature stamp in cinema. Therefore, it is artistically and emotionally pleasing, while also succeeding in being thought-provoking and socially true."

The fact that Pyaasa focuses on the human condition and how society is increasingly infested by the consumerism of the pseudo-liberal financial world, how it exacts a price and destroys intimate relationships—makes the film deep and thought-provoking. Art, when it is authentic and honest, expresses the soul's innermost cries, its passions, its angst, and its silent protest. Art belongs to the soul, while money belongs to the intellect. When money is worshiped, art suffers. The cynicism of the artist in Vijay is engrossing; his life exposes the world that consists of pretentious lovers making fake commitments, commanding false respect and leading hollow lives. When his ex-lover Meena discards him and then makes an indecent proposal to him, she falls in our eyes. It is at this point that the purist in Guru Dutt gets his opportunity to show us what truth, beauty, and love are all about: listen to this exchange:

Meena: "Main tumhi se milne aayi hoon."

Vijay: "Pichli baaten bhool jaao, Meena! Daulat ke liye tumne pyaar ko bech diya! Jab insaan ke sar pe zimedaariyaan aa jaati hain, woh unhe uthaana bhi seekh jaata hai. Apne aap ko dhokha na do, Meena, tum daulat chaahti thi, oonchi society chaahti thi, samaji naam aur izzat chaahti thi, aur aaj, woh tamaam cheezen paa kar bhi tum bechaen ho, pachhta rahi ho! Jaanti ho kyun? Tumne hamesha apna swaarth dekha hai, is liye. Meri zindagi se jaa kar meri zindagi ka khayaal nahi kiya, aur aaj, tum apne pati ki khushi cheen-na chaahti ho? Zindagi ki asli khushi doosron ko khush rakh ke hi haasil ki jaati hai. Aur ye tum kabhi nahin samajh sakogi. Isi liye naakhush ho."

Suddenly, the moral dimension of Pyaasa appears in these few lines which is an exchange between two people who once loved each other. Meena who has always been concerned with her comforts, wishes to reignite the flame between them. But the dismayed Vijay unmasks her with his scathing honesty. He reminds her that although she might believe otherwise, some things are simply not up for sale. It is as if he is explaining to her that this artist will not permit her one more selfish indulgence; he will not allow himself to become her plaything. His words signify that while he had loved her unconditionally, she had reciprocated by squashing his spirit, much like the beetle that was stomped underfoot at the start of the film. He had been mauled by her shallow materialism. There is no turning back; Vijay will not compromise, even if it means rejecting the very woman he would have given up his life for in the past.

Trivia About the Songs

Although there is a separate chapter for the spectacular songs of SD Burman's music in Guru Dutt's films, a few important pointers on a couple of songs would not be amiss here.

—According to Waheeda Rehman, the song Rut phire par din hamaare was deleted because she found this song filmed in a boat too boring, but Guru Dutt, Raj Khosla, and SD Burman all insisted on retaining it. However, it was dropped when, after the film's release, Guru Dutt observed that the audience reacted to the song by walking out of the auditorium for a break. Thus, this song is not in the film because it may have been the weak link in the narrative.

—Guru Dutt wanted Rafi to sing the song Jaane woh kaise log but after a lengthy debate, he surrendered to the pleas of Geeta

Dutt and SD Burman who had chosen Hemant Kumar for the song. As it turned out, Hemant Kumar did full justice to it, and it is one of the high points of Pyaasa.

—For the song Jinhe naaz hai Hind par woh kahaan hain, Guru Dutt wanted to shoot the scene in the red light area of Calcutta but he was prevented from doing so by the local thugs and pimps. Finally, those scenes were shot in a Bombay studio.

—Hum aapki aankhon mein was added to please the distributors since the film was found to be too dry, they didn't want their investments to sink. They requested that a romantic song be added to lighten the mood of the film and help bring crowds to the cinema hall. Thus, this song was shot in the end, and it has the distinction of being the only dream song Guru Dutt has ever included in his films.

—Johnny Walker's rendition of Sar jo tera chakraaye was a delightful piece of comic relief. Guru Dutt and Johnny Walker had gone to Calcutta and while they were at a roadside stall, they saw a maalishwaala. Guru Dutt got a brainwave and immediately asked Johnny Walker to watch the man, and start preparing for the role. The peculiar voice saying Maalish tel maalish belongs to Johnny Walker while Rafi sings the essential song.

The Symbols

—Meena is shown reading Life magazine, which has Jesus on the cross; this symbol of Jesus is brought in again when standing in the doorway, Vijay sings Ye mehlon ye takhton ye tajon ki duniya. Vijay has been identified as a pure spirit who is crucified while he lives, first at the hands of Meena, and later by society.

—Time and again, Guru Dutt used a bench as a symbol in his films. That represented his 'home', as it were, a place where the homeless poor could take refuge. The bench also becomes the platform for his discovery of Gulabo. It is when he is seated on a bench that he hears Gulabo recite his poem. Also, his poems are him, as it were, so when she sings his poems, she takes him to her heart. The poems become symbols of his pristine self, and for her to find them is destiny's way of rewarding him, never mind if society didn't.

—In the song Jaane woh kaise log the, the shawl he wears is his shield against society. It can also be seen as a symbol which represents his integrity. The poet is wearing a white shawl and standing like an angel with open wings. He spreads out his arms, which are covered entirely by the white shawl, and stands there in complete purity, moral and physical, to accuse society of its duplicity and betrayal.

—Meena uses a rocking chair, which becomes a symbol of her conflicted mind going back and forth, her thoughts like a pendulum swinging from her husband to her lover, and so on. Her heart is anguished by her lover's sharp rebuke through his song. Rehman, with his grim expression, watches both of them with contempt and disapproval. However materialistic she is, Meena still has a soft heart and lets her emotions speak volumes. Distraught, she clutches at a nearby curtain, as if she wants the drama to end and the curtain to be yanked down. But there is no escape from his sharp words or her bad situation since her anguish is guilt-ridden. She knows she has betrayed him and is the cause of his sorrow.

—Guru Dutt uses the lift symbolically to speak for their condition. At one point, Meena says, very symbolically, "Main to bhool hi gayi, mujhe toh ooper jaana hai." Ooper jaana hai was her ambition to be rich, famous, and comfortable, and it was Vijay who, for a few seconds, made her forget her goal. All this happens when we are deep in the narrative.

Nothing about Pyaasa's beginning tells us that we are about to watch a classic; if anything, it starts with awkward, childish scrawls with flowers as its titles. The mixed fonts give the credits an amateurish feel, and then there are the symbolic lotus flowers in a still pond. There is nothing spectacular about the start; in fact, it seems quite basic. But Sahir's poetry opens the first scene when Guru Dutt, speaking in Rafi's voice, recites:

Ye hanste hue phool, ye mehka hua gulshan

Ye rang mein aur noor mein doobi hui raahen

Ye phoolon ka ras peete machalte hue bhanwre

(At this point, the feet of a man in trousers trample on a live beetle, squashing him to death. His thoughts interrupted, Vijay pauses, takes stock of this thoughtless cruelty of man, and resumes his recitation with sadness)

Main doon bhi to kya doon tumhen, ae shokh nazaaro

Le-de ke mere paas kuchh aansoo hain kuch aahein

Some awkward bits of poor direction creep in from time to time. One of the poorly projected and visualised scenes was when Vijay was admitted to a mental asylum. The other inmates are portrayed in a gauche manner, the scene does not do justice to Guru Dutt's art. Another example is in the scene where Tun Tun calls upon Vijay to recite his poems. One wonders why Meena sits in the front row while her husband sits behind her to her left. It may make for good cinematography getting them in the same frame, without the wife knowing she is being stared at by her husband, but that runs against the grain of conventional seating arrangements for married couples. Besides, from where he is seated, it is simply not possible for him to see her expressions. Again, there was no ground laid in advance to let us know why Ghosh gives her an angry look and is suspicious of her right from the start. Continuity would demand this from any film. Surprisingly, this bit of poor direction got past both Guru Dutt and VK Murthy. Also, in the song Jaane woh kaise log the, the poor artist Vijay, till then, given to wearing a crumpled and shabby jacket with trousers, appears at the Ghosh home wearing a pristine well ironed white shawl with a spotless white dhoti-kurta ensemble. Once this scene ends, in the next scene he is back to his old frayed clothes, his western trouser, shirt, and jacket attire.

Another peculiarity of Guru Dutt's three epics is that in each of these films, one knows nothing about the family to which the female protagonist belongs. One sees no background, no parent of Meena, of Shanti, or Chhoti Bahu. It is as if they must exist for a limited objective. To my mind, this appears as a plot weakness; while one sees Vijay's family reject him and one feels compassion for him, one knows nothing about Meena's background and what drove her to sup with the devil.

The Ending of the Film

Ajay Chandravanshi wrote in Deshbandu that Pyaasa's ending was changed since he was pressured by financiers to change it. Guru Dutt wanted it to end at the point when he utters his last caustic words to Meena and then he is shown walking out. He didn't want a happy ending, but he had to change it. The financiers were sure the film would be rejected. So he shot the last scene where Gulabo and Vijay walk away together, away from the audience (this world) with their backs to us, moving away towards another, more honest world. Hope!

Coincidentally, in their personal lives, Sahir and Guru Dutt were going through depression; thus, the film was doubly successful in showcasing their combined angst. The entire film is imbued with a sense of foreboding. Guru Dutt's expressions project the malaise of restlessness through his eyes, through his careful, slow dialogue, through his body language and pathos-ridden personality. Pyaasa, the thirsty one, is, of course, Vijay, but every character in the film seems to be frustrated or dissatisfied with his or her life. It is not just Vijay who appears to be wanting to quench his thirst; Gulabo, Ghosh, and his family appear to be in search of something that is missing from their lives. Some who have compromised and have bent their knees to materialism and conformity feel frustrated, cheated, and angry; others who have not compromised undergo rejection, isolation, and depression. However, it is Abdul Sattar and Gulabo who, despite their difficulties, have learned to protect and insulate themselves from the blows of the world. As realists, they have developed thick skins that protect their souls from the evil of pragmatism around them.

Pyaasa was shot in 35-mm film and has a total length of 16 reels with a run time of 2 hours and 23 minutes. It was filmed mostly in

Bombay at Kardar Studio and the Asiatic Library. A few scenes were also shot in Calcutta. The film was dedicated to Gyan Mukherjee, Guru Dutt's role model, who had passed away on November 13, 1956, three months before the film's release.

How did the critics see it? Filmindia, edited by Baburao Patel, wrote, "All told, Pyaasa is an uninspiring picture, pretentious in tone and dull and confusing in effect. It is a picture that makes much noise without knowing what exactly it wants to say." Another critic recently described the film's limited appeal when he wrote, "I thought the movie was essentially a self-indulgent depiction of a frustrated wannabe poet who proudly exhibited his tormented persona as an art form, though it was (to me) a manifestation of self-pity. To me, the characterisation of women seemed too stereotypical and barely rose above caricatures, saved only by the acting prowess of Waheeda Rahman and Mala Sinha. I loved the songs by Sahir, but that's about it." Well, well, what can one say except, never listen to such critics?!

The legendary filmmaker Akira Kurosawa's words come to one's mind as one closes this chapter on Pyaasa, a classic beyond doubt.

"It is just because a director has something to say that he finds the form, the skill, and the technique to bring it out. If you are concerned only with how you say something without having anything to say, then even the way you say something won't come to anything. Techniques do not enlarge a director. They limit him. Technique alone, with nothing to support its weight, always crushes the basic idea, which should prevail."

At the risk of sounding repetitive, one understands Pyaasa's magnetism because it showcases to us in the most beautiful manner possible, how Man's spirit is corroded by the destructive power of pragmatism. The film, through its love triangle, tells us not only an artist's story but the story of us all: sometimes we compromise like Meena who is pragmatic, sometimes we are selfish and cruel like Ghosh, but at most times we are the innocent but brilliant Vijay who is wronged despite his genius, and, sadly, sometimes, because of it.

9

12 O'Clock

1958

Banner: Sippy Films Ltd.

Producer: GP Sippy

Director: Pramod Chakravorty

Script writer: Tanveer Farooqi

Director of Photography: VK Murthy

Music Director: OP Nayyar

Lyricists: Majrooh Sultanpuri and Sahir Ludhianvi (all songs by Majrooh except Song No. 3 listed below which is by Sahir)

Cast: Guru Dutt, Waheeda Rehman, Johnny Walker, Sabita Chatterjee, Helen, Shashikala, Rehman, Tun Tun and others.

Singers: Geeta Dutt, Mohammed Rafi, Shamshad Begum and chorus.

Songs: Total 7: Geeta Dutt- 5, Mohammed Rafi- 3, Shamshad Begum-1, chorus-1.

1. Ajee o, suno to—Geeta (Shashikala)

2. Arrey tauba, arrey tauba—Geeta and chorus (Helen)

3. Dekh idhar ae haseena—Rafi and Geeta (Sabita and Johnny Walker)

4. Kaisa jadoo balam—Geeta (Waheeda)

5. Main kho gaya yahin kahin—Rafi (Guru Dutt)

6. Saiyaan teri akhiyon mein—Shamshad (Sabita)

7. Tum jo hue mere humsafar—Rafi and Geeta (Guru Dutt and Waheeda Rehman)

This is not a Guru Dutt production but it has all the signs of being one. Guru Dutt has no other role in this film than that of an actor, so just a basic overview of the film is being offered.

Produced by Pramod Chakravorty, 12 O'Clock was like a home production since Geeta Dutt's sister Laxmi was married to Chakravorty. This is the last film in which Geeta Dutt sang for

Waheeda Rehman, the two songs being Kaisa jaadu balam tu ne daara and Tum jo hue mere humsafar. There was trouble brewing in the Dutt household and this film's romantic pairing of Guru Dutt with Waheeda Rehman could have been one more issue that the marriage could ill afford. The film has all the ingredients of a Dutt feature, such as the crime and the sleaze, then Rehman as the villain, along with the comedian Johnny Walker and his girlfriend, etc. Then the film also has a couple of bar dancer songs, a formula that never failed to work its magic. Add romance and great music from OP Nayyar, and it was bound to succeed!

But that success wasn't immediate. The film was off to a slow start but it picked up steam after a couple of weeks and then became a hit. The essential story was quite unexceptional. At noon at Bombay's Dadar railway station, shots are fired killing Maya (Sabita Chatterjee) who is the sister of Bani (Waheeda Rehman). Bani is accused of her sister's murder. Her boyfriend is lawyer Ajoy Kumar (Guru Dutt) and the story is about Ajoy trying to prove her innocence, with the twists and turns in the story making it an interesting film.

VK Murthy's cinematography is, as always, excellent and so is the acting of both Waheeda Rehman and Guru Dutt. Main kho gaya yahin kahin is delightful to watch as Guru Dutt is shown shaving and showering while waxing eloquent on how exhilarated he is after having fallen in love.

People were also interested in the film because of the real-life romance between Guru Dutt and Waheeda Rehman.

10

Gouri

(Shelved)

Banner: Guru Dutt Films Pvt. Ltd.

Producer: Guru Dutt

Director: Guru Dutt

Story: Guru Dutt

Screenplay and dialogues: Nabendu Ghosh

Music Director: SD Burman

Lyricist: Gouriprasanna Majumdar

Singers: Kishore Kumar, SD Burman and RD Burman

Songs: total 5, but only 2 recorded:

1. Banshi shuney aar kaaj nai—SD Burman

2. Jaani, bhromora kaino katha koy na—Geeta

SD Burman also sang the above-mentioned last song, which wasn't recorded, but please read on.

The impression many people have when writing about Gouri is that it was produced to appease an upset Geeta when their marriage began to fail. Bimal Mitra, a close confidante of Guru Dutt during the Sahib Bibi Aur Ghulam days has certainly hinted at this in his book on the genius. In any event, SD Burman had been signed on for this film that never got made, but a record with two songs on it has been found and on it is printed 1957, the year that Pyaasa was released.

Geeta Dutt was a beautiful lady with a chiselled face and a spectacular voice. Considering that she was extremely photogenic, it was only natural that she felt she needed to graduate from being a singer to a singing actress. Guru Dutt was ready; he would cast her as the film's heroine. Both husband and wife would be the lead stars.

Guru Dutt wrote the story of a sculptor who falls for a woman he sees one day because she has a striking resemblance to a sculpture he had once made of the goddess Durga. Dutt knew that Geeta, with her classic Bengali features, would suit the role well. He had decided that the film would be bilingual, in Bengali and English. It was also slated to be the first CinemaScope film in Indian cinema.

Some well-wishers advised him against making a bilingual film, and to stick to making a Hindi film, but he was determined. Once he made up his mind, nobody could shake him from his resolve. Interestingly, after the first few shoots, Dutt lost interest in it.

According to filmmaker and historian Karan Bali of the online portal Upperstall, Dutt's son, Arun Dutt, told him, "Two songs were recorded by Geeta Dutt for Gouri under music director SD

Burman's baton. One was Jani bhromora keno, a song that SD Burman also sang and whose tune he would later use in Dr Vidya (1962) as Jaani tum to dole, this time rendered by Lata Mangeshkar. The other song that Geeta recorded for the film was Banshi shune aar kaaj naai, also sung by SD Burman and again, used by him later in the Hindi film Anurag (1972) as a Lata Mangeshkar solo— Neend churaaye chaen churaaye daaka dale teri bansi.

There are very few pictures of the film. The accompanying Geeta Dutt picture is from the limited shooting of the film.

Announced after the success of Pyaasa in 1957, Gouri was to be filmed in Calcutta. As noted earlier, the story was about a sculptor who specialised in shaping idols of the goddess Durga, and who fell in love with a woman resembling one of his sculptures. The story became quite interesting because the woman who resembled his sculpture was a prostitute. The resemblance was uncanny and it seemed fortuitous, so out of compassion for her, he married her. Their blissful existence was shattered when the secret truth of her past was discovered by his family. His family began to make life difficult for her. She ran away, with the result that her distraught husband, for years, kept looking for her everywhere. He was disturbed by her face and could not get a grip on himself. A few years later when he joined a religious group on its way to immerse idols in the river, he saw her corpse being taken towards the cremation grounds.

It appears that Abrar Alvi's story about his friend, a real-life prostitute, had been utilised twice by Guru Dutt. Earlier in Pyaasa, she played the role of Gulabo, the prostitute, and later in Gouri, she played the role of a prostitute again. Incidentally, in real life, Abrar had also seen the body of that friend of his, the prostitute, being taken to the graveyard.

Writer Bimal Mitra recounted events as they happened one fateful day in his book Bichhde Sabhi Baari Baari. To sum it up, after two scenes from this film were shot, Guru Dutt stopped the film production all of a sudden. There were differences between the husband and wife over the appearance of Gouri in the film; she wanted to look made up so she could look beautiful but he wanted her to look simple.

One day, her hair was to be left open for a scene. She was to wear an old, frayed sari and have a bindi on her forehead. The shoot was ready, but Geeta Dutt had not shown up. After a long period, Guru Dutt sent Ramu Saria, a distributor, to fetch her. She delayed further as she was busy with her makeup and dressing. Finally, unable to take the delay any further, Guru Dutt stormed in, and when he saw what she had done, he was aghast. "What have you done, who asked you to do this makeup?" He had conceived the scene to show her as a poor woman in a poverty-ridden state; instead, she was heavily made up with a sophisticated hairdo. He was livid and kept shouting at her. Geeta was shocked at his behaviour in public and retorted, "Tum kya chaahte ho, yehi na ki main Waheeda Rehman se badtar lagoon?" Guru Dutt became silent. He immediately ordered the crew to pack up and leave.

He left with the distributor and they went to a bar in Chowringhee. The entire crew left Calcutta a couple of days later. The script-writer Nabendu Ghosh wrote, "Guru Dutt shot for almost three months but suddenly returned to Bombay without finishing the film …This Gouri got drowned in the water that flowed out of the eyes of a beautiful woman—who was this beautiful woman? A voice whispered, 'Waheeda Rehman,' the heroine of Guru Dutt's company."

Abrar Alvi also confirmed that it was Guru Dutt who suddenly decided to stop working on the film and who scrapped the whole project. The movie that became the first Indian CinemaScope film became Kaagaz Ke Phool instead of Gouri. The credit for the same film released in Hindi and English went to Dev Anand's film Guide.

11

Kaagaz Ke Phool

Released on 2nd October 1959, at
Maratha Mandir, Bombay

This was India's first CinemaScope film.

Banner: Guru Dutt Films Pvt. Ltd.

Producer: Guru Dutt

Director: Guru Dutt (Assistants: Shyam, Govind and Azhar)

Story: (Uncredited, but writer Nabendu Ghosh has claimed it in his autobiography 'Eka Naukar Jatri' meaning 'Journey of a Lonesome Boat').

Screenplay and Dialogues: Abrar Alvi

Director of Photography: V K Murthy (Assistants Moses, Prabhakar and Balan)

Editor: YG Chawhan (Assistants E. Shinde and S. Chakraborty)

Art Director: MR Achrekar

Production in charge: S Guruswamy

Costumes: Ramlal

Cast: Guru Dutt, Waheeda Rehman, Baby Naaz, Veena, Johnny Walker, Tony Walker, Mahesh Kaul, Sulochana Devi, Sheila Vaz, Bikram Kapoor, Mehmood, Mohan Chhoti, Minoo Mumtaz, Niloufer, Baby Farida, Tun Tun, Pratima Devi and others.

Costumes: Bhanumati (Assistant: Ramlal)

Composer/ Music Director: SD Burman (Assistant: Rahul Dev Burman)

Lyricists: Kaifi Azmi and Shailendra (only one song, i.e. No. 3 below, was by Shailendra).

Singers: Mohammed Rafi, Geeta Dutt, Asha Bhosle, Sudha Malhotra and chorus.

Total songs: 7: Rafi- 5, Geeta- 2, Asha- 1, Sudha-1, chorus- 3

1. Dekhi zamaane ki yaari—Rafi and chorus (Guru Dutt)

2. Ek do teen char aur paanch—Geeta and chorus (Waheeda Rehman and children)

3. Hum tum jise kehte hain shaadi (Oh Peter)—Rafi (Johnny Walker)

4. San san san woh chali hawa—Rafi, Sudha and chorus (group song with Mehmood, Polson, Harbans Papey, Ratan Bhushan and others)

5. Ud ja, ud ja, pyaase bhanwre—Rafi (Guru Dutt)

6. Ulte seedhe dao lagaaye—Rafi, Asha (Sheila Vaz, Manohar Deepak and Waheeda Rehman)

7. Waqt ne kiya kya haseen sitam—Geeta Dutt (a background song with Waheeda Rehman and Guru Dutt in the frame; the instrumental version of this song plays during the roll of honour at the start of the film).

In his two classic celluloid creations, Pyaasa and Kaagaz Ke Phool, Guru Dutt was expressing the suffering in Man's existence. Kaagaz Ke Phool follows Pyaasa like a sequel; one cannot, however much one tries, disengage one from the other since they both belong to Guru Dutt's pained psyche. Thus, for academic study, Pyaasa becomes intertwined with Kaagaz Ke Phool, the second being like the intellectual, financial and emotional consequence of the first.

Kaagaz Ke Phool takes Pyaasa further down the road of suffering towards its melodramatic finale. While Pyaasa examines the unfortunate state of the sensitive artist Vijay (Guru Dutt) in a ruthlessly commercial world, it still holds out a glimmer of hope because it ends with him walking away along with Gulabo (Waheeda Rehman) who offers him her unconditional love. With Gulabo's support, he is certain that they will find a well-adjusted environment. That ray of hope of Pyaasa disappears in Kaagaz Ke Phool because the unconditional love of Shanti (Waheeda Rehman) comes with a high price tag which Suresh Sinha (Guru Dutt) will not pay. His daughter Pammi (Naaz), who is a symbol of society, stands between them. Suresh surrenders to society and knows that he will be robbed of everything that means the world to him: his art and his love, Shanti. When Shanti leaves him, it is as if his creative identity leaves him as well. He loses his peace of mind and dies a broken-hearted and unfulfilled artist. In the end, when he is on the set for one last time, he looks back on his life, with his memories appearing in flashback. When he thinks about his journey from where he once was to where he now finds himself, it saddens him. By now, he has been reduced to a nondescript poor old man, a stranger beyond recognition. When the crew finds him dead on the sets, they think a beggar has accidentally died while taking shelter in the studio. The man who was once a much-applauded, successful insider ends his journey as a rank outsider, as a nobody.

Sinha finishes his race when he realises the bitter truth that everything, including fame, family, love, and work, is fleeting. He concludes that his life has been an exercise in futility. The tragedy of his conclusion lies in his death: ironically, his insignificance is proved when his dead body goes unrecognised by almost the entire crew, save for a studio hand played by Mohan Chhoti who sees through the old man's unkempt appearance. For the new film's crew and director, he becomes a costly nuisance, taking up space in the studio and delaying their shoot.

In a video interview available on the YouTube channel of Wildfilmsindia.com, when Waheeda Rehman was asked whether Kaagaz Ke Phool was a mistake, she negated it and remarked that it was a film ahead of its time. She was so right. When an artist is ahead of his time, he faces rejection and humiliation, and Guru Dutt was no exception.

We watch the story unravel. We watch Sinha's his inner struggle. In the fierce battle within his heart, he combats his flaws which impede his creative expression while he also struggles to adapt his genius to fit into the narrow constraints of society. Dealing with rejection and failure, Guru Dutt extrapolated his thoughts in Kaagaz Ke Phool, his endless questions begged for answers. He found the domination of finance over art unacceptable. Why should art be answerable to rigid orthodoxy and rank materialism?

In Pyaasa, the artist Vijay rejects the society that rejects him; if it disregards his artistic excellence, he is going to find another world which will not. Everyone, including his family, his sweetheart, and the publishing world, has contempt for him. His art almost dies because he is unwilling to compromise with it. If a painter dilutes his integrity, how can his art be pristine? The angst of just such an artist is the journey in Pyaasa. Taking the story further down the road, Guru Dutt, through Kaagaz Ke Phool, shows us the result of taking the other road: the pain of succumbing to society's demands, which makes the tragedy of Suresh even more poignant. Once Suresh decides to accept society's power over him, his art and his genius dry up. Parallels with William Shakespeare's King Lear, (the tragedy of a father who trusted his flattering greedy daughters), keep resurfacing when one watches Suresh's life on celluloid.

But the pain was not just Suresh Sinha's alone, it was Guru Dutt's too. Pain almost overpowered him at this stage in his personal life. Writer Tara Parker Pope wrote in the New York Times, "Pain doesn't show up on a body scan and can't be measured in a test. As a result, many chronic pain sufferers turn to art, opting to paint, draw or sculpt images to depict their pain." This was what Guru Dutt was also doing. It was during the shooting of Pyaasa that Guru Dutt attempted suicide for the first time. By the time the film was complete, he had the overwhelming need to project through cinema, the desire for self-annihilation which he had recently experienced. Thus, it came out in the form of a story that traced the success and sorrow of a genius, the wish to be numb to all feelings and to erase all memories.

Pyaasa is dark, but Kaagaz Ke Phool is bleak.

Because of these two films the very mention of Guru Dutt's name brings to our minds the devastating story of a passionate man who loved, who gave us his best through cinema, and who, unable to deal with the challenges of life, succumbed to despair. He let his art imitate life at first, and later, his life imitated his art. His later cinema, especially Kaagaz Ke Phool, was certainly a self-fulfilling prophecy.

Kaagaz Ke Phool, which is like a melodramatic Shakespearean tragedy on celluloid, is occasionally regarded as Guru Dutt's finest work. Not only that, some people regard it as his most uncompromising creation. But more often, it is rated lower than Pyaasa, making this a subject of much debate.

Some hold that the hugely successful Hollywood film A Star is Born (1954) was the inspiration for this film. One does see shades of James Mason in Guru Dutt when he begins to fail as a star while his protégé rises and even gets an Oscar. However, apart from this, very little is in common between the two films. Suresh Sinha is nowhere near Norman (James Mason), neither is Esther (Judy

Garland) anything like Shanti, nor do their issues, whether social or psychological, resemble each other. Some who dismiss this classic as a replication of what the West gave us, would be doing a disservice to the Indian genius. Yes, the two films also had Cinemascope in common, but that does indicate how much Guru Dutt was in sync with the cinema of his international peers.

One does wish for a more apolitical assessment of this film; it as much warrants an objective analysis as Satyajit Ray's unforgettable Jalsaghar (The Music Room) does. Both films are rich in their characterisation. Jalsaghar's brilliant actor Chhabi Biswas plays the competitive character of Biswambhar Roy, a decadent zamindar, who is so disconnected from reality that he impoverishes himself. Ray's classics always make for fascinating cinema, with Jalsaghar and Nayak topping the list. Ray did not want to associate any political or social isms with these films; these satirical films are concerned with sketching the character and showing us his intriguing thought process, his actions, and his misplaced priorities and flaws. They have little to do with reforming others, and everything to do with comprehending them, with understanding what drives them, and so on. Similarly, one must go beyond the socialist's applause earned by Pyaasa to fairly assess, through deconstruction, the magnificent cinema offered to us by Guru Dutt of the rise and fall of the protagonist Suresh Sinha in Kaagaz Ke Phool.

Pyaasa possesses the cinematic magnetism that Kaagaz Ke Phool lacks, yet, Kaagaz Ke Phool draws us to itself just as the silent, neglected child's introversion does. Such a child is a mystery because in his quietness he expresses much more than words ever can. Both films are different while being similar. While Pyaasa is all poetry, Kaagaz Ke Phool, despite its rich and subtle script and dialogues, has silence written all over it. Words are expressed, yes, but they often express the inexpressible. Somehow, it is more real because it makes no compromises and offers no easy escape doors through which the protagonist can walk out, to gratify the happy-ending seeker. It shifts the paradigm and risks being seen as too much of a bitter pill to swallow.

We suspected the tragic ending almost from the start; yet we had to suffer with him, and seated there in the darkness of the cinema hall, we were forced to sometimes experience the pain of destiny and sometimes the pain of the self-inflicted wounds of Suresh Sinha. Determined, he moved towards his tragic end, and we could not save him from himself. As helpless witnesses, we could empathise with his pain. We were made aware that, as a society, we may have also been the cause of his suffering. We watched a man go from being a successful director to becoming a non-entity. We watched how he fell in love and then how his heart broke. Society forbade their union. We were that very society. We watched him climb up the stairs, sit down on the dirty floor, go back into his past, then descend the same staircase, take his seat on the director's chair for the last time and take his last breath there. It was tragic, but it was magnetic. It was melodrama at its gentlest.

Guru Dutt was obsessed with Kaagaz Ke Phool, which he shot in CinemaScope. He spent large sums of money on it, with the cost of production running into more than Rs 50 lakhs. He pushed the envelope with this film, willing to face the risks involved in ending a film on a tragic note. The audience, on the other hand, had a mind of its own. His films had been hits in the past because they had provided entertainment, some of them like Aar Paar, Mr. and Mrs. '55, and C.I.D. had been runaway successes because not only did they have light music, there was glamour, crime, teasing, comedy, etc., all fragrant masalas for paisa vasool films. Pyaasa had been much more serious, yet it had succeeded in great part because the financiers and his co-star had guided Dutt away from making the film too serious. They had asked him to throw in a song here (Hum aap ki aankhon mein), to drop one there (Rut phire par din hamaare), to change the ending here, and so on. The film had made it, and this had emboldened Guru Dutt. Pyaasa's success made him conclude that the audience was ready for serious, thought-provoking cinema.

He was proved wrong: Hindi cinema-goers weren't ready. They didn't want to empty their pockets for a film that made them go home feeling emptier. The cloud of gloom that hung over the protagonists with whom we empathised when the film ended now settled on the audience's grieving souls. The experience was numbing, many walked out depressed, and they felt as if they had returned home from the crematorium. The deep sense of futility and grief most viewers felt for Suresh engulfed them for days.

Bimal Roy's Devdas, too, had its tragic ending, but the morose and tragic plot of the film succeeded because of the visual relief and delight offered by the brilliant performance of Vyjayantimala dancing as Chandramukhi. She lifted the film from its noir habitat and gave it the lightness it otherwise lacked; she deflected our attention from the drunken heartbroken lover for some aesthetically elevating happy moments. But here, Waheeda Rehman had no dancing numbers, nor was there a seductive or twinkle-toed vamp to offer relief from the sombre pessimism of the film. But Guru Dutt was a risk taker; he had gone into the project with no holds barred, with a devil-care attitude. He had aspired for complete freedom in the plot, and complete honesty to represent his art; he had been certain that his narration would hold the audience captive. But he was mistaken: Pyaasa had succeeded at the box office despite the gloom and doom, not because of it. Ahead of its time, Kaagaz Ke Phool was a colossal flop.

Both of these epic films were high on melodrama, yet the disadvantaged, mostly poor audience, identified more with Vijay than with Suresh. It preferred the high drama of Pyaasa where there was a socialist message about an obvious rich-poor divide, where there were obvious villains, and where the material world victimised the poor artist. Kaagaz Ke Phool, on the other hand, made no effort to dramatise the hapless condition of the poor and the middle classes, but instead focussed narrowly and intensely, on the character of one man and his dilemma. It was quite simply a character sketch of a man who was nothing like the audience because his problems, they felt, were not 'real' problems. Mental issues were dismissed as 'imaginary' issues in the '50s, and many dismissed the victims of depression as attention seekers.

The film starts with a heavy voice saying, "Jee haan, ye film studio mein daakhil hue hain, is studio mein na jaane kitni picturen ban chuki hain, ban rahi hain, aur banti rahengi, lekin ye studio nahin badla, aur na hi yahaan ka maahol badalta hai, sab kuchh wohi hai, sirf picturen badalti rehti hai yahaan, aur picture banaane waale badalte rehte hain…ek zamaana tha jab ki ye bhi yahaan picturen banaaya karte the."

Suresh climbs a staircase with a thoughtful gait. Then we see the first close-up of his bearded face, with his long, unkempt hair. He is centred on the catwalk above the studio floor, resembling a white barn owl who is looking down. He stares blankly at the studio that had once been his raison d'etre, and softly, ever so softly Rafi starts the first word of the immortal song Dekhi zamaane ki yaari. Rafi's rendition of the word "Dekhi" itself in the very first moment, is a vocal masterpiece. Then follows the rest of the pessimistic song, "zamaane ki yaari…bichhde sabhi baari baari…". It may sound like a cliché to say this, but one must admit that the magic of this film, right from the first shot, cannot be described, it can only be experienced.

Suresh climbs higher still, till he reaches the top, meanwhile, studio hands have entered the ghostly premises and are beginning to do their chores. A set is lit up, an actor is ready to face the camera, and Suresh sits down to watch the scene, but his mind goes into flashback mode. Once again, as in Pyaasa, there is a lotus pond, like the one used in the titles of Pyaasa. Guru Dutt has repeated the lotus pond as a symbol signifying how, amid so much corruption, an artist finds space to bloom like a real flower but because he is subjected to a shallow society, i.e., kaagaz ke phool, he wilts and dies.

This is no ordinary story: it is a story about Guru Dutt's personal life, his character, his angst, his flaws, and his self-inflicted wounds. He is not heroic like Vijay in Pyaasa is, because he refuses to compromise. Suresh Sinha does the unheroic, he succumbs to his daughter's emotional blackmail. Shanti's exit from his life leaves him bereft. He loses focus, loses his bearings, and he begins to make terrible mistakes at work (shown in the song Ulte seedhe dao, where he gets up from his director's chair to reach out to an actress he mistakes for Shanti). He gets drunk, turns up late at work, etc. The angst of his personal life affects his work and brings about his downfall. It is the tragic story of a man who tries to fit into society's needs while sacrificing his inner quest. The celebrity goes from being acclaimed and feted to becoming an undesirable non-entity. He is unrecognisable in his poverty, bearded, unkempt, wearing unwashed and crumpled clothes. He resembles a street beggar, a burden for society. Shanti, his muse, who has also been obstructed by social taboos, reconciles herself to her reality and becomes a well-accepted teacher in a village school. He, on the other hand, is devastated since he does not belong to his wife, his lover or his art. He belongs to nobody.

When one studies Sinha's relationship with the two women in his life, we see that it was he who was torn apart: his wife continued her upper-class life as if he did not exist, and Shanti, too, once they parted, was settled as a respected school teacher at first, and then, later, as a successful actress.

One is reminded of Sardar Vallabhbhai Patel who once said that in matters of love and war, the party that loves less has the upper hand. Although Suresh is undemonstrative and more reticent, it is he who loves more and pays the price of his emotional involvement.

Kaagaz Ke Phool's story does not have the larger dimension to it that Pyaasa has. It is not a drama portraying social evils, or attempting to showcase the wrongs of society. It has nothing to do with greed, and everything to do with character. Suresh's story was his, it was not society's, he was not preaching to change the social order or to improve the lives of film producers and directors. He was simply presenting the life and death of one genius director.

Psychiatry was yet to come to India in a big way. There were just a handful of psychiatrists around at the time, and issues dealing with the psyche were not spoken of or taken seriously. Kaagaz Ke Phool paid the price of being a psychological project which failed to resonate with the common man. Because there was no political message, it was not seen as a 'real' battle which he was fighting. Here he was not waving a leftist flag wanting to change something external in the world. If anything had to change—thanks to Kaagaz Ke Phool—it was Man, who needed to make more honest choices in his life.

Socialist countries such as France were thus the first ones to hug Pyaasa's Vijay and his angst to their hearts while disregarding the much more intense and tragic struggle of Suresh Sinha. Kaagaz Ke Phool shows us the destructive consequence of adhering to society's wishes. It shows us how surrendering to society's dictates can lead us to despair and the final desire for self-annihilation. But unlike Pyaasa, this film failed to ride both horses, i.e., it could not simultaneously appeal to the connoisseur and the common man. The audience could not fully empathise with Sinha's character.

Guru Dutt was engaged in the 'I' of the character, while the 'we' of society had a small role to play. The audience could not comprehend why he isolated himself, why he was so lonely and poor, why he would not accept the support of Shanti, and why he was so traumatised. Additionally, the audience had come to the cinema hall to witness a film that would understand and reflect their suffering which was 'real' while Guru Dutt was offering them a film with angst based on, what appeared to them, an 'unreal' dilemma. The audience reaction reflected the audience's immaturity which failed to understand that Guru Dutt was using the cinematic medium to express what Sinha/Dutt was going through. Sadly, the film that was meant to be a bridge between the audience and Dutt was the very film that the audience turned away from. People were safer when they found themselves dealing with their 'real' struggles. His struggles weren't theirs.

Ironically, when he and his film were rejected, Guru Dutt was proved right: his conclusions that the audience loves you when you are successful and dumps you when you fail were validated when the film was rejected. After its release, he was treated poorly by critics and peers alike. This aggressive and ruthless rejection by critics was recently showcased in the murder mystery film Chhup (2022), where we watched how the harsh criticism of Guru Dutt's films killed his will to direct any more ventures.

About making the film, Guru Dutt was warned by no less a person than singing-composer SD Burman. In an interview published in Filmfare, Guru Dutt's brother Devi Dutt said, "Guru Dutt had an ego and that caused problems. While he was making Kaagaz Ke Phool, SD Burman told him, 'Don't make this film, it's just your personal life'. Guru Dutt shot back, 'You concentrate on your music. Let me do my work'. The two never worked together after that."

VK Murthy's work in this film stands out as much as Guru Dutt's genius does. Murthy was like Dutt's alter ego, he filmed the latter's sadness and genius because he understood him, he also understood how much the director was attempting when he made this prophetic biopic. Murthy was on his wavelength, he knew that for Guru Dutt this was his dream project, the work he wanted to be identified with the most. Murthy expected this to be the high point of his career; when he projected the weaknesses of a deeply flawed artist and how he became a victim of his circumstances, he expected accolades. The tragedy of Suresh Sinha/Guru Dutt was that he could see it all, and yet he could not stop himself from failing.

The rise and fall of a genius, the joys and sorrows of a man of creativity, his weaknesses, his errors, the pulls and pushes of a shallow world, all these dominate the film as do the several existential questions that we are forced to ask ourselves. After all, at the end of the day, what is one's life worth? Is there any meaning or significance to anyone's life at all? Does work offer meaning or do relationships do that? Should the ones who fail to grasp its meaning, end their futile existence or should they drink their way to hedonism? Is escape through self-indulgence the only answer to life's problems? The film ends on a funereal note. When it provides no answer to Man's search for meaning, it essentially tells us that there is no meaning in life.

Guru Dutt, through Kaagaz Ke Phool, Dutt was hoping for greater success, but its colossal failure led him to reexamine his role as director. Both Suresh Sinha and Guru Dutt ended their tryst with the director's chair when Kaagaz Ke Phool ended. The last scene of the film ends with Sinha on the director's chair, breathing his last. Guru Dutt, as a director, never sat on the chair again. Like

Sinha, Dutt realised that he had failed, and the brickbats thrown at him hurt. Truly, fame and fortune were flirts who speedily left when the lights dimmed. He held that the creative artist cannot escape the angst that life brings with it and that experiences transform optimists into cynics, turning hope into despair, bringing everything down to nought. Life was especially cruel to those who felt deeply. Everyone is hurt, but sensitive artists are hurt the most.

Several unforgettable scenes in the film raise its stature higher than that of Pyaasa. One such scene is where the crowds throng him when he is successful, and the contrasting picture of how he becomes a persona non grata when he fails. Also exceptional is the incredibly symbolic dual realities scene between him and Waheeda Rehman while Waqt ne kiya is playing in the background, projecting their dual dilemmas. Then there is the stunning falling in love scene between them when they are in the car and the song San san san woh chali hawa is being sung by others. Then who can forget the scene where he goes to her home and asks her why two people understand each other so well? These are just a few obvious examples of the genius of Guru Dutt in Kaagaz Ke Phool. He simply failed to understand how far ahead of the audience he was. It would take very long, a decade or two at least, to understand that people's response to this masterpiece, while sinking his flagship Kaagaz Ke Phool, also sank the heart of its creator. They had been children in a room that was meant only for adults, so it went way over their heads. There is a beautiful line in the movie A Star is Born where the protagonist Norman Maine tells his sweetheart, Esther, "A career is a curious thing, talent isn't always enough, you need to have a sense of timing, an eye for seeing the turning point, recognising the big chance when it comes along and grabbing it. A career can rest on a trifle like us sitting here tonight, or it can turn when somebody is saying to you, you're better than that, you're better than you know! Don't settle for the little dream, go on to the big one!"

Guru Dutt went on to the big one all right, but the one thing wrong was his sense of timing. He arrived too early for a party that was scheduled to happen a couple of decades later.

Was the plot intentional? Did Guru Dutt predict his destruction through this film, or did this plot line lead him to emulate it? Did fiction finally become fact, or was the fact always present in him when he created the universe of Kaagaz Ke Phool? One wishes one had answers to these questions.

The failure of this film hit Guru Dutt hard, just as it did to the protagonist of the film. Too proud to accept charity, the man of genius preferred to die than receive alms from a loved one. Like Sinha, Dutt would live on his own terms. His aloneness, whether in life, or death defined him till the end. His protagonist died alone, and so did he.

One of the most unforgettable scenes in the film is also among its saddest ones. This is when Shanti recognises him from his sweater and begins to run after him. He runs away from the lady he had once loved. It seemed as if he was running from his flaws; after all, she had witnessed his failure. He did not want her to see him in this hapless state, reduced to a dirty, unwashed bearded old man in tattered clothes, a man with no hope in his eyes, and with no future to offer her. He was a parched, barren desert where nothing but sand existed, where nothing but sorrow and despair grew. He had failed the world, and the world had also failed him. A line expressed in the film encapsulates the philosophy of the film, the note on which the film ends: whether one rises or falls, it is all written. Ultimately, we are helpless pawns in the hands of Destiny, "Insaan har cheez se duur bhaag sakta hai, magar apni kismet se nahin."

"Be yourself" is the wise man's dictum for a man of integrity, but the wise man does not warn the seeker that when one is oneself, the path is the suryasya dhara (the razor's edge), from where one may fall if one is not strong and agile enough. Suresh Sinha was simply not nimble or thick-skinned enough to either survive the film industry and its perils, or society and its demands.

Guru Dutt's cinema was not just cinema, it was poetry in motion. He was a choreographer who understood sound and silence, light and shade, shadows and half lights, words spoken and words suggested. Through his cinema, he projected his joys, his troubled world, his angst, and his euphoria. Whatever he was going through at the time of his creation, whether as a producer or as a director, it found its way into his cinema. Like a Catholic wanting to purge himself of his guilt, he found his way to the cinematic confession booth to bare his soul hoping that the public, like the priest on the other side, would absolve him and release him from his guilt and failure. But it was because the audience was the priest that the failure of Kaagaz Ke Phool hit him hard. He wanted to exhibit the acute loneliness of an artist—to show it that void in his life. He wanted it to understand how dangerous such a void was, because when the emptiness persisted, the artist asked, "Why do I exist?" Which sometimes could lead to the solution, "I do not need to exist." With Pyaasa he was absolved of his sins; with Kaagaz Ke Phool, the sinner in him was not pardoned. The unabsolved sinner left the confession box condemned for being a failed artist. In his mind, if an artist fails to make the audience understand him, he has no business being a communicator.

In the first flashback of the film, when people are asking him for his autograph, Suresh Sinha is the successful director of a film called Vidyapati, Later, when he fails, this is contrasted with the bitter song, Bichhde sabhi baari baari. Kaifi Azmi was at his best when he wrote the lyrics of this song because it simply doesn't get more intense and real than this. In this one song, we see the rise and fall of the artist, and the truth of our tinsel world in which nothing succeeds like success, and nobody loves a loser. But more on this song in the SD Burman Kaifi Azmi chapter detailing this spectacular song.

There are many reasons for the film's failure, some of which have already been mentioned. Here is one more. In cinema, as in fiction, it pays to have an antagonist to the protagonist. Pyaasa provides us with not one, but four clear villains in the form of the vicious Ghosh, his gold-digging wife Meena, Vijay's mercenary brothers, and finally, society as a whole. Thus, it makes the honest poet Vijay a larger-than-life figure battling multiple forces that attack him physically, mentally, emotionally and spiritually. The protagonist who is rebelling against the system opposing him, thus, becomes truly heroic as he battles on with his lofty ideals and empty pockets. On the other hand, in Kaagaz Ke Phool, the real enemy appears to be his wife and her family, and his daughter Nina. This was troubling to the audience because it, too, upheld family values. One cannot hate a child who wants her father to break up with the other woman, it is only natural that she would be jealous and insecure with his new love interest. The absence, then, of a vicious enemy compounded the film's woes.

Another negative in the film was his use of Johnny Walker as a comedian. Somehow comic scenes proved to be detrimental to the plot of the film. Although Johnny Walker had proved himself to be Guru Dutt's lucky mascot, his role in this film confused the viewer and diluted Guru Dutt's vision.

In Pyaasa, Vijay rejects the society he is in, for another society which might be saner, to preserve his pristine identity and art; in Kaagaz Ke Phool, Sinha rejects this world in its entirety. At first, he leaves the known world by concealing his identity so that he, as a failure, is not recognised. Pyaasa's Gulabo accepts Vijay which shows hope and life; Shanti's acceptance of him is shameful, it is an acknowledgement of his failure. The second film goes deeper into the abyss that failures find themselves in. In this abyss, even love is not enough, it cannot cancel out the deep wounds that failure has knifed into the artist's being. He insulates himself from everything and everyone including Shanti. He becomes ostrich-like: if they don't see his failures, the failures won't be real. To his mind, defeat becomes real when someone sees him in his hapless state, but he can manage to live with his failings if nobody recognises him. In this film, Dutt, the creative director, became bold when he threw himself off the cliff and fell into the river, For that, he wanted to find out whether he would be applauded, ridiculed, ignored or whether he would sink. With Kaagaz Ke Phool he was experimenting, yet one wonders how a genius like him could miss the fact that, for the masses, cinema must be a pleasant illusion and not a grim reality.

Abrar Alvi offered brilliant dialogues for the film. One of his lines that stays with us helps immortalise the film: "Filmy duniya mein insaan ek baar gira, to girta hi jaata hai. Film line ki yehi reet hai, naam aur shohrat milte bhale hi der lag jaaye, naam aur nishaan mit-te der nahin lagti." A separate chapter on Abrar Alvi, his friendship with Guru Dutt and their work together follows in the book.

Guru Dutt used several devices to enrich our experience of the film. For example, there is the sweater and its symbolism. Initially, Shanti is shown knitting a sweater for him. Later, she becomes obsessed with knitting sweaters for him, with her sweaters becoming her vicarious way of being close to him and touching him. Because he is married, physical contact with him is forbidden, so the sweater becomes a symbol of the unattainable Suresh Sinha. She misses him and her act of knitting is a way of being with him while shortening the time and distance between them. Author Darius Cooper describes this as " her hope to embrace him even vicariously". She is aware that he will never wear these sweaters, yet she is engaged in knitting for him. Cooper aptly sums up Shanti, "Her cupboard is spilling over with sweaters. But now, it is no longer an innocent exercise to kill time. It is an obsessive act indulged in by a woman who is insanely in love with a man who is both afraid and incapable of loving her in return. It is an act of hope too. It is an escape route for a woman who is aware of the futility of her act…she knits them for a man who refuses to die in her memory."

Guru Dutt also uses doors and doorways in both these films in a subtle sense. Standing in the doorway for indecision, as in for not having made up his mind whether to accept or reject. In the opening scene there is the light coming in through the open door as he pauses there, and then in the last scene too, both being suggestive of his physical journey into the film industry and then his soul's journey out from it after his death. There are swing doors to indicate the fleeting nature of the situation, and there are large forbidding doors and doorways to indicate the enormity of the situation.

Guru Dutt's psyche during the shooting of this film would make for a fascinating study. Was he inclined, at this point, to become a full-blown workaholic with a martyr complex? Surely, when he created such a devastatingly beautiful film with unmistakable grandeur, with stunning innovations and creative flourishes, it must have drained him emotionally. It is well known that he was an insomniac, but this time, one suspect, he might not have got a minute's rest. The wizard was at his task, he was engaged in creating a magical spectacle that we had never before seen.

Sinha's tragic flaw was his cowardice combined with obsessiveness. Neither could he refuse to accede to his daughter's wishes nor could he stop loving the forbidden Shanti. He lacked the courage to stand up to society. How society saw his relationship with Shanti became his point of conflict and caused him acute stress. He was not yet ready to accept the tongue-in-cheek wisdom of Guy de Maupassant who, in one of his stories, wrote, "We marry only once, my child, because the world requires us to do so, but we love twenty times in one lifetime because nature has made us like this. Marriage, you see, is law and love is an instinct which impels us, sometimes along a straight path, and sometimes along a devious path. The world has made laws to combat our instincts—it was necessary to make them; but our instincts are always stronger, and we ought not to resist them too much, because they come from God; while laws come from men. If we did not perfume life with love, as much love as possible, darling, as we put sugar into drugs for children, nobody would care to take it just as it is." Suresh (and Guru) were resisting these natural impulses and the conflict was their undoing. But what made matters worse for Suresh was his ego, which simply would not permit Shanti to be his rescuer. He had once created her like Professor Higgins had created Eliza Doolittle in Bernard Shaw's Pygmalion (and the movie My Fair Lady). Suresh Sinha's pride and ego would not permit a role reversal. He took it to heart, and spent time dwelling on his loss, going deeper and deeper into an abyss of despair.

Two of the strengths that make this film such a work of art is its brilliance in cinematography, combined with a narrative which is close to home for the filmmaker, being as it is about the film industry and how it operates. It is finally about one man and his rise and fall, his strengths and flaws, his fears and his love, his work and his joblessness. It makes us admire Sinha for his self-respect and dignity even when he is a homeless wanderer. Today we identify with Sinha, because we are less rigid in our adherence to society's customs, and also, perhaps because we are much more mature, having seen so much more cinema than the audience of that time had.

Can one ever forget the opening scene? We watch Sinha's slow, sad movements towards the staircase which he had once climbed with excitement and hope, which he now climbs with despair and with a burden on his shoulders. This is his last visit to the studio, and we sense it too. It's heartbreaking to watch him go through the flashback, aware of his fall, aware of his despondent state, a man alone, poor, homeless, and friendless. In earlier times, he had friends and a home and considerable wealth and fame, all of which had been taken away from him. We watch him descend, his steps more despondent, the weight of his memories overwhelming him, and yet, he slowly makes his way to what had once been his refuge, his home: the director's chair. It stabs our hearts when we see him sit there. The walking stick, a symbol of his memories, is the last thing by his side. We are numbed, even as we gasp at the cinematographic triumph here. In such a denouement, when he lets his last breath go, we feel as if we, and this world, have been discarded.

Guru Dutt employs the medium he understands to expose the flaws of both, his medium and society. The safety-net for a failed artist is absent even today. The song beyond compare is Dekhi zamaane ki yaari, which encapsulates Sinha's present and past. It shows how he is thronged for an autograph by fans, who want proximity to him because they idolise him. But then there is its flip side too. The loneliness, the neglect, the barrenness and the despair of being a nobody because of a flop film.

Perhaps Guru Dutt went too far. Since the film was a critique, it exposed the audience's hypocrisy, but it was not only society in the dock: the *j'accuse* was also of the artist holding himself responsible for his ego, his marriage, his vanity, his weakness for adulation, etc. In short, everything appears rotten.

One is also reminded of the lines in Zorba The Greek (1964), where the free-spirited Zorba (Anthony Quinn) tells the intellectual Basil (Alan Bates) to enjoy life and not take it seriously: "You think too much. Clever people and grocers, they weigh everything!" Perhaps, Guru Dutt had also read this novel published in 1946. In the film that was released the year Guru Dutt died, Zorba tells Basil the writer, "You've got everything except one thing: madness! A man needs a little madness or else…he never dares to cut the rope and be free." Indeed, Suresh Sinha did not or could not cut himself off from his past, although his heart told him to do so. In some ways, Suresh was paying the price for thinking too much. Sinha did not understand the lightness of being. Because the bearded tramp was nothing like Zorba but everything like the writer Basil, he had gone deep into it, and he had decided he had seen enough. His heart was broken, and if heartbreak was all that life could offer, why should he live? His rejection of all that life could offer him was caused by his painful memories. He sat down on the director's chair for one last time, and after having found his place on that seat, he gave up the struggle for existence. He made his final exit, he escaped it all.

Can there be a better ending to this film?

Many years later, we see a similar situation in a Mrinal Sen film, Ek Din Achanak (1988). The wish to disappear, which Suresh Sinha acted upon, is also reflected in this film in which a married man with a wife and children, one day just disappears from home, leaving his family guessing about where he was and why he left. There is neither an explanation nor a letter of goodbye. The story focuses on each of the family members trying to make sense of his disappearance. The film ends with the words, "Sadly, we all live just once. The Professor possibly longed for a second life as it would help him perfect the mistakes he had made in his life and achieve a higher level in his field." A year after his disappearance, the family members sit together trying to recollect what happened in the past, and his wife recollects what he told her a few days before he had disappeared. Hurt by his own mediocrity, he had said, "Dukh sabse zyaada is baat ka hai ke aadmi ka jeevan sirf ek hi hai. Woh ek hi zindagi jeeta hai." His wife (Uttara Baokar), gets lost in thought. Was the professor (Dr Shreeram Lagoo) acting on his impulse to lead a second life, a life of greater honesty? Or was he suffocated by mundane reality and escaping from it? Or then was he running towards another, more positive, life-enhancing reality? In short, was it despair or hope that drove him out of his home? One is left guessing. As for Suresh Sinha, he was running away not from one but from three realities: his wife and daughter, his love interest and his career. He had nothing but despair left in his life. He took the step which required great courage. He released everything, letting it all go. But was his letting go an act of courage or cowardice?

In the outstanding Ruben Ostlund film Force Majeure, which deals with cowardice as one of its themes, we see the husband's cowardice when, instead of rushing to protect his wife and children from the avalanche, he runs away from it to protect himself. His wife protects the children, but after the event is over, his wife appears to feel terribly betrayed by him and he lives with guilt and shame, unable to justify to himself and the world why he had done what he did. His cowardice was his knee-jerk response to the danger he saw for himself. Similarly, we find Sinha running away from the avalanche that is Shanti, to protect his ego. She represents the world he has rejected, returning to that world (which is what Shanti wanted) would be the death of his ego, which he could never permit.

He was protecting what he valued most. For Ostlund's hero, what he valued most was his life, for Dutt's hero, it was his ego.

In Kaagaz Ke Phool the protagonist goes through self-degradation and death. In Pyaasa, the last barrier standing between life and death is the wall of love and the hope that real love brings with it. Interestingly, Guru Dutt's films don't show the last wall to be one of faith or God. However, in an article written by Waheeda Rehman, she mentioned that Guru Dutt did believe in God, only he didn't visit holy places. He had once asked her to pray for the success of BR Chopra's song-less film Kanoon because he wanted cinema to go beyond songs. This is strange coming from a man who loved filming songs. So yes, he prayed, but evidently, in his heart or in the privacy of his home. Yet, in this film, Suresh Sinha never once turns to God for answers or help. Guru Dutt probably did not want us to get distracted from the subject at hand, his film was about the character of Suresh Sinha and how he dealt with life's challenges.

Pyaasa is not the Greek tragedy that Kaagaz Ke Phool is; Pyaasa lingers over hope and wants to believe, despite the overwhelming negative social background of the protagonists. Pyaasa promotes the idea that failure can even be acceptable if a single person accepts us for ourselves, irrespective of our standing in society. That such a validation of one's existence can be so significant becomes poignant because, at the end of Kaagaz Ke Phool, Guru Dutt felt his life had become irrelevant to those close to him, and that he now stood alone in the darkness of despair. That deep sense of aloneness on Guru Dutt's wrinkled forehead, his anguished eyes, and his voiceless protest was the final silent statement from him.

More than anything else, his eyes said it all.

Conclusion

Do these two films have universal and timeless appeal, qualities that are required of a classic? The blanket of silence that lies on the protagonists in Kaagaz Ke Phool is unique. When they speak, one senses that there is an undercurrent of silent unexpressed communication. What needs to be said is left unsaid, and what does not have any importance is given speech. The subtext assumes great significance. The outstanding performance of Guru Dutt can only be critiqued with unabashed admiration. Much deeper than his role in Pyaasa is his role in Kaagaz Ke Phool, because Dutt is playing himself even more intensely. He is the disillusioned and dejected film director. Sinha was more Dutt than Vijay because the younger Dutt who created Vijay was hopeful while the older Dutt who portrayed Sinha was too proud to accept help from others.

When you are Guru Dutt, you have the unique ability to see what others miss, you see things deeper, and once you have done this, you can't later 'unsee' them. Dutt tried to forget what he had seen but there was always the morning after, when memories would return. There was the moral decadence, the shallow paper flowers that human beings had become, with their artificial beauty and fake fragrance, a two-dimensional existence where nobody really knew anyone, because everyone was wearing the conformist's mask. There is safety in being like everyone else when one is masked, because then, much to the relief of the conformists, one does not threaten their cherished false beliefs. One just quietly fits in, because one wears a mask too. However, those who don't fit in with society's strictures suffer alone and die unknown and disrespected.

Observes Avijit Pathak about Kaagaz Ke Phool's impact, "We begin to see ourselves, our collective moral decadence, our gross materialism, and our inability to see the ray of truth amidst the glitz of the outer world. In a way, these films (Pyaasa and Kaagaz Ke Phool) touch the threshold of spirituality and make us feel that it is only a poet or a mystic who can see the falsehood in the Maya of this temporal world, and an intoxicated society often crucifies these sensitive souls."

VK Murthy's stunning cinematography, Guru Dutt's brilliant visualisation, Waheeda Rehman's outstanding portrayal of Shanti, Guru Dutt's stunning portrayal of Sinha, Abrar Alvi's smart script, SD Burman's ethereal compositions, Kaifi Azmi's gut-wrenching lyrics, and Mohammed Rafi and Geeta Dutt's brilliant renditions, all come together in this film which one must see during one's lifetime. There is one certain thing about this film, unlike its title, this film is no paper flower.

The film highlights, as no other film has done before or since, the sense of alienation Sinha experienced as a man constantly in search of 'shanti' and his never attaining it except for a few moments in his life. In the end, he was an outsider, a nomad. That's why Guru

Dutt went through his later life in a haze of depression, with a deep sense of otherness.

The then-popular cinema journal Filmindia too, in its November 1959 issue, failed to appreciate what the story was trying to express. Its critic wrote a facile couple of lines to dismiss the film with, "Script laboured and slow tempo. Excellent technical values." That was it. The classic was done and dusted! Such reviews tell us a few things that Kaagaz Ke Phool has already shared. The critics and society, both are kaagaz ke phool; they understand little, but they have much power, while the artist understands a lot and still gets crucified.

Kaagaz Ke Phool received two Filmfare awards in 1960, the Filmfare Best Cinematographer award which was given to VK Murthy and the Best Art Director award to MR Achrekar.

In the end, one is reminded of these lines from Ahmed Faraz, which speak for both Guru Dutt and his creation Suresh Sinha:

Kisi ko ghar se nikalte hi mil gayi manzil

Koi humaari tarah umr bhar safar mein raha

Kuchh is tarah se guzaari hai zindagi jaise

Tamaam umr kisi doosre ke ghar mein raha

12

Chaudhvin Ka Chand

Released on Friday, July 15, 1960

Banner: Guru Dutt Films Pvt. Ltd.

Producer: Guru Dutt

Director: M Sadiq

Story: Saghir Usmani's story, Jhalak

Screenplay & Dialogues: Saghir Usmani and Tabish Sultanpuri

Director of Photography: Nariman Irani (2 songs, i.e., Chaudhvin ka chaand ho, and Dil ki kahaani rang laayi hai were later re-shot in colour by VK Murthy)

Editor: YG Chawhan

Choreographer: Sohanlal

Art Director: Biren Naug

Cast: Guru Dutt, Waheeda Rehman, Rehman, Minoo Mumtaz, Johnny Walker, Tun Tun, Mumtaz Begum, Pravin Paul, Zebunissa, Baby Farida, Aruna and others.

Composer: Ravi

Lyricist: Shakeel Badayuni

Singers: Mohammed Rafi, Geeta Dutt, Asha Bhosle, Shamshad Begum, Lata Mangeshkar and chorus

Total:10 songs: Mohammed Rafi- 5, Asha Bhosle- 3, Geeta Dutt-1, Shamshad Begum-1, Lata Mangeshkar-1, and the chorus in 2.

1. Baalam se milan hoga—Geeta and chorus (filmed on uncredited stars)

2. Badle badle mere sarkaar nazar aate hain—Lata (Waheeda Rehman)

3. Bedardi mere saiyaan—Asha (Minoo Mumtaz)

4. Chaudhvin ka chaand ho—Rafi (Guru Dutt)

5. Dil ki kahaani rang laayi hai—Asha (Minoo Mumtaz)

6. Mera yaar bana hai dulha—Rafi (Johnny Walker and an old man)

7. Mili khaak mein mohabbat—Rafi (Guru Dutt)

8. Sharma ke ye kyun sab pardanasheen—Asha, Shamshad and chorus (unknown stars)

9. Yeh Lucknow ki sarzameen—Rafi (Background song playing during the film's titles)

10. Ye duniya gol hai— Rafi (Johnny Walker)

After the failure of Kaagaz Ke Phool, Guru Dutt went through a deep depression. It was a traumatic period for him. He was so shell-shocked by the disaster of Kaagaz Ke Phool that he lost confidence in his directorial abilities. After some reflection, he made up his mind that he would never direct a film again but that he would continue in the industry either as a producer or as an actor. As such, this film, Chaudhvin Ka Chand, was his maiden effort at taking a back seat and letting someone else take the driver's seat. He would never sit on a director's chair again. For this film, he handed over the job to his friend M Sadiq.

Based on Jhalak, an Urdu story written by Saghir Usmani, Chaudhvin Ka Chand was a super hit. It turned out to be Guru Dutt's best money-spinner, but he took no credit for any part of it, not even as the director of its songs. In his book on Guru Dutt, "In Black And White", Darius Cooper observes "This time he did not ghost direct, the results are obvious. Though this was his most successful commercial film, on artistic and aesthetic grounds, it is his worst."

This was a peculiar story filled with innumerable coincidences and implausible twists that could be regarded as silly if it had not been such a visual and aural delight. A man wishes to transfer his wife to his best friend, who, the best friend that he is, chooses to commit suicide rather than let his friend sacrifice his most precious wife to him! And what of the wife? It never strikes either of them that the woman has feelings too! Surely she is not a share certificate of a flat or an inanimate object to be transferred, but a woman of flesh and blood! Did it strike him that a woman who can be repulsed by the idea of being touched by another man? Anyhow, this was a Muslim social drama which the audience lapped up!

The essential idea of a love triangle, with two buddies in love with one woman but both also caring so much for each other that one of them sacrifices his life for the other, was repeated four years later by Raj Kapoor in Sangam (1964). The latter film impressed Guru Dutt so much that even a day before he passed away he wanted to meet Raj Kapoor to ask him for his advice on how to make a colour film. Incidentally, many years later, we also see the Chopras re-working some part of this Guru Dutt film in Nikaah (1982) where two men (Deepak Parashar and Raj Babbar) decide to treat Salma Agha like a 'tohfa', a gift to be transferred to someone as one deems fit. Coincidentally, both Chaudhvin Ka Chand and Nikaah were Muslim socials and both had music by composer Ravi.

The film was a melodramatic romance, and the audiences loved it because of its music and the love scenes. Muslim socials became a genre that found a captive audience; later even Dil Hi To Hai, Mere Mehboob, Bazaar, etc. had tremendous success at the box office.

A significant aspect of Guru Dutt's later films was that there was an increasing contribution and dependence on Muslim stars and on projecting an Urdu style of communication. For example, if one were to look at his penchant for Urdu in his films, one realises that he needed Urdu poets, especially Muslim poets because they would correctly represent the feelings of his characters. In Pyaasa, although the protagonist was Vijay, an obviously Hindu character, his expression was in chaste Urdu as was his poetry. Then again, Suresh Sinha in Kaagaz Ke Phool was not a Muslim protagonist, yet his grasp of Urdu was stunning. This was because consistency was not as much of a concern as entertainment was. His poets were Majrooh Sultanpuri, Sahir Ludhianvi, Kaifi Azmi and Shakeel. His dialogue and screenplay writer was mostly Abrar Alvi. The singer on whom he depended the most to reflect the chief protagonist's feelings was Mohammed Rafi. The heavy concentration on Muslim actors was also evident. Shyama, Waheeda Rehman, Meena Kumari, Johnny Walker, Rehman, Mehmood, Naaz, Minoo Mumtaz, Shakila, Kum Kum, etc. dotted the landscape of his films constantly. Even the minor stars, strangely, were so often mouthing chaste Urdu even when they were street urchins from a metro like Bombay or Calcutta!

However, the chaste Urdu of Chaudhvin Ka Chand was perfectly in order, since the film was located in Lucknow and all the families were Muslim. Their diction, vocabulary, attire, tehzeeb were perfectly in sync with the story, making the whole film credible. Because of the strict purdah observed by Muslim families, the story of a man falling in love with a woman in such an atmosphere of conservatism made sense. Thus, when we saw Waheeda sleeping without her purdah, we, too, were inspired like Guru Dutt, to burst into the song Chaudhvin ka chaand ho ya aftab ho! In the song Waheeda Rehman looked like a fairy tale princess, quite in contrast to her drab black burqa which she wore when she stepped out into the world.

Also, an interesting bit of trivia for this film is the role of Johnny Walker who got to sing two songs in the film. Guru Dutt increased his dependence on the comedy angle of the film to make sure it gained popularity.

For the first time, we got to hear a Lata Mangeshkar song in a Guru Dutt film. Her exceptional rendition of Badle badle mere sarkar nazar aate hain moved many listeners to tears. Sadly, this was also the only song Lata ever sang for a Guru Dutt production. Geeta was Dutt's first choice, but, by this time, the Guru Dutt and Waheeda romance had become public knowledge. Thus, we have only one song by Geeta in this film. It appears that Geeta refused to sing for Waheeda, and thus, Lata was invited to render the sad song.

When the writer Nasreen Munni Kabir asked Lata Mangeshkar, "Which film directors, for you, have a good understanding of music and how the song can work on screen?" Lata answered, "Guru Dutt and Vijay Anand were the best. Although I did not sing many songs for Guru Dutt, I sang a few songs in his films 'Jaal' and 'Badle badle mere sarkaar' in Chaudhvin Ka Chand—the film was produced under his banner. But I really liked the way he visualised songs. He gave importance and weight to every song line. He was careful about camera angles and how the actor should mime the song to make it work. He performed to 'Ajee dil par hua aisa jaadoo' in Mr. & Mrs. '55 so well. He was so natural. I'll never forget it. Guru Dutt was an intelligent and quiet man. During the recording sessions, he'd sometimes explain the way he intended to film the song, but we communicated, by and large, through SD Burman." Of course, Jaal was not a Guru Dutt film although Guru Dutt did direct it, so for the record it is just this one song in this film, Chaudhvin Ka Chand that has been sung by Lata for Guru Dutt Films Pvt. Ltd.

Incidentally, several people wonder why this film's cinematographer was Nariman Irani and not VK Murthy. This was because at that time Guru Dutt had sent VK Murthy to London to understand the art and science of colour cinematography. He had been assigned to learn it on the sets of the film The Guns of Navarone whose production was underway at that time. Since Irani had been assisting Murthy, he was given the charge while his boss was away. This film was received well and went on to become a Silver Jubilee hit. VK Murthy had returned by this time, so, to celebrate that success, Guru Dutt asked Murthy to put his learning to work by re-shooting two songs in colour. Those songs were the title song, Rafi's Chaudhvin ka chand ho, and the Asha Bhosle rendered Dil ki kahaani rang laayi hai. Both versions of these songs are available for viewing on YouTube.

Amlan Chowdhury, described it perfectly in his piece, "Enchanting Star of All Time", published by The Afternoon Despatch and Courier dated June 27, 2008, "Perhaps one of the very few actors, directors, producers, and writers of Bollywood whose creations are marked by high sensitivity, has poetic touches, and casts electrifying effects on their viewers, Guru Dutt has rolled into filmdom as a person who really can move minds and hearts simultaneously. Whether it was Kaagaz Ke Phool or Chaudhvin Ka Chand, a web was created by him which caught us all…He had an extraordinary acumen to cast magical effects on viewers…his work proved that he not only was able to entertain people but to provoke their thoughts too."

Mohammed Rafi and Shakeel Badayuni received their first Filmfare awards thanks to Guru Dutt's Chaudhvin Ka Chand. More details on the music of this film can be found in the chapter on Ravi later in the book.

13

Sahib Bibi Aur Ghulam

Released in 1962, at Eros Cinema, Mumbai

"Ye film mere liye ek chunauti hai"

– Guru Dutt

Banner: Guru Dutt Films Pvt. Ltd.

Producer: Guru Dutt

Director: Abrar Alvi (All songs were directed by Guru Dutt)

Story: Bimal Mitra's novel, 'Saheb Bibi Golam' (1953)

Screenplay and Dialogues: Bimal Mitra & Abrar Alvi

Music Director: Hemant Kumar

Lyricist: Shakeel Badayuni

Director of Photography: VK Murthy

Editor: YG Chawhan

Cast: Meena Kumari, Guru Dutt, Waheeda Rehman, Rehman, Dhumal, Nazir Hussain, Sapru, Haren Chattopadhyay, Pratima Devi, Sajjan, SN Bannerjee, Ranjit Kumari, Jawahar Kaul, Krishan Dhawan, Minoo Mumtaz and others.

Costumes: Bhanu Athaiya (Assisted by Ramlal Maheshwari)

Dances: Sohanlal and Sudarshan Kumar

Singers: Geeta Dutt, Asha Bhosle, Hemant Kumar and the chorus.

Songs: Total 8. Asha Bhosle-4 solos, Geeta Dutt- 3 solos, Hemant Kumar- 1 solo, and the chorus in 1.

1. Bhanwra bada naadaan, haaye—Asha (Waheeda Rehman)

2. Koi duur se aawaaz de chale aao—Geeta (Meena Kumari)

3. Meri baat rahi mere man mein—Asha (Waheeda Rehman)

4. Meri jaan, o meri jaan—Asha (a courtesan to Sapru)

5. Na jao saiyaan chhuda ke baiyaan—Geeta (Meena Kumari)

6. Piya aiso jeeya mein samaaye—Geeta (Meena Kumari)

7. Saaqiya aaj mujhe neend nahin ayegi—Asha & chorus (Minoo Mumtaz)

8. Saahil ki taraf kashti le—Hemant Kumar (deleted song)

In Guru Dutt's first phase of films, we find him deeply influenced by Hollywood's melodramatic techniques as well as the song and dance musical routines. Despite their difficulties, his characters in these early films find light, hope and joy. They appear to resolve their problems with a sense of enthusiasm. In the second half of his oeuvre, represented by just Pyaasa, we find the dimming of that hope and an increase in pessimism. In his last phase, the joylessness is stark and intensified. In this phase, his cinema increases the black quotient of scenes. Sahib Bibi Aur Ghulam belongs to this last phase of his career.

In Sahib Bibi Aur Ghulam, when we do see light and beauty in Chhoti Bahu's (Meena Kumari's) life, it is not outside of her but within her. Her eyes, her smile, and her kindness radiate outwards and are portrayed to emphasise her beautiful soul in the contrasting sombre and loveless environment she is trapped in. She represents the white to the evil black in this black-and-white film. Her vulnerable beauty is as fragile as a Ching vase perched dangerously close to the table's edge. Her beauty intensifies our foreboding because she is too alone to withstand the onslaught of the socially endorsed ugliness around her. This is the nature of the dark pessimism which reigns over hope in Guru Dutt's last phase. Chhoti Bahu is the victim in a repressive domestic setting. She is pure, but the good and beautiful are damned from the start, while the bad and the ugly continue being destructive.

A departure from his previous escapist film, the super-hit Muslim social drama Chaudhvin Ka Chand (1960), Sahib Bibi Aur Ghulam focuses on the decadent feudalism of 19th century Bengal. The story focuses on the marital life of the zamindar's beautiful wife, Chhoti Bahu, a woman who is neglected and humiliated, despite being a paragon of virtue. She asks only that her healthy and innocent human needs be met, but, instead of getting what she wants, she is spurned with contempt.

As the neglected and abused wife of the spoilt hedonist Chhote Babu (Rehman), Chhoti Bahu attempts to make sense of her marital status in the sequestered and strict confines of a patriarchal environment which places restrictions on the women in the feudal family. The film maps her emotional descent from that of a free girl to that of an abused and neglected slave of a coarse libertine. Imprisoned by orthodoxy, she tries her best to make her marriage work. She attempts to seduce her promiscuous husband. She becomes pathetic in her desperation to win the attention of an amoral man who has neither the patience nor the inclination for her. Chhoti Bahu learns that her husband is too set in his habits to succumb to domesticity or her charms. While he is unworthy of her in almost every way, his boorishness and his libertine lifestyle are truly repugnant. His repulsive self-indulgence extends to spending lavish sums of money to buy the favours of garishly made-up prostitutes/kothewaalis. His life is convoluted: in his perverse universe, he treats his loyal and loving wife with disdain, while he treats cheap prostitutes like queens. He respects the unworthy, which, consequently, makes him unworthy of our respect.

The ethos of the period condoned such dalliances since rich feudal lords were accepted as 'bigde nawabs' entitled to have their 'fun'. Their lack of empathy for those loyal to them, whether they were their underlings or their wives, was considered normal. Essentially,

Chhote Babu was following tradition, 'reet-riwaaj'. It was a hallowed tradition to ape the libertine ways of his promiscuous, self-indulgent forefathers and his elder brother, Majhle Babu (Sapru). This was power at its worst: at home, he would kick the faithful and good, and then go outside and reward the undeserving and ghastly. Society recognised that this was the inevitable consequence of being too rich and powerful for one's own good.

However, feudalism was not unique to India in the period addressed by this film. In many parts of the world, feudalism created such inequality. Not only were the poor hapless, they were often subjected to abuse, violence and exploitation. Whether one looked at the West or the East, the situation was the same.

Let's now look at Satyajit Ray's Jalsaghar, which was released in 1958, four years before Sahib Bibi Aur Ghulam. Jalsaghar has a story with the same background and ethos. A little about the Ray film might throw some light on the subject of landowners and their character flaws and style of living. Jalsaghar, while being a masterpiece in characterisation, is also a classic because of the way it presents the decadent life of a self-obsessed landowner. The desire to continue with one's grandiose lifestyle, even if it resulted in one's downfall, appears to be a theme common to Ray's Jalsaghar and Dutt's Sahib Bibi Aur Ghulam.

This Guru Dutt film, running into 17 reels, was based on a novel by Bimal Mitra and began with the message, 'Thanks to Gaine Brothers of Dhankuria for filming at their residence.' To make the film credible, the film was set in an old, dilapidated palatial structure which represented the crumbling age and was projected as its symbol. The mansion was forty miles away from Calcutta, and five miles away from the border India shares with Bangladesh. The structure belonged to the Gaine family. This mansion was also used to represent the corrosion and downfall of the feudal mindset. There were innumerable problems in restoring the mansion and a lot of time was spent in making it appear authentic. There was no electricity in the structure, but, with some pull, electrical power lines were put in place, without which the film could not be shot. Walls were plastered, tube wells dug. The place went through a complete change so that it would reflect the crumbling nature of the family symbolised by the structure. They created a fountain at the entrance, and some horses were even sourced from Calcutta. Guru Dutt was in considerable stress, expenses were mouthing and not a day's shoot had been done yet. Finally, when it was ready, the shoots had to be done at breakneck speed and everyone had to work long hours, so they would end at 3.30 am and be back to work at 6 am. Abrar Alvi credited Guru Dutt for the success of the shots of the film, especially the one with Sapru at the top of the stairs. Said Alvi "Guru Dutt told me two things. One was to shoot with the third eye that I possessed as the man who had written and recorded the entire film. And the second was to ignore Murthy's laments. He said, 'Murthy ki bilkul nahin sunna, bahut kun-kun karega, but direct him properly and he delivers the goods.' " The choice of this structure and location was so brilliant that it authenticated the film with the solid feel of the period, intensifying the experience of the audience and making it a delight for connoisseurs.

In sum, the film documented the narcissism and amoral permissiveness of rich feudal landowners; it unraveled how their ruthless hedonism imprisoned an innocent woman, robbing her first of her freedom, then her dignity, and, in the end, her very life. The lordly brothers gambled, drank and squandered their wealth on garish, coarse prostitutes who seduced them with song and dance, and who offered their fleeting obedience in exchange for huge sums of money. The ruins of the family, its property and the degradation of the beautiful woman were the inevitable consequences of this reckless amorality.

Here, Guru Dutt repeated his favourite theme of the victimisation of the pure in a corrupt world; about how the powerful misuse their power to exploit those without it. The film draws brilliant character sketches, those of Chhoti Bahu, Chhote Babu, Majhle Babu and Bhootnath.

Heavily influenced by Bengali cinema, Guru Dutt chose the Bengali story in an attempt to capture the evil of the feudal times. Incidentally, the same novel of Bimal Mitra had been filmed in Bengali earlier in 1956, in the film titled Sahib Bibi Golam. Directed by Kartik Chatterjee, that feature had Sumitra Devi playing the role that Meena Kumari played later, while Uttam Kumar played the role of Bhootnath. The Bengali version is regarded as one of the best Bengali films ever made. The resemblance of Sapru in the Hindi film to the outstanding Bengali actor Chhabi Biswas in the Bengali film was no coincidence, Sapru practically looked like Chhabi's brother! On his part, Guru Dutt imitated Uttam Kumar's innocence as Bhootnath. The dances, the atmosphere, the old edifice, the similarities were too many to miss. Where the Hindi film scored over its Bengali counterpart was in the performances of Meena Kumari and Rehman. The tragic relationship between the pathetic Chhoti Bahu and the contemptuous Chhote Babu was remarkably realistic. One wonders if Meena Kumari was playing herself, while Rehman was playing her husband Kamal Amrohi, because it was common knowledge that Amrohi was insufferably dominating and abusive to Meena. This actress's true-to-life portrayal of a woman who adopts desperate means to get her husband's love was superlative. She was soft and kind but her life was pitiable. If one were to look at the message of the film it would not be too far-fetched to conclude that Guru Dutt wanted to show us how evil, when it begins on the journey of self-indulgence, goes on to destroy others, and, finally, it ends up devouring itself.

Sahib Bibi Aur Ghulam also has shades of the Apu trilogy of Satyajit Ray. The Apu trilogy, beginning with Pather Panchali (1955), followed by Aparajito (1956), and culminating with Apur Sansar (1959) also captured the class divide, while showcasing the struggle between the rich and the poor, and the heavy hand of fate that fell on the poor. In the trilogy we see the destruction of the home along with the death of Apu's sister which is caused not by her misdeeds, but by her condition of acute poverty; Nature finds her at the wrong pace and the wrong time. Additionally, his father dies of a high fever, his mother has an illness that wasn't treated and Apu's wife dies in childbirth. Similarly, if one sees these three films of Guru Dutt (Pyaasa, Kaagaz Ke Phool and Sahib Bibi Aur Ghulam) as a trilogy, there is Vijay in Pyaasa being admitted to an insane asylum, there is Suresh in Kaagaz Ke Phool who becomes a failure and gives up, and finally, there is Chhoti Bahu in Sahib Bibi Aur Ghulam who gets murdered.

Guru Dutt's depressive trilogy reflected his personal melancholia, and it signified his battle with depression. He was suicidal right from his youthful days. If one were to ignore his first effort when Dev Anand prevented him from carrying out his wish to kill himself (his mother shared this at a get-together of her community), he had probably attempted suicide thrice. It was during the making of Pyaasa that he attempted suicide for the first time. The second time was when he was shooting Sahib Bibi Aur Ghulam. He took 36 sleeping pills and was admitted to Bombay's Nanavati hospital in a coma. After a couple of days he came around. Arguably his third effort, in 1964, roughly a year after he had gone to showcase Sahib Bibi Aur Ghulam in Berlin, sadly, was successful. The three films, Pyaasa, Kaagaz Ke Phool and Sahib Bibi Aur Ghulam, coincided with these three highly creative stages and revealed their destructive consequences on his psyche. He was engaged in showing us situations that were too difficult for his protagonists, and they, tragically, became too difficult for him as well.

The idea in Sahib Bibi Aur Ghulam was that the world of a poor woman was completely different from that of the privileged men who were landlords. Although that 19th-century world had begun to disappear when Bimal Mitra wrote his novel, the microcosm of the feudal families headed by two libertine brothers made for a fascinating watch, especially since we could see how, as a woman, Chhoti Bahu was silenced by patriarchal double standards.

The story of Chhoti Bahu who was married to Chhote Babu was tragic. Coming from a lower-class background, she was chosen as the bride of the Chhote Babu because she was beautiful. Earlier, in Pather Panchali, Satyajit Ray showed us how a sweet daughter was treated as second grade when compared with her younger brother because of her gender. Ray showed us how often her needs were ignored, but that, she was, nevertheless, expected to perform her duties cheerfully. Her life was devoid of joy, she was even denied education while her younger brother was sent off to school. It is the girl who must suffer for society's biases and traditions; this was the imbalance in society which reinforced patriarchal stereotypes. Ray's little girl paid with her life, and so did Dutt's Chhoti Bahu. They were both victims of a misogynistic and patriarchal mindset.

Sahib Bibi Aur Ghulam owes a lot to VK Murthy's brilliant capture of the era and the inhabitants of the mansion throughout the film. From the first scene where the shy Bhootnath sees Chhoti Bahu's feet first (because he dare not raise his eyes), to all the scenes connected with Meena Kumari, Rehman and Sapru, the film is a cinematographer's delight. Yet, the humble VK Murthy credited his success to Guru Dutt. He told Govind Nihalani, "Guru Dutt was the person who pushed me to do anything I wanted. He wouldn't stop me from doing whatever I wanted to do. That's the main thing. If a person wants to do some creative work, but he doesn't have support from the main people, the opportunity, and the equipment, then he can't create. Therefore, don't give me the credit. That credit should go to the persons who have encouraged me and given me the equipment I wanted." Sapru was brilliantly projected through the film as a person who hardly ever spoke but his body language and face spoke for him. If that is not the success of VK Murthy, Guru Dutt and Abrar Alvi in the film, what is? Luckily, today we can watch this film on OTT platforms and pause it from time to time. We see, more often than not, that almost every frame of this film is aesthetically presented and is a photographer's delight.

Sahib Bibi Aur Ghulam was not much of a commercial success because of its stark realism and the dark hopelessness of the macabre reality of Chhoti Bahu. Also, the audience was uncomfortable seeing Meena Kumari as an alcoholic. This is because, till then, cine-goers had placed her on a lofty and pristine pedestal. What was more scandalising was the fact that she expressed her wish for sexual intimacy. In the early '60s, a woman did not overtly seek fulfilment through sex. But Guru Dutt was showing Chhoti Bahu as a normal woman, wanting her husband to physically desire her. Her efforts to seduce him also did not go down well with the uneasy patriarchal mindset of the audience. The mindset that Guru

Dutt was attempting to portray as negative in the film was the very mindset that proved to be the stumbling block in the film's acceptance. After Pyaasa and Kaagaz Ke Phool, Guru Dutt was again trying to show the audience the mirror. While he succeeded with Pyaasa, with Kaagaz Ke Phool and Sahib Bibi Aur Ghulam he absolutely did not.

The Casting

Originally Guru Dutt had decided to cast a beautiful young woman named Chhaya Arya as Chhoti Bahu. Chhaya and her husband Jitendra Arya, the ace photographer, were living in London those days. She was working with the BBC at that time. Guru Dutt, then on a visit to England, met the couple and offered her the role of Chhoti Bahu. But when his friend, script-writer Abrar Alvi saw her photographs, he was not impressed. Guru Dutt had his heart set on Chhaya Arya, so he persuaded the couple to move from London to Bombay. After they moved, Dutt arranged a photo shoot for Chhaya. "One look at those stills and after a couple of rehearsals with her, I was convinced Chhaya would be completely miscast," noted Abrar. "She was a beautiful girl, fair with chiselled features and a good voice, but I needed a face that mirrored the 'mamta' (love) she felt for mankind, despite all the trials she had endured." Then they thought of casting Waheeda. But when they tried to see her in those heavy sarees, Guru Dutt laughed and said "Tum to chuha lagti ho". So they settled on Meena Kumari who had always wanted to do a Bengali woman's role.

However, Chhaya Arya told this writer why she was dropped. It appeared that initially the role had been offered to Meena Kumari but she wanted to be paid a higher sum. Then the role went to Chhaya who moved from London with bag and baggage to set up residence in Bombay. One day, when Chhaya was in the studio rehearsing for her role, Meena Kumari, visiting the studio for another shoot, ran into Jitendra who had come to meet his wife. Since they knew each other, they chatted and Meena learnt from him that the role of Chhoti Bahu had been assigned to Chhaya. The very next day Meena Kumari reached out to Guru Dutt, agreeing to the earlier amount that Guru Dutt had offered her. Chhaya Arya was a newcomer while Meena Kumari was an already established popular actress; also, Meena had been his first choice from the word go. Additionally, her name would draw both film financiers and audiences. The delighted Guru Dutt signed her on after her belated acceptance. Chhaya Arya was dropped, Meena Kumari was in. As Abrar once said, Guru Dutt could be ruthless and he would spare nobody when it came to his art. He simply dropped Chhaya who wondered why she was not being called anymore. Guru Dutt dropped her without so much as an apology.

Guru Dutt had first chosen Biswajit for the role of Bhootnath because Dutt saw his performance in the play based on the same Bimal Mitra book. Biswajit, on his part, was willing but he did not want an exclusive contract with Guru Dutt Films, so he did not sign on for the project. Guru Dutt next chose Shashi Kapoor for the role. As it turned out, Shashi Kapoor arrived three hours late for their first meeting. Not only did Guru Dutt find this disrespectful, he also found it unprofessional behaviour. He felt it was a sign that Shashi Kapoor would delay them during the rest of the shoots. In the end, Guru Dutt acquiesced to his wife Geeta Dutt who wanted her husband Guru to play Bhootnath. After Pyaasa, this was, once again, a role he played when he failed to get a suitable actor to play the role of the male protagonist.

For the director's job, according to Abrar Alvi, Guru Dutt had first approached Satyen Bose, then Nitin Bose, before finally persuading Abrar Alvi to take on the responsibility. When Abrar directed the film, he felt Waheeda Rehman was miscast as Jaba. Of the five Guru Dutt Productions in which Guru Dutt and Waheeda had acted together, in three of them, her role was of the supporting actress, this being her last. This was also the last film in which they worked together because their relationship had come to an end and even for the last scene that remained to be shot, Abrar had to beg Waheeda to turn up for the shoot. She obliged but only after several conditions were met.

VK Murthy's creative cinematography, combined with Guru Dutt's vision, had some excellent shots of Meena Kumari, who arguably, never looked more beautiful. 'Chiaroscuro' in art is characterised by strong contrasts between light and dark as they affect a whole composition. VK Murthy gave us an excellent example of chiaroscuro in the song Saaqiya aaj mujhe, sung by Asha Bhosle and the chorus. Minoo Mumtaz as the dancer was shown in light, in stark contrast to the other dancers who were in darkness. All the bright light fell on her form while she danced, while the forms of the supporting dancers were seen in darkness. The contrast made the song enticing and mysterious, enhancing the allure of the dance. VK Murthy, the first Dadasaheb Phalke award-winning cinematographer, was the genius behind this visual spectacle. The hand-held fans or 'pankhas' and the huge sweeping ceiling pankha add to this song's visual, zamindari splendour. In a meeting with a few film lovers, VK Murthy shared what had happened about this filming. There had been heavy rains in Bombay on the day the shoot was to take place; the selected dancers could not make it to the studio, and alternate dancers who replaced the original girls, however, had not been photogenic. The camera could not possibly focus on their faces. Then Murthy had improvised: he had chosen to keep their faces in the darkness, which, as luck would have it, enhanced the impact of the shot. Their faces were shrouded in darkness, so the audience saw only their form, while the focus remained on the faces and expressions of the beautiful Minoo Mumtaz. It was this creative genius of VK Murthy to think on his feet and come up with brilliant solutions that Guru Dutt respected and admired.

Sensuousness and Self-destructive Decadence

The two female characters of the film are polar opposites of each other. Meena Kumari who plays Chhoti Bahu is a melancholic and unfulfilled wife who pines hopelessly for her unavailable and decadent zamindar husband 'Chhote Sarkar', played by Rehman.

She uses desperate ploys such as the magical 'Mohini Sindoor' to rescue herself from her dilemma. Waheeda Rehman, playing the modern Jaba, on the other hand, is the playful and talkative daughter of Suvinay Babu (Nazir Hussain), a member of the Brahmo Samaj movement. While Guru Dutt has shown Chhoti Bahu as a slow, buxom and full-bodied woman, Jaba is contrasted with her, she is thin and sprightly; Chhoti Bahu appears in brocaded or heavy saris while Jaba is shown with plain cotton Bengali saris worn by ordinary women. Chhoti Bahu's way of talking is sensuous while Jaba speaks in plain language without any overtones to her speech. Guru Dutt often contrasted his women in films, as can be seen also when he contrasted Meena with Gulabo in Pyaasa. Waheeda Rehman, it appears, was very keen to have a scene where the two women meet in this film, but Guru Dutt, after some thought, did not accept the idea since it would not be congruent with the story. One wonders how that scene would have played out. Perhaps, Guru Dutt already suspected that Waheeda would be eclipsed by the beautiful and seductive Meena Kumari in her brocade sarees and heavy jewellery. For certain, it would not have served Waheeda Rehman well because Meena Kumari's character was truly the most overpowering one of all in the movie.

Sadly, the existential angst Guru Dutt portrayed, was in tandem with his personal life as well, where the outcome was equally distressing. His passion and romance with Geeta Dutt had ebbed; now there was distrust and anger that ripped them apart.

For Meena Kumari, the role of Chhoti Bahu was a career-high. She was now placed firmly at the top, along with Nargis who had won millions of hearts in Mother India, and Nutan whose performance in Bandini was par excellence. A few years later, Suchitra Sen rose to the challenge with her double role in Mamta, and Waheeda Rehman who was superlative as Rosie in Guide.

The audience knew that a Guru Dutt film required a lot of mental engagement. One was never the same after seeing a sad film from Dutt's second and third phases. Yet, because the pain was depicted so beautifully, we kept the films close to our hearts.

That was us, the audience. But what about insiders? What did they think? When Raj Kapoor saw the film with Guru Dutt, he praised him effusively. However, with tears in his eyes, he followed it up with, "But will it run?" He couldn't have been more on the ball.

The crumbling structure that Guru Dutt had chosen for the film and in which he perfected the *mise en scene*, symbolised his confused and chaotic personal life as well. According to Abrar Alvi, he kept directing and interfering in the scenes which involved Waheeda, since he was very possessive about her. Abrar Alvi complained that Guru Dutt would have "the final say on decisions pertaining to camera placements, shots, close-ups. The cameraman would merely follow his instructions."

After the Release

In 1963, Dutt and Waheeda had grown apart. Guru Dutt, Abrar Alvi, and Waheeda Rehman attended the 13th Berlin Film Festival in June 1963. Meena Kumari could not attend it because her husband did not want to let her out of his sight. Since many had found this film a bit too long, it was truncated and shown on June 27, 1963. The thin 25-member audience didn't grasp the Indian ethos; it especially could not understand why Chhoti Bahu could not just leave her abusive husband. The film failed to impress them. A little over a year later on October 10, 1964, Guru Dutt was found dead.

In an interview, Waheeda Rehman said that she met Guru Dutt last in Berlin when this film was screened. She noted that it was her lucky day since a few good things happened to her. For the first time in her life, she had watched TV on that day. Then she had seen John F Kennedy, the President of the United States, from the roof of a cafe, and in the evening she had attended the screening of the film at the festival, which was followed by a banquet too.

The next day Guru Dutt left for Bombay, while Waheeda left for Paris where, accompanied by her sister Saeeda, she stayed for two days and then went to London. This was her first trip abroad.

On this very trip, Guru Dutt, Satyajit Ray, BR Chopra, and Abrar Alvi were also photographed together in Berlin. Later BR Chopra said some shocking things about Guru Dutt, including that he was heavily drunk on the flight home. Recalled Chopra, "That man, Guru Dutt, drank from Berlin to Bombay while keeping all to himself in a corner seat. We knew all about Waheeda having told him, point-blank that she had made up her mind about him and that was it. Guru Dutt was heading towards turning into a mental and physical wreck…I instinctively knew that it was the beginning of the end." In his book on Dutt, Bimal Mitra wrote, "Guru Dutt used up all the sleeping pills that he had carried with him to Berlin. He didn't sleep for the next four nights. He said to me, 'I think I will go mad' ".

In his book on Guru Dutt, Bimal Mitra has recorded his conversation with Geeta Dutt which he had with her on January 1, 1961, the day of the pooja and mahurat of Sahib Bibi Aur Ghulam. He was surprised to see her there, but Guru Dutt said he had specially called Geeta to help Waheeda tie the sari the Bengali way. When they were alone and Geeta was sure that Guru was not nearby, she told Bimal Mitra that she had asked Guru Dutt not to do the film because it was their life on celluloid. Essentially Meena Kumari was playing Geeta, Rehman was playing Guru Dutt, and the nautch girl Minoo Mumtaz was playing Waheeda.

Incidentally, Guru Dutt, who believed in God, had been very keen to adhere to the original idea in the story which had about a hundred pages with references to Swami Vivekananda and his spirituality. However, since the agnostic Abrar Alvi was directing the film, he did not want to include the Swami Vivekananda angle.

Sahib Bibi Aur Ghulam met with mixed reactions from the audience at that time. Film historian Firoze Rangoonwala reported that it performed badly, but not as badly as Kaagaz Ke Phool. Meena Kumari excelled as Chhoti Bahu and received Filmfare's Best Actress award for her performance in the film. Meena Kumari had gone so deep into her role that she had written in her diary, in exasperation,

"I am sick to death of Chhoti Bahu!" Incidentally, in that year, Meena Kumari was nominated as Best Actress for three films, so the finalist was her, whether she won it for Sahib Bibi Aur Ghulam or Aarti or Main Chup Rahungi. Abrar Alvi received the Best Director Award and VK Murthy received the Best Cinematographer award too. The film won the Best Feature Film award as well. Waheeda Rehman was nominated as Best Supporting Actress but the award was won by Shashikala for her role in Aarti. Rehman was nominated as Best Supporting Actor but he lost to Mehmood who won it for his role in Dil Tera Deewana.

It was much later that appreciation for this film intensified and it is today regarded as one of the three best films made by Guru Dutt.

14

Baharen Phir Bhi Aayengi

Released on Friday, September 9, 1966

The film has a posthumous tribute to Guru Dutt who passed away on October 10, 1964.

Banner: Guru Dutt (Atma Ram).

Producer: Atma Ram

Director: Shahid Lateef (Assistants: Shyam, Govind and Shinde)

Story/Screenplay/Dialogues: Abrar Alvi

Director of Photography: KG Prabhakar

Editor: YG Chawhan

Cast: Mala Sinha, Dharmendra, Tanuja, Rehman, Deven Verma, Johnny Walker, Madhavi, Badri Prasad, Moni Chatterjee, Mumtaz Begum, Geetanjali, Radheshyam and others.

Composer: OP Nayyar (Assistants: Sebastian and GS Kohli)

Lyricists: Aziz Kashmiri, Anjaan, Kaifi Azmi, SH Bihari and Shewan Rizvi (the last was not credited in the film, but several logs, including the generally accurate Hindi Film Geet Kosh Volume 4 credits him for song no.3 mentioned below)

Singers: Asha Bhosle, Mohammed Rafi and Mahendra Kapoor

Songs Total: 6. Mohammed Rafi-3, Asha Bhosle-4 and Mahendra Kapoor-1.

1.   Aap ke haseen rukh pe—lyricist Anjaan. Rafi (Dharmendra)

2.   Badal jaaye agar maali—lyricist Kaifi Azmi. Mahendra (Dharmendra)

3.   Dil to pehle hi se madhosh—lyricist Shewan Rizvi. Asha and Rafi (Tanuja & Dharmendra)

4.   Koi keh de keh de zamaane se jaake—lyricist Aziz Kashmiri. Asha (Tanuja)

5.   Suno, suno, Miss Chatterjee—lyricist Aziz Kashmiri. Rafi and Asha (Johnny Walker and Madhavi)

6.   Woh hanske mile humse—lyricist SH Bihari. Asha (Mala Sinha)

The film's story was a version of the earlier 1937 New Theatres Hindi film called President. The story is a love triangle, or rather a love quadrangle, set in a Calcutta newspaper office (in the Hindi version of President the setting was a cotton mill). The fourth angle of the quadrangle was the character portrayed by Rehman who was in love with Mala Sinha who was bin love with Dharmendra who was, in turn, in love with Tanuja. At the end of it all, Rehman's love remained unrequited because Mala Sinha had to die, permitting the two lovers, Dharmendra and Tanuja, to unite.

Guru Dutt had completed filming 11 reels of the film before he died in October 1964. He had the lead role in the film but his unexpected death put a brake on the project. The film was re-shot after his death. Yet, some scenes which were shot during Guru Dutt's lifetime, like those in the office, or some parts of the song Aap ke haseen rukh pe appear to have been included in the re-shot film.

The film was later re-shot with Dharmendra who replaced Guru Dutt in the lead role. Earlier in 1958, the owners of Filmfare magazine had set up a competition to discover new talent and called it the Filmfare New Face Award. Dharmendra was one of the six finalists. (The sponsors of the talent contest were Guru Dutt and Bimal Roy, who were also the main jury members. The event received an overwhelming response). The six finalists were brought to Bombay and lodged in a home. But before the finals Bimal Roy became unwell, so Abrar Alvi replaced him and screened the six along with Guru Dutt. They selected Dharmendra since he was clearly the best. It was Bimal Roy who cast him later in Bandini.

Because Guru Dutt had been one of the selectors, it is said that Dharmendra had felt obliged to him for having selected him. Dharmendra accepted the role because he thought he had to return the favour to the genius even if the filmmaker was no longer alive. Incidentally, the role had earlier been offered to Dev Anand and Joy Mukherjee; both had refused the assignment. But it was filmmaker Arjun Hingorani who signed Dharmendra on first, offering him the lead role in Dil Bhi Tera Hum Bhi Tere which had the famous Mukesh song Mujh ko is raat ki tanhai mein awaaz na do.

Baharen Phir Bhi Aayengi was being ghost-directed by Abrar Alvi. When Guru Dutt was alive, it was well known that Shahid Lateef was the film's director only in name. After Guru Dutt's death, his brother Atma Ram took charge of the film.

When Guru Dutt heard the songs that OP Nayyar had composed for the film, he remarked that OP Nayyar composed not just music, he composed feelings! Originally, it was SD Burman who had been signed up for the film's music. He had already composed a couple of songs when he fell seriously ill. These songs were not used for the film since the project was then handed over to OP Nayyar. But one of those SD Burman songs was re-used in Dev Anand's film Jewel Thief. That song was re-jigged and made into Ye dil no hota bechaara and recorded by Kishore, while the original version in Baharen was rendered by Rafi. This tune was heavily influenced by Colonel Bogie's Theme, i.e., the title song of The Bridge on River Kwai. The lyrics of the Baharen Phir Bhi Aayengi song were Koi na tera saathi ho, dagar kahin bhi jaati ho, ae dil ke raahi chal akela, chal akela chal!

So many regulars were missing from this Guru Dutt film, there was no Guru Dutt, no Geeta Dutt and no VK Murthy either. This is the only film in which Geeta has no song to sing despite the fact that the music had been chosen during Guru Dutt's lifetime. While Geeta and Guru had begun to live separately, OP Nayyar was keen that only Asha sing his compositions.

Unfortunately, it was while this film was being shot that Guru Dutt took an overdose of sleeping pills and combined them with alcohol, which led to his death. Tragically, the death scene of Mala Sinha in the film was being discussed and shot at that time, where a depressed Mala Sinha dies of a broken heart. Known to take his films too seriously, Guru Dutt, too, was morose and his last conversation with Abrar Alvi reflected his despondent mindset. Mala Sinha, who was supposed to shoot that day, was held up in Madras and could not return in time for the shoot.

On her part, Mala Sinha was all praise for Guru Dutt. In a radio interview, she remarked, "He was an actor, a director, a genius!" After all, it was Guru Dutt who had given her a role nobody can quite forget, the role of Meena in Pyaasa, the beautiful woman who spurns love for wealth.

Now that we have arrived at the last film produced by Guru Dutt, we see the tragedy of a protagonist when he loves too much and his love is unrequited. The hero or heroine suffers from this tragic flaw, and excessively seeks the love of another, much like an alcoholic needs excessive alcohol, and ends up paying the price of this excess. Such a price can be death. For example, in Kaagaz Ke Phool his ego and his obsessive love for Shanti destroy his career and he succumbs to death. In Chaudhvin Ka Chand, it is Rehman who pays the price (by committing suicide) of pinning his hopes on a beautiful woman who he discovers is his best friend's wife; in Sahib Bibi Aur Ghulam, it is Meena Kumari as Chhoti Bahu who loves the wrong man and suffers death because of it. Her husband is unfaithful, but it is she, the innocent who must be killed. In Baharen Phir Bhi Aayengi, it is Mala Sinha who pays the price for loving someone who loves her sister. Her heart cannot stand the pain, and she dies of a broken heart.

Although the film was shot with Dharmendra in the lead, somehow the story didn't ring true. The audience did not find it interesting and gave it a thumbs down. The direction of the film was poor in parts for which Shahid Lateef and Abrar Alvi were responsible. Especially badly directed was the death scene of Mala Sinha, which was terribly artificial in its melodrama. Such a scene would have made Guru Dutt turn in his grave!

The film did not have one or two lyricists, it had five! Never in a Guru Dutt film had there been more than two. All the songs, nevertheless, are stunning creations, with the waltzing Aap ke haseen rukh pe, being its most popular melody.

There was a tendency to have a romantic waltz in many of Guru Dutt's films, so Aap ke haseen rukh pe was added in the film. His lucky mascot, Johnny Walker was also found playing his usual impish self. He was given stunning lyrics by Aziz Kashmiri in the irresistible Suno, suno, Miss Chatterjee…the English words in the song made it even more delicious and comic…

Suno, suno, Miss Chatterjee, mere dil ka matter jee

Calcuttewaali rooth gayi kyun, baat nahin ye better jee!'

…

Ban-than ke kahaan chali ho fifty ki raftaar se

Dil waala koi kood na jaaye chalti motor-car se!

Chalte chalte padti jao dil ka open letter jee!

Probably the most tragic and also most ironic song in the film is the Asha rendered Woh hanske mile humse, hum pyaar samajh baithe. It was almost as if it had shades of his personal life in it, as if Guru Dutt had mistaken someone's shallow affection for him for romance. SH Bihari underlines her sorry plight when he writes, "Aisi to na thi kismat apna bhi koi hota, apna bhi koi hota…kyun khud ko mohabbat ka haqdaar samajh baithe?"

The deep philosophy in Mahendra Kapoor's song Badal jaaye agar maali is rich both in melody and thought. The lines, Hawaaien aag bhadkaayen, fizaaen zeher barsaayen, baharen phir bhi aati hain, baharen phir bhi aayengi…The film ends with a couple of initial lines sung by a teary Asha Bhosle of the same song, singing Badal jaaye agar maali, chaman hota nahin khaali, baharen phir bhi aati hain, baharen phir bhi aayengi…

Somehow, the note of positivity that was struck by this song didn't resonate with the despondent Guru Dutt who was going through a lot of turmoil in his personal life. He even felt he was losing his mind, something he shared with Abrar Alvi a few hours before he overdosed.

15

Guru Dutt in Films Produced in Madras

As a young man, Guru Dutt had travelled a great deal, going to places like Bangalore, Calcutta, and Almora, to finally settle down in Bombay. Later, he would journey to several parts of India as a successful director and producer, flying a few times to Europe as well. In the last couple of years of his life, Guru Dutt spent a great deal of time in Madras, making visits there from his base in Bombay.

The Madras film industry had an excellent reputation for its professionalism and was also well known for its prompt and generous compensation to film artists. Because of this, Madras attracted many film stars from Bombay's cinema world. After Kaagaz Ke Phool's monumental failure dnd the tepid response to Sahib Bibi Aur Ghulam, Guru Dutt accepted acting roles from Madras where he starred in a few Hindi films, some of which were remakes of already successful Tamil or Telugu films.

Bharosa, released in September 1963, was Guru Dutt's first film from Madras. It was released a year before he died. The film was made under the banner of Vasu Films and was produced by N Vasudeva Menon, while the director was K Shankar. The music was by Ravi while Rajinder Krishan wrote both the lyrics and dialogues for the film. Guru Dutt was cast as the love interest of Asha Parekh who sang the unforgettable Lata Mangeshkar song, Woh dil kahaan se laaoon.

The composer Ravi was then known in Madras as 'Bombay Ravi' because he composed many extremely popular songs for Tamil films. He had a wide, committed fan following in the South. Working on this film was easy for Guru Dutt because neither was his role demanding nor was he the director. Unlike in his own films, there weren't innumerable re-takes; most shots were done in a take or two. The entire crew was professional and punctual, which resulted in improving the quality of the cinema. However, the film received mixed reviews, some critics praised it while others found that it lacked depth in its narration. Still, it was successful with audiences. Bombay Ravi continued to compose music for many more Madras films, and, with every film, he cemented his place in the Tamil film industry.

An interesting anecdote is shared by the author Sathya Saran. In her interview with Abrar Alvi, the latter revealed that he, Guru Dutt and Ravi would relax together in Guru Dutt's room, drinking, chatting and having dinner together. One day, the composer ordered three Chicken a la Kievs to be sent to the three of them via room service. When Abrar Alvi woke up from his drunken sleep the next morning, he discovered a woman sleeping in his bed! Then he realised that the chicken was not a dish but a woman who was to service each of them. He could not recall what Guru Dutt did with his Chicken a la Kiev though. The strange thing is, since Abrar's name does not feature in any of the Madras films Guru Dutt worked in, why was he there in the first place? Perhaps Guru Dutt was in the habit of taking his buddy Abrar along for out-station shoots to help with the dialogues.

Bahurani was next in 1964. It was a remake of the Telugu and Tamil films Ardhangi and Pennin Perumai respectively, both being based on the novel Swayamsiddha by Manilal Banerjee. Ardhangi was released in 1955 in Telugu and in 1956 was released the Tamil Pennin Perumai. The music for Ardhangi was composed by B Narasimha Rao and Master Venu, while the latter film had music by PM Rao, A Rama Rao and Master Venu as its composers. In Ardhangi the cast was headed by Savithri, A Nageswara Rao and K Jaggaiah, while in the latter film, the cast had Savithri, Gemini

Ganesan and Sivaji Ganesan. The same roles were later played in the Hindi film by Mala Sinha, Guru Dutt and Feroz Khan in Bahurani.

1964 was also the year that Guru Dutt left this world. In Bahurani, which was released in January 1964, ten months before his death, Guru Dutt put in a brilliant performance in the role of a mentally challenged son who is completely cured of his condition through the commitment and love of his good wife played to perfection by Mala Sinha. The film was directed by T Prakash Rao, and produced by M Azam, with dialogues by Yogesh, while the music was composed by C Ramchandra with lyrics by Sahir Ludhianvi. Bahurani was one of the two Guru Dutt starrers (the other being Sahib Bibi Aur Ghulam) in which Rafi did not figure in the singers' list.

Later, in the same year, 1964, came Suhagan. Producer AL Srinivasan had signed Guru Dutt for the lead role in the film, which was the Hindi version of his Tamil hit Sarada. Although the director KS Gopalakrishnan was tense about working with Guru Dutt, the highly acclaimed director, his fears were soon laid to rest. Guru Dutt who was then staying at the five-star Hotel Ashoka, reassured him that he had come there as an actor and not as a director and that since KS Gopalakrishnan was his director, he was duty-bound to follow his instructions to the T, without any ego. The humility in both, Guru Dutt's words and tone, dispelled all Gopalakrishnan's misgivings. Moved to tears by his modesty, the director hugged Guru Dutt.

Soon they became good friends, so much so that Guru Dutt was even invited to spend a week fishing with Gopalakrishnan in Malliam, his village. Guru Dutt was extremely fond of fishing right from his youth so this was an enjoyable week for him. The film, which was certified for viewing on Dec 3, 1964, a couple of months after Guru Dutt's demise, began with the dedication, "I humbly dedicate the film Suhagan to the everlasting memory of late Shri Guru Dutt, my friend and your favourite—AL Srinivasan."

The film starred Guru Dutt, Mala Sinha, Feroz Khan and Nazir Hussain, among others. The music was composed by Madan Mohan, while the story, screenplay and direction were by KS Gopalakrishnan. Since the film had neither great production values nor an exceptional narrative technique, it was doomed to failure. Worse, Guru Dutt looked haggard and over the hill in a few scenes, and the film's tragic ending also turned people off. Also, the idea of a woman's remarriage was ahead of its time, especially if the reason was that the marriage had not been consummated.

At this point, Guru became interested in a story by Silappadhikaram and took back with him a translated script titled Madhavi for a future film project. He must have been far from suicidal because he was preparing himself for a fresh project. Meanwhile, AL Srinivasan, the producer, praised Guru Dutt, saying that, unlike other Bombay stars, this actor was always punctual and readily acceded to the suggestions of the film's producer and director.

AL Srinivasan's daughter-in-law, Jayanthi Kannappan, revealed that on the last day of his shooting for this film, Guru Dutt requested the director to take several different shots of his, in case the need for such shots arose later. His commitment to work and the project was admirable. While working with them, Guru Dutt was like them, a true professional.

Suhagan, which was released a few months after Guru Dutt left this world, was advertised as Guru Dutt's 'last and best' film. One wonders what must have been running through Guru Dutt's mind at the time the film was being made. He could have been conflicted in those days: on the one hand, he was preparing himself for a new project for the future, on the other hand, aware of his tendency to despair and get suicidal, he did not want to leave the makers of Suhagan in the lurch. That may explain his need to take the additional shots mentioned above. After all, even when he was an actor, he was empathising with the producer and director, having been one himself for so many years.

Guru Dutt's Family and Friends

1. Geeta Dutt

2. Arun Dutt

3. Dev Anand

4. Abrar Alvi

5. VK Murthy

6. Waheeda Rehman

7. Bimal Mitra

8. Raj Khosla

9. Johnny Walker

10. Rehman

1

Geeta Dutt

(November 23, 1930-July 20, 1972)

"To rehne do, aur kabhi poochho mat ki main unhappy kyun hoon. Zindagi to yunhi kat jayegee--bas kaam kiye jao… mujhe sirf do cheezen pyaari hain, ek mera kaam aur doosri tum…"

The writer of these emotional words was Guru Dutt. In his letter to Geeta Roy dated August 21, 1951, he spelt out to his sweetheart that only two things really mattered to him: his work and Geeta.

To attempt to understand Guru Dutt, his life and his work is no easy task, yet one catches a few glimpses of his personality through his relationship with Geeta and through the letters he wrote to her before and during their tempestuous marriage. That he was depressed often becomes clear when one watches his later films or when one reads his letters to her. The gloom that Guru Dutt projected in his films came naturally to him, it was seeded in his conflicted soul. In his films of Phase 1, Guru Dutt used the joy he felt during the start of his cinematic career and the happiness he experienced after he got married. When the darkness began to overshadow their relationship he observed it, understood it, and represented it in his cinema in Phases 2 and 3. The artist in him was like an alchemist, who quite often, turned the base metal of his life-experiences into cinematic gold.

What drew Geeta and Guru apart? Why could they neither live together nor away from each other? Why was their relationship so painful and tempestuous that both of them resorted to self-destructive methods? Let's laser in.

Geeta Dutt was born on November 23, 1930, in Faridpur, now in Bangladesh. Her father, Devendranath Roy Chowdhury, was a wealthy landowner. In the early '40s they left their properties and moved first to Calcutta then to Assam, to finally settle in Bombay. She was one of ten children and she was a musical child. One day, when he was passing below her Dadar home, music composer Hanuman Prasad overheard the 15-year old teenager Geeta Roy sing. He was impressed, knocked on her door, and offered her a singing assignment for his three films, Bhakt Prahlad, Nai Maa and Rasili (all 1946 films).

When composer SD Burman heard her sing the Bhakta Prahlad song, he signed her on for Do Bhai (1947), in which she sang the hit Mera sundar sapna beet gaya, and also Yaad karoge yaad karoge ik din humko yaad karoge. She had other songs in this feature too, like Humen chhod piya kis desh gaye. All these songs became very popular. After this, she sang for several Hindi films before she met Guru Dutt. She had arrived.

Geeta Roy met Guru Dutt during the recording of Tadbeer se bigdi hui taqdeer bana de for the Navketan film Baazi (1951). Guru fell in love with her immediately. They began seeing each other.

Since they lived close to each other (he lived in Matunga which was near her home in Dadar, two miles away), she often dropped in at his home to visit him and his family.

But although Guru Dutt had been crazy about Geeta, she had been unsure of marrying him. It is said that her family was reluctant because Guru Dutt was neither rich nor famous, while she was already established in her career as a successful singer and she was very rich. She was conflicted for another reason too. In an article in Mumbai Mirror (November 23, 2018), writer Roshmila Bhattacharya wrote that Geeta's family had been insisting that she choose a Bengali suitor. Finally, one day, after two long years of waiting, an exasperated Guru Dutt took her to the Haji Malang shrine near Bombay and asked her to decide. There she said yes to him. They married in her mother's home on May 26, 1953. Their marriage was attended by several friends which included Dev Anand, Smriti Biswas, Lata Mangeshkar, and Talat Mehmood.

For three years, things were wonderful.

In a 2020 interview to Seniorstoday, Guru Dutt's sister Lalita Lajmi shared, "After almost three years of rendezvous, when Guru got some success he asked for her hand in marriage. They bought a house in Pali Hill and were so much in love. A happy couple, working together, hosting dinner parties. They had two beautiful sons. Their first-born child, Tarun, was born on the same day as Guru, 9th July and Arun, the second-born on the 10th, so Geeta always celebrated the birthday of all three together. Those were their happy days. As time passed, Guru became more and more engrossed in his work. He would stay back at the studio working late. Geeta, on the other hand, would wait for him and this became a usual thing. The distance between the couple began to grow, he kept busy at the sets and she just kept herself busy with friends. The days Geeta didn't have a recording she would catch up with her friends over cocktails. Guru began spending more time on the sets with his heroines, and rumours got out. The house that was once filled with laughter began getting populated by insecurities. Night after night of verbal arguments and loud fights—Geeta would often fight and pack up with the children to her mother's house. Helpless and lonely, Guru would ring me up, crying, asking us (my mother and me) to come right away. My husband would drive us to Guru's bungalow in Pali Hill. We would spend the night there and would leave the next morning when things looked better. Guru was very close to our mother but, like me, he was an introvert. He never expressed his emotions. He was always quiet, always living in his mind. He never said there were problems, he never said he was sad, he never said anything. As time passed the environment of their house became distressful – the fights grew. Geeta took to alcohol and Guru got into depression, and this cut the already frail thread between them. At the end they got separated."

Much has been written about the Guru Dutt-Waheeda Rehman affair, Abrar Alvi confided as much to Sathya Saran when she interviewed him for her book on Guru Dutt. Their relationship became common knowledge, but neither of the two infatuated stars let thoughts of Geeta and their two sons deter them.

If we are to believe Abrar Alvi in Saran's book, Waheeda Rehman's sister's husband Rauf attempted to rush Guru Dutt into an Islamic marriage. Sathya Saran wrote, "A strange incident happened during the shooting of Sahib Bibi Aur Ghulam. Waheeda was sure of her status as a practising Muslim. She was also sure that she would marry only a Muslim." Abrar Alvi then told Sathya Saran, "Rauf, in fact, went to the extent of announcing it at the Jama Masjid in Bombay. It was a Friday, and at namaz time there was quite a gathering of the devout there. Taking the opportunity, Rauf declared publicly, 'Listen, my friends, there's good news. The famous director Guru Dutt is going to become a Muslim and marry my sister-in-law Waheeda.'" In India, polygamy is permitted to Muslim men while to Hindu men it is not. Guru Dutt was a Hindu while Waheeda was a Muslim. The idea was for him to convert to Islam and then marry her after that religious conversion. There would be no need to divorce Geeta or even consult with her if he converted. Guru Dutt was horrified, he panicked at the turn of events. He turned to Abrar Alvi to rescue him from the tight spot. "Rauf drove up in a Fiat with a friend. He stomped up to us and said, 'Get him now, I need to speak with him.' An altercation ensued. But once he realised he was beaten and had no leg to stand on, Rauf went away." Luckily for Guru, Geeta was in London and did not know of all this until much later. Had Geeta been in Bombay, perhaps, such a daring step from Waheeda and her family could not have been taken. Evidently, Guru was not about to forsake his whole family and culture and adopt another way of life for Waheeda. Clearly, he was unhappy in his marriage but he did not want to convert and betray Geeta in this manner.

Guru Dutt was intensely passionate about Geeta when he was not extremely disturbed. It was how much she meant to Guru that really shaped his life after marriage.

From the start of their courtship days, Geeta Dutt and Guru Dutt shared a stormy relationship reminiscent of Catherine and Heathcliff from Emily Bronte's classic novel Wuthering Heights (1847). They knew very little peace when they were together or when they were apart. A roller-coaster ride, up one day, down the next. The Guru Dutt letters that Nasreen Munni Kabir has published in her extraordinary collection "Yours Guru Dutt" are significant for someone who wishes to study the mindset of Guru Dutt. They had frequent fights, yes, but they also shared scintillating moments of intense and vibrant love. Their marriage was never a steady boat, it was always facing storms and dangers. There was chaos and there was passion too.

In these letters, Guru Dutt, who fell in love with Geeta Roy during the shooting of Baazi, can be seen making fervent appeals to her, begging for her love, "Lekin kaam karne se mujhe jo tassali milti hai wo tassali tum mujhe nahin de sakti ho, bas is wajah, shaayad, main shaayad, unhappy hoon. Agar main unhappy hoon to tumhe kya?" He wanted her to accept his proposal, he badgered her because he was obsessed with her. That was the Guru Dutt who would have stopped at nothing to get Geeta to marry him. While he would have crossed the seven seas for Geeta, for Waheeda he did not feel as deeply or else he would have gone ahead with the conversion and subsequent nikaah. The risk-taker in Guru Dutt was courting danger on both fronts. Guy de Maupassant observed brilliantly, "It is better to be unhappy in love than unhappy in marriage, but some people manage to be both." Guru Dutt managed to be both, unhappy with his wife and unhappy with his love interest.

When Pyaasa was being shot, he became depressed and attempted suicide for the first time. Luckily, he was quickly brought out of it. The film was released and, after a slow start, it gathered momentum. He was happy to see the film succeed at the box office. Then he stuck his neck out further and took a bigger risk with Kaagaz Ke Phool. It flopped. Geeta had already realised that her husband was deeply involved with Waheeda by this time, so things were not playing out well on the home front too. As mentioned earlier, she would leave with the children to stay at her mother's home. Both setbacks were hard on him, with his family (especially Geeta) and work appearing to fade from his horizon, so, once again, Guru Dutt hit bottom. The futility of his existence hit him hard. The two things that had given him meaning had deserted him. He was adrift, and he lost the will to swim against the tide.

Had the recognition of his genius come during his lifetime, Guru Dutt would have been encouraged to create more masterpieces. But sadly, he was discovered much later, when it was too late for Guru Dutt. Lalita Lajmi, in an interview, revealed that, after his second suicide attempt when he came out of a coma at the Nanavati Hospital, the first word on his lips was, "Geeta!" Considering that this was subsequent to the conversion fiasco, his uttering his wife's name after being in a coma for a couple of days, tells us an eloquent story. He had only one love and her name was Geeta.

To make matters worse, what he saw around him was dismaying. The film industry was full of hypocrisy and backstabbing, more than other professions were. Waheeda Rehman had already let him down when she quickly went to work with Sunil Dutt without a nod from him. BR Chopra also said a few nasty things about him. Like other successful directors, he, too, was surrounded by so many users and sycophants that he lost his ability to differentiate his friends from his foes.

Paradoxically, while Hindi films projected a certain joy and truthfulness, they were being created by people who had long ago abandoned those ideals. The hypocrisy of the fake film fraternity hit him hard. Most of them upheld great values in their cinema but they derided those deep values through their actions in their real lives. They wore genial masks that concealed ambitious, ruthless and materialistic minds. Things were never what they seemed. Idealism had buyers, so they sold stories with pure idealists as protagonists, while their own lives were far from idealistic. He saw the crudity, the hollowness, the materialism and was disturbed by what he saw. So much vanity, ambition, greed, self-vaunting, it was a challenge to a sensitive spirit all right. Guru Dutt tried hard to remain unspoilt by it all, so he tried to bury himself in his work. He often returned home late to Geeta and the children. Some nights he did not return, preferring to sleep in the studio. Obsessed with his art, he sometimes took off for Lonavala without informing Geeta. He became self-indulgent, often choosing to escape life by immersing himself in his art, which was also his way of running away from his reality. But that escape eluded him too. He could not sleep at night and took to combining sleeping pills with alcohol to try and get sleep.

Nothing made sense to him anymore since he felt that he had failed in the two areas that mattered most to him, his work and Geeta. In light of this, his two suicide attempts were important because they signify his decision to end it all. The second time was during the shoots of Sahib Bibi Aur Ghulam, after which he was rushed to Nanavati hospital where he was in a coma for two days. With such repeated attempts at self-destruction, it was a matter of time before he succeeded.

When Sathya Saran interviewed Abrar Alvi, he told her that Geeta's suspicious nature was one of the reasons why Guru Dutt drew closer to Waheeda Rehman. Once Geeta dropped in at his home to share her fears with him. Abrar Alvi and Guru Dutt were planning to travel together soon. He told Sathya that she pleaded, " 'Please understand me,' she said, 'I am at my wits' end, helpless. You are travelling with him, please try to reason with him, he is crazy about Waheeda.' I told her, 'I know Waheeda very well by now. There is nothing between them. Please understand that if he does anything that breaks the sanctity of married life, there are at least two people in his unit, Niranjan and me, who will not work with him after that. He has become a father, and we will not brook any irresponsibility on his part towards his children.' She listened quietly and left. But before she went, she dried her eyes, and said in a very calm voice, 'Don't tell him I was here.' I believe she came only to verify her suspicions. And though I gave Guru Dutt a clean chit, it did little to allay Geeta's doubts. She was influenced a lot by Smriti Biswas, who also taught her ways to test whether her suspicions were valid and, if possible, to catch her husband red-handed."

On another occasion, Abrar told Sathya Saran that Guru Dutt had received a letter which was signed, "Yours Waheeda." In the letter, the writer said that she wanted to meet him in the evening at Nariman Point. The letter was, in Abrar's words, a torrid declaration of love. 'I said, 'You meet her every day, have enough opportunity to meet her in private, in her make-up room. Why would she write this, and why would she want to meet you in a public place like Nariman Point? Why call you there?' We decided on a plan. He would drive towards Nariman Point and stop near the Cricket Club of India. I would, in my car, take another road, and check out who came there. I took my second-hand khataara car and parked it in the by-lane next to the CCI. I knew where Guru Dutt was waiting and watching. I saw a car approach and slow down near Nariman Point. Geeta Dutt and Smriti Biswas were sitting in the backseat of the chauffeur-driven car. It moved to the Nariman Point area, waited and watched and then moved on to Marine Drive. I followed the car and went back to Guru Dutt who had seen the whole drama. I think this was the first time, that night after going home, that he confronted Geeta with the episode and, as he confessed to me later, raised his hand on her."

Their marriage was falling apart now that Guru Dutt had resorted to physical abuse. Still, Geeta was keen to save her marriage. However much Geeta tried to persuade Guru Dutt to pay attention to her and the children, Guru Dutt would not oblige. Even his mother had observed that her favourite child would heed nobody once his mind was made up.

Then came the film Gouri. When they were shooting for this film, things took an ugly turn. Geeta and Guru had a major fight, once again involving Waheeda. The film was shelved and the couple became even more estranged. During the making of Sahib Bibi Aur Ghulam, writer Bimal Mitra saw their tension from very close since he would often be staying at their home. Geeta did not want Waheeda to be in Sahib Bibi Aur Ghulam but Guru Dutt was determined to include her in it.

By the time Sahib Bibi Aur Ghulam came to an end, the Waheeda chapter of Guru's life had ended. Geeta and Guru tried to reconcile with each other. They even went to Srinagar together. Nina was born after this. Yet, there remained a lot of tension between them.

Bimal Mitra, who was a close friend of Guru Dutt's at that time and was living in their home for several weeks, wrote about this phase at length in his book Bichhde Sabhi Baari Baari. He saw their tempestuous relationship. One morning when Bimal and his wife woke up, they discovered that Geeta Dutt had left the bungalow at two a.m. the previous night and had requested both of them to visit her at her mother's home. They had been together till twelve a.m. the previous night and there had been nothing amiss. They learnt later from Geeta Dutt what had happened later. Guru Dutt downed a bottle of whiskey in the night. Then the couple had got into a major fight. Guru Dutt asked his driver Ramjee to take Geeta out of the house. With all his strength, Guru pushed Geeta into the car. Geeta's wrist was bleeding. Bimal Mitra recounted: "Geeta asked him, 'Tum mujhe yoon ghar se nikaal rahe ho? Maine tumhaara kya bigaada hai?' Guru replied, 'Tum roz roz mujhe yoon hi sataati rahogi? Tumhaari wajah se main so bhi nahin sakta, tum jao, yahaan se chali jao. Is ghar mein apni shakal kabhi mat dikhaana. Ye ghar hi to tumhaare liye zeher ban gaya hai…' Geeta replied, 'Is makaan ne meri taqdeer mein aag nahin lagaayi, aag lagaayi hai tumne! Tumne aur Waheeda Rehman ne!' Waheeda ka naam sunte hi Guru maano aur nirmam ho gaya. 'Ramjee, le jao!'"

After this major fight, they were never the same. After some time, Guru Dutt moved to a rented flat at Peddar Road while Geeta began living with her children in Santacruz. Guru decided to break down his beautiful home and rebuild it. Geeta had been worried that their unhappiness could also be caused by an evil spirit in their house. So many terrible memories were associated with this house that he, too, wanted it ripped apart.

It was tragic indeed. The genius Japanese filmmaker Akira Kurosawa was once asked whether his films have a common theme. He answered, "I suppose all of my films have a common theme. If I think about it, though, the only theme I can think of is really a question: Why can't people be happier together?"

A few hours before he passed away, Guru had fought with Geeta Dutt over the phone. He wanted her to send the children to him, but she refused because it was already late and they were asleep. The bitter fight ended with Guru Dutt warning her, with words to the effect that if she didn't send the children to him she would see his dead body the next day. Such words are often expressed at emotional moments by angry people, Geeta thought, and she ended the conversation without acceding to his emotional outburst.

Whether he intended to kill himself or not is still a mystery, but the words disturbed Geeta a lot. The next morning, as was his routine, his doctor dropped in to see him at 9 a.m. But the door was locked from the inside. He returned again at 11 a.m. Still no luck.

He called Geeta, who asked for the door to be broken. When they broke open the door, they found him dead.

Guru Dutt's brother Devi Dutt, in an interview with Filmfare, said, "Bhabhi was shattered at his sudden death. When they were taking away his body, she cried, "Mat le kar jao!"

According to Devi Dutt, Guru Dutt didn't like the fact that Geeta's family influenced her a lot. Both husband and wife tended to believe what others told them. Rumours found their way to Geeta Dutt and they upset her. He said, "Actually, Guru Dutt was happy-go-lucky. He was fond of women. Women were attracted to him, one reason being that, through him, they could become actresses. Women were ready to do anything for him. He was as fond of alcohol as he was fond of creating. But when Kaagaz Ke Phool flopped he was devastated. He felt that his career as a director was over."

Devi Dutt lamented that Geeta Dutt had given up on life. "More than loneliness, it was joblessness that troubled her. Lata Mangeshkar and Asha Bhosle had taken over. But one couldn't blame anyone. She'd take drugs like charas during the day and alcohol in the evening. Her tongue used to be swollen. She couldn't sing. Once, she went for the recording of Basu Chatterjee's Anubhav (1971). The song was Mujhe jaan na kaho meri jaan. She couldn't stand, so disoriented she was. Sound recordist BN Sharma sent for me. I asked her what the problem was. She said she didn't feel like singing. BN Sharma ne phir chai pila pila kar unhein jagaaya (he made her have cups and cups of tea). Mar mar ke she completed the song." This comes as a surprise to music-lovers because she sang the song perfectly. How could she have rendered it so beautifully if she had been unwell?

Of all the female singers that Guru Dutt had in the films produced or directed by him, Geeta Dutt was at the top: she sang most of the songs, 51 to be precise. If one were to exclude Baazi and Jaal (because they did not belong to the Guru Dutt banner), then the total would be 42 songs. All the songs that she sang are covered in the chapter on the singers of Guru Dutt films.

Geeta Dutt died on July 20, 1972, when she was only 42 years old. She had cirrhosis of the liver. Not only did her marriage come in the way of her career, her personal life was reduced to rubble.

Tarun, Dutt's eldest child, committed suicide as well in 1989 when he was only 35 years old. Arun, their second child also died early, on July 26, 2014, when he was 58 years old. Kalpana Lajmi shared that he had several complications arising out of excessive alcohol intake. Thankfully, Nina, their youngest, is happily married to Production Designer Naushad Memon (Minoo Mumtaz's nephew) and has a son and a daughter.

2

Arun Dutt

(July 10, 1956-July 26, 2014)

Thanks to the advent of social media platforms, one is fortunate to access interviews of friends and family members closest to Guru Dutt. Some of the most fascinating interviews are those of his son Arun Dutt, who was eight years old when his father passed away. Although he has only a few sketchy memories of his father, he holds that his father had all the hallmarks of the world's most creative artists. This chapter is a collection of his thoughts from his several interviews available online, i.e. on YouTube and other platforms.

Arun Dutt recalled that his father was a quiet introvert. He was also inclined to be impulsive and hot-tempered. He was so private that even his closest friend Abrar Alvi could not be his confidante.

Arun respected that his parents were protective of their children and refrained from quarrelling with each other in their presence.

As such, the children were insulated from the upheavals in their lives. Guru Dutt was not a demonstrative father. There was always some reserve and restraint. Arun could not recall a single instance when his father had hugged him or held him close. Since Guru Dutt was a workaholic, he was inclined to be moody when he returned home, so the children were afraid of him. He said that the only family member his father was comfortable with was his younger brother Atma Ram. None of the other family members spoke to Guru Dutt unless he addressed them but when he initiated a conversation, they would respond.

Going down memory lane, Arun recalled that the last time he met his father was a week before his death on October 10, 1964. Guru Dutt loved flying kites and on that day the children and he flew kites. They were supposed to meet him again on the 9th of October when they were to go directly from school to his home in Ark Royal building at Peddar Road. But this did not happen. On that fateful Saturday evening Guru Dutt was with Abrar Alvi from six p.m. to work out a scene for Baharen Phir Bhi Aayengi. Since this was a rented flat without a telephone, Guru would go down in the same building to a distributor's flat to make a telephone call to his family. On that day he called their mother Geeta around 9.30 or 10 p.m., asking for the children to be sent to him. Since the children were already asleep she said she could not send them there so late.

Arun Dutt stressed that he did not believe his father committed suicide because when he had attempted suicide twice before he had left a suicide note. This time around there was no suicide note, so he may have been accidentally had too much to drink and overdosed himself.

Arun regarded his father as a creative filmmaker who sought excellence and, thus, became a demanding perfectionist. When asked about his preference for Guru Dutt's films, Arun mentioned that his favourites were Pyaasa, then Saheb Bibi Aur Ghulam, and

Kaagaz ke Phool, in that order. He held that Kaagaz Ke Phool was technically a superior film but subject-wise it fell short; for example, Arun observed that his father should not have included Johnny Walker in the film because in such a serious film, a comedian would dilute the seriousness of the tragedy. "Somewhere the screenplay went wrong", he observed.

On the subject of the film's finances, Guru Dutt sometimes had to compromise because financiers and distributors wanted his films to include certain scenes and he had to concede to their requests.

Arun Dutt felt that his father was a combination of two film characters, Vijay from Pyaasa and Suresh from Kaagaz Ke Phool. Incidentally, he shared that his father had written Pyaasa in 1946 or 1947, the period when he was out of work for eight to ten months.

Arun shared that he had the original handwritten script of Pyaasa with him. It was written on the letterhead of Pramukh Films, a film company Guru Dutt would go to in search of work. He made that film ten years later, once he became successful. In those ten years, he had become an actor, a filmmaker, a director and a producer. He knew Pyaasa was a risky project and he also knew distributors would not be keen to finance the film.

After Guru Dutt passed away, for more than a year, Geeta, their mother, suffered a nervous breakdown. Arun asserted that because she had loved Guru deeply, she had refused offers for marriage after becoming a widow. She answered everyone with a negative, telling them that Guru would be the only man in her life.

Arun felt that Guru never got the critical acclaim that was his due during his lifetime. Guru also had, from childhood, a very 'negative thought process', and was 'into morbid thinking'. Plus 'he was never satisfied with anything.' Even when he got what he wanted he was dissatisfied. Because his work was not acclaimed by critics, it discouraged him. It was only in the 80s, much after he had passed away, that his films went to France and Guru Dutt's oeuvre got the recognition it deserved.

Geeta and Guru, who met during the making of Baazi in 1951, separated in 1963, ten years after their marriage because they were unhappy with each other.

He observed that his father was a reluctant actor. The first film he acted in, Baaz, was because of financial reasons: they could not afford a star. It so happened that KN Singh spotted his good looks and asked him if he wanted to act. So one day KN Singh took him to a photographer and got his pictures clicked. Then he took the pictures to Geeta Bali's sister who was one of the co-producers of the film, and they could not believe these pictures were Guru Dutt's because he used to wear very thick glasses. That is how Guru became the lead actor in Baaz. Again, for Aar Paar, Guru wanted a couple of stars but their dates clashed, so he himself took on the lead role. Then for Pyaasa, he wanted Dilip Kumar but the latter refused, because he felt the role was too close to his role in Devdas (the film had already been released), and he didn't want to do a similar role again. Some say there was a financial disagreement between them, but Arun was unable to confirm or deny this. But in Kaagaz ke Phool, Guru wanted to cast himself, because it was a semi-autobiographical film. As such, he never approached anyone for that role. For Sahib Bibi Aur Ghulam however, he initially wanted Shashi Kapoor to star in it. Again, for reasons beyond his control, the role of Bhola was enacted by Guru himself.

Guru Dutt's Nature

Arun Dutt shared that Guru Dutt was impulsive. When he got something in his mind, he would act upon it. One day he wanted to travel on a scooter from his home to the studio in Andheri. When he was in the middle of his trip, he was recognised and mobbed. He quickly abandoned the scooter and got into his car which had been tailing the scooter. He would often act first and think later. For example, Arun said that since they used to go for holidays to Kashmir, his father had been fascinated by the Kashmiri shikara. He placed an order for it, got it dismantled and reassembled it for use in Bombay's fishing area in Powai. When the shipment arrived, he was unable to get permission to ply the shikara, and thus it rotted in the studios.

Guru had several hobbies, such as fishing, flying kites and photography. But because his bungalow had a slanting roof, he could not fly kites from there. A solution was found: since Johnny Walker's bungalow was near their home, they would get together and fly kites from the comedian's terrace. Guru Dutt later wanted the bungalow to be broken and re-cast; one of the reasons was so that it would have a terrace from where he could fly kites.

In an interview with P. Rajendran of Rediff, on Oct 23, 2009, Arun Dutt said that his favourite film was Pyaasa. "He wrote the script of Pyaasa in English. He thought in English too…" He added that their father didn't encourage the children to visit him on the sets. If he had been alive, he guessed that their father would not have allowed them to come anywhere close to the cinema world. He was very disillusioned by the film industry and found it a very insecure business.

About Guru and Sahir, Arun said that Sahir used a lot of Farsi, much more than Urdu. Because it was not understandable, Guru asked him to simplify the lyrics. "Sahir saab, after Pyaasa, said that if it was not for his lyrics the film wouldn't have worked…it is teamwork, and even if it is true you don't go around saying that. Just lyrics couldn't make a film. It had to be picturised (well) also. Sahir has written lyrics of so many films but none of them was Pyaasa. Most of the strong songs he wrote were about himself. Even Jinhe naaz hai Hind pe kahan hai is based on his own original Chakley. Actually, Jinhe naaz hai Hind pe was printed in his book. From that book, my father had taken out this song. And he said, just simplify this line, "Sanaa-khwan-e-taqdees-e-mashriq kahaan hai?"

Arun Dutt admired both his parents and, in all the interviews he gave, he spoke of them with respect.

In Nasreen Munni Kabir's book Yours Guru Dutt, she shared a letter written by Guru Dutt to his sons Tarun and Arun from Shimla on 6/2/1958. In the letter, he offered a bit of advice to them: "When you grow up, I want you to remember that work is the most important thing of all. A person who doesn't work is a fool. So let me finish the work I am doing here and then I'll be back".

Arun Dutt and his wife Kavita parented two daughters, Gouri and Karuna. Arun Dutt passed away in 2014 when he was 58 years old.

3

Dev Anand

(September 26, 1923-December 3, 2011)

"Guru Dutt was my only true friend in the film industry."
– Dev Anand

Dev Anand, born in Gurdaspur on September 26, 1923, was a couple of years older than his friend Guru Dutt who was born in Bangalore on July 9, 1925. But while they were only two years apart in age, Guru Dutt died very early, when he was just 39 years old, while Dev Anand lived till December 03, 2011. Perhaps because they saw life differently, with Dev Anand full of pep and Guru Dutt inclined towards melancholia, their lives turned out the way they did.

Dev Anand and Guru Dutt were both handsome young men, with many shared interests, including international cinema. Interestingly, Dev Anand who was born Devdutt Pishorimal

Anand, dropped Dutt from his name, while Guru Dutt, who was born Vasantkumar Padukone, adopted Dutt as his second name.

They met each other quite by accident. In 1946, during their days of struggle, they were working in Hum Ek Hein made by Prabhat Film Co. Ltd, whose producer had lodged them in a Pune guest house. Their roles were quite different though; Dev Anand was the hero of the film while Guru Dutt was credited in the titles with 'Dance composition'. But destiny was about to smile on both young men through a comedy of errors!

Since they were both staying at the same guest house, they had a dhobi in common who used to carry their clothes to the ghat for washing and ironing. The dhobi was probably having a confusing day, so he mixed up his deliveries and exchanged their shirts.

In his autobiography, Dev Anand recounts what had transpired. By his admission, Anand was at that time involved in a clandestine affair with a married woman. She wanted to meet him the next afternoon since it was her birthday. She persuaded him to meet her for lunch, wearing his best clothes. Here's how Dev Anand recounted his first meeting with Guru Dutt:

"The next day I was looking inside my cupboard for my best shirt, but it wasn't there. I called my elder sister. "It's there, your shirt," she pulled it out from the cupboard. "But that's not my shirt," I insisted.

"But this is the one the washerman brought back," she said. "Perhaps the washerman has brought me back the wrong shirt! And I have to wear that today," I murmured, half cursing the washerman.

"Wear this one then, looks just as good, and seems to be your size," she suggested. I entered the portals of the studio in the afternoon, with somebody else's shirt on. A young man, roughly my age and almost the same build was leaving as I entered. As we crossed each other, he stopped to say, "Hello...you are the new leading man they are all talking about in the studio?" "You have recognised me!" I said with humility. "My name is Guru Dutt, I'm assisting Mr Bedekar." We shook hands, "Hope to see more of you, Mr Guru Dutt," I said. "Sure," he said, and was about to move on when he stopped abruptly to look at me...He was looking at the shirt I was wearing, I looked at it too, and then suddenly at the one he was wearing. Our eyes were glued to each other's shirts. Then he raised his eyes and said, "I like that! It is beautiful!" He was pointing at the shirt I had on. "That is beautiful too," I said, pointing to the shirt he was wearing. "Where did you buy it from?" He was keen to know. "You tell me, where did you buy that one from?" I asked too. "I stole it, for it is so elegant," he smiled. "And my washerman presented mine to me!" I joked back. "To wear it on somebody's birthday," I said on the side. We both laughed like we had never laughed before. We hugged each other, wearing each other's shirts, and became the greatest of pals, of all time."

That fateful meeting marked the start of their lifelong friendship. They often met and confided in each other about their professional and personal lives. Both men fell in love during the making of Baazi. Dev Anand married Kalpana Kartik while Guru Dutt married Geeta Roy.

In a DearCinema interview of Dev Anand with Laalit Lobo published on June 11, 2007, titled "Dev Anand Remembers Guru Dutt", Dev spoke about his friendship and the pact between the two of them. He said, "I think if I can call anybody in the movie industry my greatest pal, it would be Guru Dutt…We struck a great friendship jaise langotiya yaar kehte hain hum waise dost the. And we struck a deal over a glass of beer and then he said, 'Dev…if I ever become a director you are my star' and I said, 'If I ever form a company and I invite a director to direct a film you're going to be THE one'. So I brought him in for Baazi… that type of friendship. Then he made C.I.D. He invited me to do the picture…"

Incidentally, Navketan, established in 1949, was owned by Chetan Anand and Dev Anand. Navketan's first film Afsar (1950), directed by Chetan Anand, flopped. The film Dev made next was Baazi (1951) for which he signed Guru Dutt as the Director. What a risky gamble that was!

But they won their bets!

The film was a hit because it was a refreshing change from the standard fare that the audiences had been offered till then. This crime noir film had many interesting twists and turns in the plot, combined with some exhilarating songs from SD Burman. The racy film with Dev Anand and Geeta Bali's sparkling performances under Guru Dutt's direction, fascinated the audience.

About Guru Dutt's sudden death, Dev Anand, in a video interview on YouTube, said, "It was a very sudden death and I had met him five or six days earlier when he had invited me. He said, 'Come over let's do a picture together,' but at that moment I also realised when I saw him that he was looking very frail, very feeble… yellow on the face, he had lost his hair. This was not the same Guru Dutt because he had made some very beautiful films…the film that he made Kaagaz Ke Phool was very brilliant but it didn't do well. He could not take it, after that, he never directed a picture, so that was the start of his physical downfall. Even his creative downfall. Sad…I think he was very melancholic. He was a young man and he should not have made depressing pictures…Guru Dutt always made depressing pictures. I don't know why because he was a brilliant man. He was a good thinker. He had that dogged perseverance to go on and on but he used to shoot a lot but when he found success he was wonderful, on top of the world and the moment failure hit him hard he could not take it."

On the day of Guru Dutt's death, Dev Anand was at work. He writes in his autobiography, "I was on the sets of Teen Deviyan and I was ghost directing for Amarjeet, a friend of ours, and I got news that Guru Dutt is dead. I packed up. I went straight to his apartment. I was probably the first visitor and was ushered into the room where his body lay. There was nobody else in the room, just me and him. His face turned blue perhaps because of the blue liquid in a glass lying next to him on his bedside table which he had drunk to kill himself, seemed to say, "Goodbye, my friend. I have been missing you. I have to go. But you keep going!"

Dev Anand added about his friend, "He wanted to make some great films, and I wanted to be a great star. We saw masterpieces of outstanding filmmakers together, both of us earnest to make our mark on the sands of time. We were inseparable. Together we tramped and cycled the streets of Poona, looking for books and magazines that excited our creativity…often for hours we would climb up the hill, struggling through rough patches of overgrown grass and wild jungle flowers, to watch the gold on the horizon melt into the pale yellow of twilight, our dreams dancing back and forth, getting ready to form a shape that the world would take note of one day."

They chose plots in which the hero was a street-smart urbane individual, whether it was in Baazi, Taxi Driver, Aar Paar, or Mr. & Mrs. '55. Urban characters and landscapes also made their work move fast. For example, Dev Anand's Taxi Driver was shot in just 30 days on a shoestring budget!

Many Hindi films then were morality plays with exaggerated emotional scenes. On the other hand, Navketan's and Guru Dutt's films were Westernised and city-centric, with very little moral messaging. There was a lot of modernity projected that bore the class and sophistication of Hollywood movies. Their films were great to watch from the edge of the seat because they were edited so well. They were thrilling from start to finish, with never a dull moment. The heroines were often strong and impish, so they were not projected as victims. There was a focus on technical excellence and an overwhelming need to entertain the audience through catchy songs.

On the personal front, Guru Dutt was quiet and depressive, yet he would surround himself with people. He would be with others and yet he would be aloof. Chhaya Arya, who was chosen to do the role of Chhoti Bahu in Sahib Bibi Aur Ghulam, found that when they were working on the script in Guru Dutt's home in Lonavala, he would keep to himself and wander around lost in his thoughts, always quiet and introspective. Quite his opposite was Dev Anand who was always upbeat and enthusiastic. He would pick himself up the moment he fell and move on to the next project. He would not waste time brooding. Both of them detested parties, but Dev, despite being an extrovert, did not drink unless it was unavoidable, while Guru Dutt became dependent on alcohol. Both faced life's challenges differently.

Dev Anand fulfilled his end of the bargain with Baazi but regretted that his friend Guru Dutt did not direct him in any Guru Dutt film. Guru Dutt produced C.I.D. which featured Dev, but it was directed by Raj Khosla. Because there were creative differences between Guru Dutt and Navketan's Chetan Anand, it made collaborations with Navketan difficult for Guru Dutt. Also, one can't ignore the fact that Guru Dutt became successful as a lead actor in roles that Dev Anand and he were both good at. His success as the lead actor in Aar Paar, Mr. & Mrs. '55, 12 O'Clock, made him realise that it made more financial sense for him to play the lead role in his films.

Later, after Guru Dutt's death, when Abrar Alvi offered Dev Anand the lead role in Baharen Phir Bhi Aayengi, Dev Anand refused. They needed to replace Guru Dutt who had died midway through the shoot. Was he uncomfortable replacing his friend or was his diary full of commitments at that time? Nobody knows.

In 1978, Prabhat Chitra Mandal held a ceremony to celebrate Guru Dutt's birth anniversary in Marine Lines, Mumbai. The function was attended by Guru Dutt's mother, Vasanthi, as well as Dev Anand. Guru Dutt's mother shared a touching story about the friendship between Guru Dutt with Dev Anand. In his youth, she said, Guru Dutt was about to commit suicide; it was Dev Anand who succeeded in preventing him. She added, "This Guru Dutt you all know is not the son I gave birth to but the one whose life Dev Anand saved." One can only imagine how much she must have loved Dev Anand because of this.

4

Abrar Alvi

(July 1, 1927-November 18, 2009)

Guru Dutt's closest friend was Abrar Alvi, who was not only the script-writer of many of his films but also the director of Sahib Bibi Aur Ghulam.

Their work together is fascinating because it was during his association with Guru Dutt Films that Abrar did his most creative work. Guru and Abrar laughed, fought and even had serious discussions with each other. Quite often, when they held opposing points of view, they would close the argument by agreeing to disagree. If there was one person who knew and understood Guru more than anyone else, it was Abrar.

Their films together included such unforgettable movies as Aar Paar, Mr. & Mrs. '55, Pyaasa, Kaagaz Ke Phool, Chaudhvin Ka Chand and Sahib Bibi Aur Ghulam. Abrar and Guru became so close that when Kaagaz Ke Phool flopped, Guru handed over the charge of directing Sahib Bibi Aur Ghulam to Abrar.

Their last film together was the incomplete Baharen Phir Bhi Aayengi, which was re-shot because Guru, the lead actor of the film, died and they had to recast with Dharmendra playing the protagonist's role. Abrar also did small bit parts in three of Guru's films, i.e., Mr. & Mrs. '55, C.I.D., and 12 O'Clock.

Two years younger than Guru, Abrar was born in Ayodhya, Uttar Pradesh. Apart from having an M.A. in English, he was, like his father before him, a qualified lawyer. He began to work as an amateur writer for radio for which he wrote plays and stories. In his youth, he had fallen in love with a girl and had written her 300 love letters, so his pen was truly flowing with delightful words. In 1951, he left Ayodhya for Bombay with the dream of becoming an actor.

Abrar joined IPTA (Indian People's Theatre Association) where his cousin (and college senior) Irshad Hussain gave him company. Incidentally, Irshad had renamed himself 'Jaswant' for his career in the film industry. Jaswant got Abrar a job as Assistant Director to CL Dheer for the film Bahu Beti (1952) in which Jaswant had a role. Jaswant then got a role in Baaz (1953), which starred Geeta Bali and Guru Dutt. This film was jointly produced by Geeta Bali's sister Haridarshan Kaur and Guru Dutt. During the making of this film, Jaswant and Haridarshan Kaur fell in love. Although Jaswant was already married, he took Haridarshan as his second wife. Abrar loved to drive, so he would drive Jaswant to the studios for Baaz in the latter's Hillman. They would meet the film's cast and crew which included Raj Khosla, the assistant director, and Guru Dutt who was the actor, director and co-producer of the film.

Initially, Raj Khosla and Abrar Alvi hit it off, but later they would have differences. One day when Khosla discovered that

Abrar was a writer, he asked his opinion on a scene and requested him to re-do its dialogue. "I gave my opinion to Raj Khosla and Guru," Abrar remarked. Guru was impressed and put him through a seven-day script test. Every day Guru would ask him to write a script for a scene, and then disappear with what he wrote. Later Abrar learnt that Guru would take his script to his mother whose opinion he respected immensely, and who would then approve the flow of Abrar's writings.

At one point, Guru narrowed down his choice to two writers: Abrar and Rajinder Singh Bedi. Finally, he opted for Abrar. Guru said to him: "I have met Bedi and listened to him because Majrooh insisted I should do so. But now I am convinced that you will write for me. Bedi says directors don't even bring ten percent of what he writes to life. He might say that of me as well if I direct what he writes; I have heard you for seven days, I want you to write my next film." The film was Aar Paar.

In Aar Paar, four characters had to speak Hindustani in their separate dialects. Abrar rose to the challenge: the heroine's father was a Punjabi which was easy, Johnny Walker was a Parsi so he gave a Gujarati accent to his diction, then there was a Qazi from U.P., and then there was Kaalu, the hero played by Guru, who was from Madhya Pradesh. For example, Kaalu would say 'Main nahin kehta, yaaron ne kaha…ab yaaron ka waqat dheela hai to aap laal peela ho rahe ho…' in Madhya Pradesh, it was commonly understood that when they said the word, 'yaar' they meant themselves.

However, in time, there developed a lot of tension between Khosla and Abrar. They would get into heated arguments, with Guru siding with either one of them, and then Johnny Walker would pitch in, making matters worse. Somehow, Guru managed these temperaments and brought out a blockbuster film.

In an interview available on YouTube, Abrar said, "With Aar Paar, we started the trend of modern writing which is followed even today. Earlier it was theatrical language. The script was a refreshing change, it was street talk, real and delicious, very easy for the audience to accept." In another interview, he remarked, "I found the earlier films' dialogues artificial and stilted. Again, Raj Khosla had issues with this, because he believed that language should not be pedestrian but chaste…I told Guru and his team that the best way to write dialogues for films, so that they would be remembered, was to break away from the theatrical tradition. I told him you have to write wrong to write right."

Alvi added that Guru hired him because he felt his Urdu was weak since he was from Bangalore, while Abrar spoke chaste Urdu. Yet, even if Guru found him brilliant at his work, Abrar was not popular with many crew members who found him quarrelsome.

"When Atma Ram said to Abrar, 'You cannot work with anybody,' Abrar retorted, "I cannot tolerate anyone talking like an idiot." Guru admired Abrar's refusal to be a yes-man. Abrar would stand his ground no matter what others said. He held that a character's dialogue must be consistent with his background and that the choice of words should reflect that background too. The credibility of the film often rested on such minute attention to detail.

Guru, Abrar found, was quite transparent. For example, when he lied, his ears would turn red! Also, Guru had a young man's romantic vision. He shared that, "He was not a very communicative person." As a director, he was continually dissatisfied with the shots and re-did them. Guru was a demanding colleague, a moody perfectionist who would not settle for second-grade work.

About Gulabo in Pyaasa, Abrar told writer Shishir Krishna Sharma, "The son of a Hyderabad-based landlord who was one of the Reddys studied with me in Nagpur. Through him, I met a prostitute who was the daughter of a Gujarati temple priest. She had run away with her lover and finally, after being cheated by him, she became a prostitute. I was quite impressed by the girl's way of speaking and values. I wrote the character of Gulabo (in Pyaasa) keeping her in mind."

When Abrar got to know her, he was poor and he used to visit the prostitute and talk with her through the night. She was generous-hearted and would feed him from the goodness of her heart. Abrar told writer Sathya Saran that she had a husband and a daughter too. Later when he learnt she had TB, he used to give money to her husband, but she was hurt that he had stopped visiting her. This was because he had become deeply engrossed with his work for the film, Mr. & Mrs. '55. One day, he accidentally saw a corpse being carried to the cremation grounds, and when he looked at the face, he recognised it, it was hers. Abrar was shocked. He carried a lot of guilt because he had not visited her in the end.

Later, he told Guru about his guilt in this relationship. "Guru was quite captivated by her and asked me if I could make her the basis of a story. It was a challenge I felt I could take on. I told Guru that I would like to bring out the selflessness of the streetwalker by contrasting it with the selfish greed of the socialite character that he had thought of using in the film...I transferred much of my relationship with Gulabo into the script, even taking some of her lines verbatim, and the rest was easy." Abrar's personal experience was put on celluloid with Waheeda Rehman portraying the role of Gulabo in one of the most unforgettable performances of her career.

About Pyaasa, Abrar told Sharma, "I always used to be on Pyaasa's film's set and monitor the artists' language and pronunciation. However, due to some reasons, I was not able to attend the film's shooting for a few days. Actors Radhe Shyam and Mehmood were playing the roles of the elder brothers of the hero Vijay, played by Guru Dutt. On the first day of the movie's shoot Mehmood had requested to be permitted to speak his dialogues in a Bengali accent which was agreed to. If I had been on the sets, at that time, I would have never let that happen because in Pyaasa, this was the one family of Benares where all members spoke Bhojpuri mixed Hindi and where the youngest brother Guru was a poet of Hindi and Urdu. In such a family, it looks odd that only one member speaks in a Bengali accent but unfortunately, an ace director like Guru did not pay attention to this anomaly. My aim of saying all this is to remind people of those contributions of mine to Guru's creations which have been ignored by everyone till date."

Talking about Sahib Bibi Aur Ghulam, Abrar said that he wrote the screenplay and dialogues for the story written by Bimal Mitra. "I was busy with some movies outside this banner and it was difficult for me to be available for the movie's shooting. Due to this, the script of the movie was recorded in my voice on a spool running for nearly four hours so that it could become easy for Guru to understand the story and its characters. However, due to personal troubles and heavy mental tension, Guru decided not to take up direction." He asked the reluctant Abrar to direct it. After much resistance, Abrar acceded to his request. The film went on to receive the President's Silver Medal and also the Filmfare Award for Best Film.

In Sathya Saran's interviews, she learnt that Chhaya Arya was dropped despite Abrar's efforts to retain her for the film Sahib Bibi Aur Ghulam. "The stills of Chhaya Arya displeased Guru. He found her "jawline too pronounced, her face too harsh on camera. "She was glamorous and beautiful in real life, but Guru wanted Chhoti Bahu to look wanton and motherly and beseeching, all rolled in one at different times, and Chhaya's face seemed incapable of at least some of the softness and yearning that the character demanded...I told Guru that I would get her to emote and that he should not drop her, that I will be blamed for dropping her after she has uprooted herself from her home in London... but he was ruthless, I have never known a more uncompromising director. He spared no one, not even his wife, whom he had cast in a film called Gouri, only to scrap it when it did not measure up to his expectations, (he did) not even spare himself when he found his acting inadequate in Raaz, of which he had shot 12 reels!"

Abrar was against casting Waheeda Rehman for Sahib Bibi Aur Ghulam because he found her unsuitable for the role. Abrar said, "Waheeda is a fine artist and I could get almost anything out of her, but I still believe she was miscast as Jaba. Meanwhile, the relationship between the two had blossomed and Guru was very possessive of her and kept directing her through the scenes." Thus, apart from the scenes which included Waheeda, and apart from the songs, the film was directed by Abrar. Guru was pleased with the way the scenes involving Sapru had been filmed by V K Murthy and also by the first appearance of Meena Kumari whose face was made to appear elongated rather than broad. This was achieved by the brilliant VK Murthy, thanks to some brainstorming between him, Abrar, and Guru. One day Abrar shot the song Bhanwara bada naadaan. When Guru saw the way it was picturised, he was shocked. He asked Abrar, "What have you done?" Then he re-shot the whole song, adding a lot of comedy to it. It was during the making of Sahib Bibi Aur Ghulam that Guru and Abrar fought a few times. Once, when he lost his temper, Guru told Abrar to remember that the film was Guru's and not his. At that point, Abrar decided to leave Guru Dutt Films, he wrote a letter to Guru saying he did not even want to be credited as the Director of the film. Guru replied to him that no matter what, the film was Abrar's. They continued to be friends right till Guru's last day.

After this, Guru decided to remake President, the New Theatres' hit movie, as Baharen Phir Bhi Aayengi. Since Abrar was busy at that time, Ismat Chughtai wrote the script for Baharen Phir Bhi Aayengi. On her suggestion, Ismat's husband, Shahid Lateef, was made its director but the film's shooting stopped after three reels had been recorded. Abrar told Sharma, "Guru called the movie President's writer Benoy Chatterjee from Kolkata to make necessary changes to the script and decided to direct the film himself. Meanwhile, through K Asif, Lateef put pressure on him. Guru told him that he himself would direct the film but Lateef was welcome to come and sit on the sets and also get his payment as per the contract. Lateef agreed to this, but suddenly Guru passed away. Twelve or thirteen reels of the movie had already been made by then…Considering the situation of the movie's distributor BM Shah and Guru's brother Atma Ram, I had to complete the movie Baharen Phir Bhi Aayengi. Since Guru was also the hero of this movie, I reshot all his scenes with Dharmendra. For doing this I had to leave the writing assignments of lyricist Shailendra's production Teesri Kasam, and Director Lekh Tandon's Jhuk Gaya Aasman. However, as per the contract, the dummy Director Shahid Lateef got the credit as the Director of the film."

About Sahir, Abrar told Sharma, "Sahir was very straightforward and curt. He used to say very undiplomatically of his fellow composers that they used to listen to English records and prepare the tunes of their Hindi songs after lifting them, while the lyricists wrote with their hearts and minds. Hence, the status of lyricists is above that of the composers. He used to ask the producers to pay him one rupee more than the composers and this had made many of the top composers of the era against him. Once he went to SD Burman's house in an inebriated condition and talked to him in such a manner that Burman swore never to work with Sahir again in his lifetime."

At that time, Pyaasa was being made and its last song was yet to be written and recorded. Guru and Abrar tried to convince Burman to work with him. After a lot of effort, Burman relented and agreed to record the song if they could bring the written song from him. He, however, refused to participate in any sitting with Sahir.

Abrar recalled, "The climax of this film was yet to be written when I had to be admitted to the hospital for an operation. I explained the situation of the movie to Sahir and asked him to write the song while I would write the climax after returning. When I got discharged after three weeks, I came to know that the song had already been recorded. The lyrics of the song were, 'Yeh takhton, ye tajon, ye mehlon ki duniya' upon hearing this I was quite troubled. It had been ten years since India had got independent and kingdoms no longer existed. The days of takhts, taajs and mahals were long gone. I was finding it difficult to come up with suitable dialogues for such a senseless song. I asked Sahir what stopped him from coming to the hospital and making me read the song but he silently stood smiling there. What could he tell me anyway? After three days of scratching my mind, I finally wrote this dialogue for actor Rehman, "Agar aaj Vijay zinda hote to hum unhe apne dilon ke takht par bithaate, shohrat ke taj pehnaate, aur gareebon ki galiyon se utha kar mehlon mein raaj karaate."

Abrar felt that Guru and he were on each other's wavelength, and that they both loved their work. Yet, Abrar admitted that Guru was a private person.

When Guru moved out of his bungalow into a flat, his troubles with Geeta continued. Finally he moved to a rented flat on Peddar Road. Abrar, knowing the state he was in, would make it a point to spend as much time with Guru as his workload would allow. Bimal Mitra wrote that once he even stayed at Guru's home for a week or two, just to give him moral support and be there for him.

On that fateful day, Abrar was with him till late at night. This is what Abrar recalled: "He (Guru) began drinking at five p.m., he had very morbid thinking, the scene was morbid and we were discussing the last scene, the scene of Mala Sinha's death. I was involved with the scene I had to write, but while we were discussing the scene he would stray from it to other things unconnected with the scene, things about madness...he discussed how he had received a letter from a friend who was in the insane asylum, and from that letter, it did not appear at all that he was insane, and then he went back to himself, saying that it felt as if he might go mad...". Then Abrar reassured him with why would you go mad, etc. "He was very, very disturbed. I was with him till 1 a.m., he didn't open up. I had no clue that he would do this mad thing. Otherwise, I would not have left him alone."

Abrar could not believe that Guru had died. When he saw his body, he felt, "He must have pulled one of his stunts, taken a tablet to worry us, to trouble all of us ...Guru lay on his bed in his kurta pyjama, on the bedside was a glass with a little pink liquid still left in it. Of course, I knew he had killed himself, we had discussed it so many times. "It's Sonaril" I told them, he used to get it through his driver from a chemist in Khar. We used to talk about it: the ways to kill oneself. I had even tried it once, and he had too, at least twice before. We realised a man cannot kill himself by swallowing sleeping pills…Guru had worked it out. He told me, "You must take it like a mother gives medicine to her child…crush the tablets and dissolve them in water."

The film Sahib Bibi Aur Ghulam won four Filmfare awards: Meena Kumari won the Best Actress Award, Abrar received the Best Director Award, VK Murthy received the Best Cinematographer Award and the film also won the Best Feature Film Award.

Apart from the work he did with Guru, Abrar wrote for nearly 20 films including Saathi, Prince, Professor, Chhoti Si Mulaqat, Bairaag, Laila Majnu, Do Phool, Sabse Bada Rupaiya, etc. His last film was Guddu, released in 1995, starring Shahrukh Khan and Manisha Koirala.

Abrar Alvi passed away in Mumbai on November 18, 2009. He was 82 years old.

5

VK Murthy, Guru Dutt's Eyes

(November 26, 1923-April 7, 2014)

Guest article by film and music historian Manek Premchand

"If I can't picture it, I can't understand it"
– Albert Einstein

Many Kannadigas have made a name for themselves in various fields of endeavour. One thinks of the physicist Raja Ramanna, the life guru Sadhguru Jaggi Vasudev, the 'human computer' Shakuntala Devi, the co-founder of Infosys Narayan Murthy, and many more. Our story will engage with a few other people from the region, mainly the actor-filmmaker Guru Dutt, and his famous cinematographer, VK Murthy—"Guru Dutt's eyes" as he was called. "Neuroscientists have found that roughly two-thirds of the human brain is dedicated to visual processing", says a report. Both these gents knew that fact, and both wanted the camera to capture astonishing images for people to remember them by.

Dutt and Murthy bonded deeply, not only because both Kannadigas spoke the same language—which usually helps—but also because both were Brahmins and utterly in love with cinema. Such bonding started in 1951 and went on till Dutt passed away in 1964. The filmmaker's journey has been beautifully plotted at length through this book. So let's connect VK Murthy's dots from the beginning.

VK (Venkatarama Pandit Krishna) Murthy was born in Mysore on November 26, 1923. Impressed with the sounds of the violin, especially as it was played by a senior Mysore musician, T Chowdiah (who later became legendary), young VK went to Lakshmipuram School, Mysore, chose Music as his central subject, and learned to play the violin. After school, he started playing a bit here and there. But soon it was 1942, the year Gandhiji was galvanising many young Indians to participate in the Quit India Movement. Like millions of Indians, VK Murthy agitated and went to jail.

When he was released, he reconnected with another music-loving friend he had met in Lakshmipuram School, the older-by-one-year S Krishnamurthy who would go on to become a vocalist of much fame in the future. This young man was the grandson of Mysore Vasudevacharya, the Palace Vidvaan working in the court of Mysore's king Wadiyar. One day, young VK went with his friend to the palace, where he came face to face with Sri Jayachamarajendra, the current young king of Mysore. In fact, he would be the last king of Mysore, acceding, as all rulers did, to the Union of India when the Constitution was ready in January 1950. Sometimes you just need a nudge in the right direction. It was this king who was a heaven-sent man for VK.

To understand why he was heaven-sent, we need to quickly fly over the legacy of this prince who had become king at the young age of 21. Jayachamarajendra was a multi-talented personality. He was born in 1919, but by the time he sat on the throne (in 1940), he had built an enviable reputation as a sharpshooter, having conquered or killed a few wild animals. By 1944, he was also a competent polo and tennis player. In addition, he was deeply in love with classical music, both the Carnatic and the Western kind. If all this wasn't enough for young people to admire him, his enormous wealth and interest in India's literature permitted him to sponsor the translation of several classics into Kannada. He even found the time and enthusiasm to author many books.

Add to that another important detail. In the early 1940s, a positive wind was blowing in the direction of cinema. So, with a substantial donation from Jayachamarajendra Wadiyar, a new college called Sri Jayachamarajendra Polytechnic was set up in Bangalore in 1943. (It is now known as Film & Television Institute, Bangalore.) This was the first government body to offer technical courses in filmmaking. Under the young king's advice, VK Murthy joined the Polytechnic in 1944 and a year later, received a Diploma in Cinematography. The young man was now full of ideas about capturing moving images.

At this time, a Bombay-based director named Jayant Desai was making a film called Maharana Pratap, for which Murthy was hired as an assistant cameraman. The 1946-released film disappeared, even if it lives on through its many songs.

The disappointed young cameraman started doing some other work in films. For instance, in the 1950-made, Nitin Bose directed Mashaal, VK Moorthy (credited that way) was a Production Secretary. Then VK got a job with Famous Studios, Bombay, as an assistant cameraman. Soon, he began assisting a cinematographer named V Ratra for a Nav Ketan film titled Afsar (1950). Ratra was the director Chetan Anand's cousin but this camera chief was hardly interested in creative photography. He was a happy-go-lucky man who just wanted to pack up as soon as possible so that he could spend his evenings more satisfactorily. So it was Murthy who ended up doing a lot of thinking about camera angles and other inventive ideas. Upon this scene arrived Guru Dutt with his blueprint for Baazi. When that happened, Ratra and his assistant Murthy were signed up for Baazi which, like Afsar, was a Nav Ketan product. In the credits of Baazi, VK Murthy was mentioned under Photography as the Assistant with the name Murty.

But if in Afsar, Chetan Anand had looked the other way when his cousin Ratra was doing his work frivolously, the exacting Guru Dutt was going to offer no such luxury to his camera team in Baazi. For one, he was not related to Ratra. Besides, he had an intense personality that didn't subscribe to too much humour, especially irrelevant Punjabi jokes on the sets.

As for the story, Baazi was a crime thriller and hence Dutt decided to give it the film noir treatment. Film Noir (French for dark film) has to do with stark lighting, say a single source of light, with a lot of dark shadows, as was popular in many Hollywood crime films of the time. To shoot footage for such a subject handled by a director who wouldn't smile at your jokes meant Ratra would have to punch above his weight. CK Muralidharan did a long interview with Murthy, who said this:

"He (Ratra) would always say to me, 'Murthy, tum kar do na' (Murthy, you please do the work). That gave me a very good opportunity to do everything. I was doing lighting, camera placement and operation—everything. Ratra was simply enjoying.

One day, during shooting, it so happened that Guru Dutt was trying to find an angle to take a shot of a particular portion of a song. (Author's note: That song was Suno gajar kya gaaye). This portion had a lot of music. He was thinking about how the music could be covered up with camera movement. So I told Guru Dutt, 'If you don't mind, I could suggest one thing; see there is a big mirror we can use to create a great sense of movement.' He asked, 'How?' I said, 'Put the camera on the mirror and make Dev Anand start here from his reflection. I will move the camera as he walks towards it to the dance. I will follow him until he goes and sits on the chair.' The camera used to have a dolly. I placed the camera according to the music, I rehearsed the timings and all that and said to Guru Dutt that if you like it I will take the shot."

The shot was executed masterfully. But even otherwise, during the rest of the feature, Dutt and Murthy would often spend a lot of valuable time discussing *mise-en-scene* (the visual arrangement between the people, props and sets), during the shoots.

This film clicked and how! The next thing we know, the camera responsibility for Dutt's next film, Jaal (1952) went to VK Murthy, independently. By this time, Murthy and Dutt had become very close and had much respect for each other's art. Murthy went on to handle the camera in most of the subsequent films produced or directed by Guru Dutt. These films were Baaz (1953), Aar Paar (1954), Mr. & Mrs. '55 (1955), Pyaasa (1957), Kaagaz Ke Phool (1959), and Sahib Bibi Aur Ghulam (1962). The cinematography of Guru Dutt's Chaudhvin Ka Chand (1960) was handled by Nariman Irani because VK Murthy had been sent to study colour photography on the sets of the film The Guns of Navarone. When Chaudhvin Ka Chand celebrated its silver jubilee, VK re-shot two songs in colour, the title song Chaudhvin ka chand and Dil ki kahaani rang laayi hai.

Murthy also worked with other banners, including many directed by Pramod Chakravorty, Guru Dutt's brother-in-law (Geeta Dutt's younger sister, Lakshmi was married to Pramod). For Chakravorty, Murthy filmed 12 O'Clock (1958), Ziddi (1964), Love In Tokyo (1966), Naya Zamana (1971), Jugnu (1973), Nastik (1983), and Deedar (1992). Murthy also worked with director Govind Nihalani in Tamas (1988) and with director Shyam Benegal in the TV serial Bharat—Ek Khoj (1988-1989).

Guru Dutt, too, worked with other people, such as with director Mahesh Kaul in Sautela Bhai (1962), the cinematographer was Ratan Nagar; K Shankar in Bharosa (1963), photographed by Thambu; Bahurani (1963), director T Prakash Rao, the Director of Photography being Marcus Bartley; Suhagan (1964), director KS Gopalakrishnan, photographer M Karnan; and Sanjh Aur Savera (1964), director Hrishikesh Mukherji, cinematographer Jaywant Pathare.

But most film buffs and experts remain awestruck by the extraordinary results achieved by these two artists when they came together in three landmark films: Pyaasa (1957), Kaagaz Ke Phool (1959), and Sahib Bibi Aur Ghulam (1962). Hard-wired into our sensibilities is the silhouetted image of Guru Dutt, standing with a light behind him, at a door in an auditorium in Pyaasa. But, asks a learned view (in WordPress.com), "How can there be light? Pyaasa went on to be understood as a creative cinematic expression stemming out of the disappointment regarding the failure of Nehruvian socialism and the independence of India beyond the story of Vijay a tragic poet."

Murthy used innovation in Sahib Bibi Aur Ghulam too. In the mujra Saaqiya aaj mujhe neend naheen ayegi, there was a need to utterly anonymise the girls singing and dancing with Minoo Mumtaz, so that the latter could stand out alone in an audience comprising of men. VK Murthy achieved that, showing us only females dancing, with their identities subsumed in the music. Today simple apps let you airbrush the backdrop in seconds. But in the 1960s, this was quite a feat.

Earlier, in 1959, Guru got together with Waheeda in a lead role in Kaagaz Ke Phool, a story with strong autobiographical touches. This narrative, told in flashback, was about a once-famous director who fell in love with an actress he had discovered, with her career on the ascendant as he was on his way down. The film, sadly, was a commercial failure. Guru Dutt never directed a film again. But Director of Photography VK Murthy did go on to win the ultimate honour for contribution to Indian cinema: he won the Dadasaheb Phalke Award. The award salutes an artist's life's work of course, but if one film could be found—in fact if just one sequence could be found—as Murthy's greatest moment under the sun, it would be for the filming of the song Waqt ne kiya kya haseen sitam, Tum rahe na tum hum rahe na hum.

Guru Dutt had laboured for weeks over this song. He wanted to dramatise the moment with heavy contrasts in lighting as he had seen in some Hollywood films, and he had seen quite a few of these imports. One film came particularly to his mind. It was called The Cabinet of Dr Caligari, a silent horror film made in Germany in 1920.

Chiaroscuro

The lighting technique which Guru loved in that German film is called chiaroscuro. In this method, most things are put in the shade, as a single light source lights up specific objects. Guru discussed this with Murthy and used this technique in several situations in Kaagaz Ke Phool. For instance, when he, as the director in the narrative accidentally sees Waheeda in such a light, he is so enraptured that he thinks she is Paro, the embodiment of the woman he has imagined. It is a similar lighting effect near the end of the film when Guru Dutt is about to die in a chair.

But as observed before, the apex of the film's cinematography is perhaps during the song Waqt ne kiya kya haseen sitam, Tum rahe na tum hum rahe na hum. During this song, the light source alternates between a huge open door and a beam coming from the top. Into this beam walk the souls (or is it the desires?) of the two protagonists, even as their physical bodies stay grouted outside the spotlight, highlighting the gulf that now separates them. The song with its evocative poetry underscores an existential crisis that identifies Time as the central culprit of their once-beautiful relationship, with the stark setting and lighting combining to create an electric effect.

Will there be a scene as captivating as this one? Will there be another Guru Dutt? Will there be another creative cinematographer such as VK Murthy? Rhetorical questions. I'd say forget it.

In 2001, when he was 78, Murthy moved back to Bangalore city. From time to time, he would be toasted on many platforms as a person of exceptional ability in cinematography. He had such an extraordinary understanding of his art, that he has today become a guru for other film cinematographers who study his creations so that they may replicate his art.

VK Murthy passed away at age 91, on 7th April 2014. He has a daughter he named Chhaya, which means shade, a function of light.

6

Waheeda Rehman

(Born on February 3, 1938)

"The film industry has lost a great director, humanity
has lost a man of compassion and I lost a great friend who had
made the first and the greatest contribution to my success as a film
artist. I will always be grateful to him for this."
– Waheeda Rehman

When most of us think of Guru Dutt and Waheeda Rehman, a scene from Kaagaz Ke Phool comes to our minds. The extremely emotional scene with Waqt ne kiya kya haseen sittam playing in the background is one of Hindi cinema's most memorable moments. This is not only because of the brilliant direction of Guru Dutt and the innovative cinematography of VK Murthy, but it is also because of the closeness shared by Suresh Sinha (Guru Dutt) and Shanti (Waheeda Rehman) which is so subtly filmed that, even today no other intense and bitter-sweet scene comes anywhere close to it.

The scene begins with the actress Shanti, knitting a sweater for the film director Suresh Sinha who is a married man. He begins by asking her who she was knitting the sweater for. She answers that it was for someone who was as alone as she was. He understands that she is knitting it for him, and, without saying another word, he walks away from her into the darkness. With his back to her, he informs her that he is a married man with a child. She answers that she knows about his marriage. Then, when he gropes around to light his pipe with his injured arm, she rushes to him, joins him in the darkness and then lights his pipe for him. This symbolic act of hers of lighting the flame between them and, simultaneously, partnering with him in his act of self-destruction, remains etched in our minds. We know that smoking is harmful to health and yet here she is, facilitating his smoking. Guru Dutt didn't want us to miss the symbolism, he made it clear that she would support him even if he was engaged in doing something harmful. The idea that she had surrendered to him and that her love for him was unconditional was beautifully portrayed. Through that act of lighting the flame, she was, as it were, setting on fire many taboos that stood between them. She had already defied society when she accepted him as a married man, but she was also ready to go through the fire for him. The subtle symbolism enhances the romance of the song; the pathos of their love is intensified by the beautiful composition of SD Burman and Kaifi Azmi in combination with Geeta Dutt's sensuous yet painful rendition. The agony expressed by Geeta here is gut-wrenching,

Beqaraar dil is tarah mile, jis tarah kabhi hum juda na the

Tum bhi kho gaye, hum bhi kho gaye

Ek raah par chalke do qadam…

The visuals of the two lovers who are apart because they are constrained by society but who, in their souls, meet each other, are captured by the magician VK Murthy who uses the play of light and darkness to intensify their doomed love. Dressed as Paro (they were shooting a film about Devdas) she is bejewelled and fully made up. Waheeda Rehman's face is a sea of expressions; at one moment she expresses courage, at another despair, at a third, she offers him a beautiful smile, and so on. In this one scene, Guru Dutt and VK Murthy get the best out of Waheeda. We see, apart from her beauty, her breathtaking ability to completely immerse herself in the role. She is authentic, and since the film is autobiographical, it reflects the off-screen love of a single woman for a married director. Their emotions, their hurdles, their intense understanding of each other, everything comes together in the song in which we watch the two grapple with the social dilemma they find themselves in. When Guru Dutt moves from light to darkness, we understand that the extra-marital affair (in the secrecy of the darkness which envelops them) would exact its price. But Guru Dutt does not stop there. He goes a step further to boldly project the "other self" of the two lovers who move into the light to come together for a few intimate moments. The symbolism of the light into which both of them move is, at the same time, surreal and spiritual. They meet, even if it is only in their imagination, but even this imaginary union between two souls will soon set his life on fire.

This is the scene that has immortalised Waheeda Rehman: it has shown us what she is capable of, and why Guru Dutt was so convinced of her talent that he contracted her to act in his films.

Born in 1938 in Chingleput, on the outskirts of Madras, Waheeda Rehman belongs to a traditional Muslim family. Her father, Mohammed Abdul Rehman, was a district commissioner from Tamil Nadu. As a child, she used to be quite unwell with asthma. As the youngest of four daughters (Zahida, Shahida and Sayeeda were older), Waheeda had been trained in Bharatanatyam from a very young age. By the time she was seventeen years old, she had acted in a couple of films. One of them was a 1955 Telugu film called Rojulu Marayi. Abrar Alvi shared in his video interviews that when Guru Dutt was visiting Hyderabad, he had spotted her in a song in that Telugu film. In Sathya Saran's study of Abrar Alvi, she described their first encounter in which destiny played its part. "Guru Dutt, Abrar Alvi and production controller Guruswamy had landed up at the offices of a distributor in Secunderabad. While they were talking to each other, a car pulled up and some urchins were following the car. Waheeda Rehman got out while trying to avoid the fans, she entered a building across the road. They were told that she was a dancer in a super hit film. She had become very popular thanks to her song-and-dance number." Since they had time on their hands, a meeting was arranged. A reel of her dance was fetched for so they could watch it. Guru Dutt was impressed. They met briefly and then when he returned to Bombay, he sent for Waheeda later in 1955. She, her mother and a family friend landed in Bombay and their stay was booked at the posh Ritz Hotel. The contract was signed by Waheeda's mother since the actress was only seventeen then. Waheeda was part of Guru Dutt Films.

Trying to come to grips with Waheeda's impact on Guru Dutt's life, one comes across a piece written by her on Tumblr, titled, 'Guruji and I'. In that write-up which has also been shared in film historian Feroze Rangoonwala's monograph of Guru Dutt, she observed a few things about him which are insightful. She found that Guru Dutt was an extremely sensitive, quiet and complex person which is why he was often misunderstood. After meeting him in Hyderabad she met him in Bombay when he had sent for her. She signed a three-year contract to work with him. She observed, "C. I. D. and Pyaasa were being shot simultaneously at Kardar studios and he had advised me to come and sit on the sets and watch the shooting when I had nothing else to do. One day I saw him losing his temper with a senior artist and I was shocked that day I told him not to shout at me like this otherwise I would quit. I can't face it." "I have told you I won't lose my temper with you". He did not get angry with me even in the most trying circumstances. The shot of Pyaasa where I come running down the staircase and speak a dialogue was taken 20 times and every time I failed; by the time I came running down the staircase, I was too exhausted to speak the dialogue. He noticed it and came and told me that I should take rest for some time but I was not prepared to admit that I was tired and the shot could not be okayed till lunch break but he did not seem to be angry at all. After lunch, I had to give 14 more takes till the 34th take was okayed. It was perhaps a record for me and also a record of the patience of Guruji…"

She admired him because he "enjoyed every moment of the work". Yet he wanted to destroy himself, which was difficult to understand. He believe in God, she said, and once he had asked her to pray for the success of Kanoon, a B R Chopra film, because he was a song-less film. "I asked him, "Why do you want me to pray for the success of Kanoon? You have nothing to do with it". He answered, "At least someone is trying to make a movie without songs which I could not. If he is successful someone else could be inspired to go a step ahead. You must pray for the success of this film without songs." Guruji was considered one of the best directors for picturising songs, (yet) he was not a man who would be jealous of others' success; on the contrary, he enjoyed the success… He was a great lover. He loved his work. He loved his fellow beings, he loved his creations and he loved death too…He was never satisfied and I think he knew that he would never be satisfied…I explained to him that no one could ever get everything in life but that even death is not a solution, but he was a perfectionist who could not be easily satisfied; perhaps he refused to accept that life can never be perfect. He wanted to get everything…Some things are destined. Some patterns in life cannot be broken. You simply cannot change them. We must accept them… His death must have been just an accident but I know that he had always wished for it, longed for it and he got it."

About her beauty Waheeda said that she was not beautiful but that she, "just photographed well," for which she thanked the cameramen. Waheeda Rehman was very firm about how her costumes were designed. She never wore revealing clothes and initially, she had a lot of difficulty even with the Oscar-winning Bhanu Athaiya who told her that she must try to wear sleeveless or backless clothes. Waheeda Rehman later told her interviewer, "I said if people are going to sign me after seeing my arms and back, then I have failed as an actress."

Not only had she been firm about the decency of the costumes she was to wear, but she had also been very firm that she would not change her name from Waheeda Rehman to something else. Despite their efforts, neither Guru Dutt, Raj Khosla, VK Murthy nor Guruswamy had been able to persuade her to change her name. This self-confidence from Waheeda makes one thing clear: she was self-assured and centred, but she also knew from the start how Guru Dutt felt about her. She knew she would have her way with him. As has been revealed by his friends, including Abrar Alvi, Guru Dutt was transparent with his emotions and she was extremely perceptive.

For quite some time, Guru and Waheeda were in a serious relationship. Writer-director Abrar Alvi shared what had happened. Waheeda's sister's husband Rauf had gone to a mosque and announced to all and sundry that Guru was converting to Islam to marry Waheeda. When he heard of this, Guru Dutt was shocked and the whole thing was scuttled. Also, Geeta had earlier persuaded Abrar to put some sense into Guru's head. Waheeda has studiously avoided speaking on this sensitive subject.

In an interview, Guru's brother Devi Dutt said, "The relationship between Waheeda Rehman and Guru Dutt was that of a teacher and a student. Her mother's health was fragile as she suffered from a heart problem. She passed away around the time Pyaasa was released. Waheedaji, with her older sister Saeeda, wanted to return to Hyderabad. But Guru Dutt insisted they stay back. He shifted them from Khar to a more comfortable house in Colaba and gave them a car. He believed she was lucky for us. And she was. There must have been something emotional between them. When people work together, a bond, a friendship develop. But it was a temporary phase. There was nothing serious. My brother hardly went home. He stayed back at the studio to finish his work. Bhabhi suspected it was because of Waheedaji, which wasn't right. There were rumours that he wanted to divorce Bhabhi, become a Muslim and marry Waheedaji. None of it was true. Guru Dutt, no matter what, would never have left the kids. He had no guts to do that."

There were also several issues Guru was dealing with at that time. It was rumoured by some that he had discovered the presence of another man in Geeta's life, and he had wanted to preserve his marriage at any cost. Their last meeting was at the showcasing of Sahib Bibi Aur Ghulam in Berlin, but even before this, Waheeda and Guru had not been in touch. This has been reinforced by three people, Abrar Alvi, Waheeda Rehman and Lalita Lajmi.

While Guru and Geeta patched up after his breakup with Waheeda, their lives were still stressful. They quarrelled incessantly. They took to drinking. His rise in the film industry and her fall, with her reluctance to give up singing, heightened the tension between them. But the two worst things to happen were Guru's dalliance with Waheeda and his obsessive involvement with work. He was, perhaps, so driven by his art that he could not be a devoted family man.

Waheeda Rehman and Guru Dutt worked together in C.I.D., Pyaasa, 12 O'Clock, Kaagaz Ke Phool, Chaudhvin Ka Chand and Sahib Bibi Aur Ghulam. But surprisingly, she was the lead heroine in only three of them, 12 O'Clock, Kaagaz Ke Phool and Chaudhvin Ka Chand. They did work together in the film Raaz as well, but the film was shelved after about 12 reels had been shot.

Waheeda Rehman shared that the first shot she did with Guru Dutt was for Pyaasa when she, as Gulabo the prostitute, was thrown out of a car by a man who had slept with her. Her last shot with him was in Sahib Bibi Aur Ghulam when she visited Guru Dutt at the site at which he had just discovered Chhoti Bahu's corpse. They sat together in a horse-and-carriage and she reassured him with her smile by putting her hand on his while he looked lost and broken. She was unwilling to do this last scene with Guru because, by this time, they had broken up, but she finally agreed to Abrar's pleas with the condition that she would not say anything to him in the scene. Abrar heaved a sigh of relief because something was better than nothing!

Waheeda Rehman's ability to perform her role to perfection was seen in so many scenes that one was left awe-struck. But two scenes stood out, one in Pyaasa and another in Kaagaz Ke Phool. One was when she heard some wandering sadhus sing a Krishna Bhajan and her face expressed her deep love for Vijay. Her face showed us the anguish of her one-sided love for the poet who had no real feelings for her. Her tears, her love, her fear, everything was on her face while the song Aaj sajan mohe ang laga lo spoke about her Radha-like devotion to the abstracted Vijay.

The other scene was her brilliant performance in the car in Kaagaz Ke Phool while the song San san woh chali hawa was sung by Mehmood and friends. Some songs just pass us by, and we don't pay too much attention to them because anything growing under an oak tree doesn't get noticed. Kaagaz ke Phool has been so much discussed for its oak tree songs, Waqt ne kiya and Dekhi zamaane ki yaari that we simply don't notice a song that is spectacular in its performances by both Guru Dutt and Waheeda Rehman.

The filming of San san san woh chali hawa, its direction, its ability to show you the exact moment when two people are falling in love with each other, all of it leaves you agape! One can only gasp when one watches these few minutes in isolation if we forget the other two epic songs. The filming of this song showed us how Suresh Sinha was falling in love with a woman who adored him. He seemed conflicted, yet, the moment was so heady, the strong breeze so full of promise, the beauty of the damsel next to him so simple and so magical, that he let himself feel the love. The song by itself is not a magnificent creation from SD Burman or even from Kaifi Azmi, but what is magical is VK Murthy's artistic capture, Guru Dutt's natural magnetism, and, of course, Waheeda Rehman's doe-eyed shy, romantic glances at her companion. The direction of the scene is brilliant. We have a group in an open truck out for a picnic, and we have a young male and female in a chauffeured convertible.

The camera flits between the two vehicles, one full of gaiety and the other resplendent with romance. The car in front has three people, a driver whose back is visible but not his face, a handsome well-dressed man who is Guru Dutt and the pretty Waheeda Rehman with her long hair flying in the breeze. The camera watches their expressions change while Waheeda's hair flies away from her. She is clearly blushing because she senses how magnetic he is for her. She is overcome by her attraction to him. He watches her face go through those emotions and hesitates. VK Murthy intentionally lets the camera move away from Guru's face as he begins to consider the possibility of a liaison with her, and then, after showcasing the merry picnickers, the camera returns to him. By this time his conflict has been resolved, and now relaxed, he turns around to look at the happy truck, and then exchanges an intimate glance with her. At this point Waheeda is relieved that his moment of doubt has passed and, feeling secure in the knowledge, she smiles and they are once again comfortable with each other. Both the actress and director combine to create a scene of intimacy between two people without a hand touched, without an embrace, without even a single loving word exchanged between them.

It is all in their body language, especially in their eyes. Guru Dutt always said, "It's in the eyes." And one sees how beautifully he has captured Waheeda Rehman as she shows her shy love to him! A truly brilliant actress like Waheeda Rehman convinces us that one does not need revealing clothes, ornamental words or too many physically intimate scenes to perform well. A true actress emotes and says it all through her face and body language.

Waheeda had earned a lot of respect from her peers too. In an interview, Shyama, the actress of Guru Dutt's Aar Paar, spoke highly about her, "She was my neighbour. She lived here with her mother and sister Sayeda. She was very photogenic and loved wearing saris. She was good-natured but kept to herself largely. Guru Dutt was very fond of her. He was a good director and she was a good actress. I don't know about their personal lives but we knew that Geeta Dutt had stopped singing for her. I worked with Waheeda in many films." Shyama hinted at Waheeda Rehman's romantic feelings for Dilip Kumar too because they had worked together in Dil Diya Dard Liya. "Yusuf bhai (Dilip Kumar) was the hero. Often she'd be reading on the sets. Once I asked her teasingly, 'Whom are you trying to impress? What can you see in the dark?' She'd smile. She'd also be knitting a sweater. I'd ask her mischievously, 'Whom are you knitting it for?' They made a good pair. But ultimately, love and marriage is a matter of naseeb (destiny)."

Incidentally, Vyjayanthimala wrote in her autobiography 'Bonding' that she was shooting for Ram Aur Shyam in 1964 but suddenly Dilip Kumar had Vyjayanthimala removed from the film even though she had completed shooting for a few days. He wanted her to be replaced by Waheeda. He again tried to do the same with Sunghursh but this time he failed. Dilip Kumar was insisting on being cast with Waheeda since they were seeing each other at that time. However, Dilip Kumar switched his affections to Saira Banu and proposed to her.

Sometime around 1968/69, Waheeda got engaged to Farid Ahmed Siddiqui, from Najibabad in U.P. Later, she broke the engagement because she thought it was a mistake. In 1972, Waheeda got engaged to the actor Shashi Rekhi whose screen name was Kamaljeet. They were married in a nikaah ceremony on July 26, 1974, in Waheeda Rehman's bungalow, Saahil. He was introduced in Son Of India by Mehboob Khan. Waheeda and Shashi had acted together in Shagun which had flopped despite its excellent musical score. Then he also acted in Heer Ranjha, Tamacha, Mr. India, Kismet Ka Khel and Mr. Lambu. He then moved to London and from there to Toronto. Then on one of his visits to Bombay, he proposed to Waheeda Rehman. They moved to Bangalore after marriage. They had two children, a son Sohail, and a daughter Kashvi. When he had a stroke in 1997, the family moved back to Bombay to be close to Lilavati Hospital which was near their home. He was in and out of the hospital several times since he had diabetes along with other health conditions. He was 67 years old when he died of a brain haemorrhage on November 21, 2000. Waheeda continues to live in Bombay.

Controversy has always followed Waheeda Rehman throughout her life. Only this year, 2024, a book by Shailendra's daughter Amla Shailendra Mazumdar ('Shailendra, A Love Lyric in Print') shows Waheeda Rehman in a poor light. On the actress's association with Shailendra for the film Teesri Kasam, Amla writes on Page 214:

"We eavesdropped on their (parents) whispered conversations and gathered that Waheeda Rehman was refusing to go for the outdoor shooting (for Teesri Kasam) until she was paid for the dates. As mentioned the unit had already travelled out to Bina at considerable expense. In conversation with Nasreen Munni Kabir, Waheeda Rehman mentions that Shailendra went to her and pleaded for her to join the unit as soon as possible. I sensed from my parents' conversation that Baba may have approached her asking her to reconsider her decision not to go for the shooting, assuring her that she would be paid after a few days or so, but she did not relent; what is more shocking is to read her claim that she took no money at all, while Raj Kapoor took only a single rupee..." Since they had no money to pay Waheeda Rehman at this time, their family was in a crisis. "Then Mummy stood up, pulled out her bunch of keys, and opened her cupboard slowly. She pushed all the saris on the floor, shook each one vigorously allowing several hundred rupee notes to fall from their folds…Both Baba and Mummy counted the notes, their smiles radiating contentment. Believe it or not, Baba now had enough money to pay Waheeda Rehman…Looking back I feel anger and sadness at the same time: anger towards those who created these unnecessary situations around Baba and sadness when I reflect on his vulnerability to such manipulation."

About Guru Dutt's death, Waheeda said pensively, "Whatever God does is for our good only. He knows what is best for us. As Rabindranath Tagore has said, 'We cannot choose the best, the best chooses us'. His death has been a great loss to us; but whatever happened was, perhaps, best for him! That is the only consolation left."

The world lost a genius, and all we can say is, 'If only he had been less sensitive.' But then, was it not his sensitivity that defined him and made him the genius we salute?

7

Bimal Mitra

(18 March 1912-02 December 1991)

Guru Dutt, voracious reader that he was, used to order books by the dozens from all over the world. He would go through them quickly. His mother Vasanthi said that he had a very strong memory and he would never forget important things. He would store the memory of these books in his memory bank. One day, he ordered a copy of Bimal Mitra's Bengali novel, 'Saheb Bibi Golam', from Calcutta. Since he had studied in Calcutta from a very young age, he was accustomed to reading and writing Bengali.

He read the novel which had taken Mitra many years to write. The story was originally carried as a weekly serial in a Bengali newspaper and had become so popular that later it was published as a novel in 1953. Mitra wrote that Guru Dutt liked the novel and so he read it again. He liked it even more the second time. Then he read it again. In this manner, he read the novel five times! Then when he was considering making it into a film, he would ask people what they felt about the novel; some would praise it while others would discourage him. A few years later he decided to go ahead and film it.

The novel was first filmed in Bengali in 1956. It starred Sumitra Devi, Uttam Kumar and Chhabi Biswas. When the Bengali film was being made, Bimal Mitra did not visit the studio even once. However, now that he was dealing with Guru Dutt, matters were different. Guru Dutt sent for him to come to Bombay sometime in March or April of 1960. Bimal Mitra was afraid because he had never flown before. Moreover, his health wasn't good. Guru Dutt called him long distance and charmed him into accepting.

When Mitra met Guru Dutt he found the filmmaker extremely affable, he had a beautiful smile and a friendly manner. Both of them loved reading and had a lot of interesting discussions on varied subjects which included the meaning of life, the role of society, about loneliness or God. Bimal Mitra also got along very well with Geeta who was sweet and would arrange for the right Bengali food to be cooked for him. She attended to his every need and made him feel at home.

He saw Guru Dutt from close quarters and grew very fond of him. He saw both his flaws and his strengths since they spent days together in Bombay, Lonavala and Mahabalipuram.

The mahurat of Sahib Bibi Aur Ghulam took place on 1st January, 1961. Mitra, who was in Bombay for some work was invited by Guru Dutt to attend the mahurat puja. After the puja was completed, Guru, Geeta, Waheeda and Mitra sat down together for lunch. Mitra was surprised to see both ladies together at the table since he knew, from Geeta, how much she detested Waheeda's presence in Guru Dutt's life. Guru, meanwhile, told him that he had dragged Geeta to the studio because he had wanted her to help Waheeda wear the saree in the Bengali style. Geeta had earlier confided in Mitra that she had been betrayed by Waheeda since Geeta had trusted her implicitly. She even told Mitra that she had asked Guru not to make this film because, "Sahib Bibi Aur Ghulam humaari hi zindagi ki kahaani hai." Geeta confided in Mitra that she had come to the studio after very long; earlier she used to regularly visit the studio but then she stopped because she said, "Mujhe laga in sab par mera haq nahin hai." Geeta also did not want Waheeda to play Jaba in the film, but Guru had been adamant. In constant conflict, the couple could not see eye to eye on anything.

Mitra witnessed their fights and sometimes tried to help. For example, Geeta told him that Guru was constantly fighting with her to give up her singing career but she would not comply because his reasons didn't make sense. When Mitra confronted Guru about this, he said there was no need for her to work, and that the home was being neglected. Mitra asked him where then was the need for Guru to make films. Guru, instead of answering his question, asked him why he was comparing his films with her singing. He said the servants were stealing, the furniture was getting old, the flowers in the garden were not being tended to, etc. Through all this Bimal saw that the patriarchal mindset he was attacking in the film, was the mindset Guru shared.

In the middle of 1963, Guru Dutt ordered their Pali Hill home to be demolished and rebuilt, so all of them moved to Sun N Sand Hotel. But this did not suit them, so they rented an apartment at Pali Naka. The reason for the destruction of that beautiful bungalow was because Geeta had felt that there was an evil spirit there. "Is bangle mein kisi bhoot ka vaas hai, jisne hamaari zindagi ashanti se bhar di hai!" Mitra felt bad because the house had been beautiful but he was optimistic. But his hopes were soon dashed. He wrote, "Lekin, sukh to Guru ki kismat mein hi nahin tha. Wahaan bhi jhagde shuru ho gaye. Is baar, woh jhagde is hadd tak ja pahunche ke Guru woh ghar bhi chhod kar chala gaya aur Peddar Road mein ek flat kiraye par lekar akela rehne laga."

Mitra had seen Guru struggle with sleep. He would drink and also take sleeping pills, but sleep still eluded him. Night after night this was his biggest challenge. His mind would be racing on and sleep would be nowhere on the horizon. Because of the deadly mix of alcohol and drugs, he would sometimes wake up with such terrible agony and pain that a doctor would be sent for. The doctor would give him very painful detoxification medicines and injections to alleviate his suffering. But he refused to stop playing with his health.

Mitra said when Guru moved to Peddar Road, Abrar Alvi tried to be with him every evening when he was in Bombay. On that last night in this world, Guru was in a disturbed state of mind and he had kept a bottle of whiskey in his hands. "Guru ko drink karne se mana karna Bhagwan ke liye bhi asambhav tha! Asal mein Guru ka man kachhue jaisa tha." What he meant was that once he decided to withdraw from everyone, nobody could bring him out of that decision.

Books had created an unbreakable bond between the two of them. While Guru was generous to a fault, what Mitra found attractive was that he was an engaging conversationalist. He would be willing to discuss any subject under the sun, God included.

Guru's commitment to excellence fascinated him. Yet, Mitra wrote that he was also deeply flawed. "Woh to aisa insaan tha, jo ek baar jis kutte ko paalta tha, wohi insaan ye khabar lene ki zaroorat bhi nahin samajhta ki woh kutta zinda bhi hai ya nahin. Jo shaks apne alaava aur kisi ko nahin pehchaanta, wohi shaks jab achaanak apne aamne saamne khada hota hai, tab woh apne ko bhi nahin pehchaan paata...". He also observed, "Jab kabhi use apni marzi, apni khushi ke liye kisi aur ka samarthan nahin milta tha, tab wo naaraaz ho jaata tha. Gusse mein woh apne ko hi takleef deta tha, aas paas ke logon par zulm karta tha. Jisse bhi woh apne saamne paata tha, ussi par tohmat jad deta tha. Ant mein jab usse apni galti samajh mein aati thi, tab tak kaafi nuksaan ho jaata tha. Uske baad uska aatamnigrah shuru ho jaata tha. Us waqt woh yathasambhav apne ko behlaane ki koshish karta tha aur apne ko bhulaane ki ekmaatr raah thi aur aur zyaada kharch karna. Us waqt woh vilayat bhaag jaata tha, ya jo bhi mil jaaye, uske saath adebaazi karne baith jata tha." Mitra observed that he would be surrounded by users and false friends and his circle of friends would constantly keep changing. They would praise him just so they could exploit and loot him. Mitra was dismayed to see Guru mixing with such crooked characters. He concluded that since he was constantly restless, he settled for this kind of company because when he was with others, he could manage to forget himself and his troubles.

When Mitra heard that Guru Dutt had died, he was stunned. For days, he just could not believe it. In the end, his most beautiful observation was, "Mere liye Guru ka jaana, kabhi na poore hone waala nuksaan tha."

Bimal Mitra wrote over a hundred novels and short stories. Filmfare nominated him for the Best Story Award for Sahib Bibi Aur Ghulam. He passed away at his residence in Calcutta on December 2, 1991.

These recollections of Mitra are sourced from his book, Bichhde Sabhi Baari Baari published by Vani Prakashan in 2010. The translation from Bengali to Hindi is by Susheel Gupta.

8

Raj Khosla

(May 31, 1925-June 9, 1991)

In an interview available on YouTube, Raj Khosla spoke very highly of his friend Guru Dutt. He observed, "He would often get lost, from all the people he loved, and then he would feel lonely; he was a lonely person but he was never alone. He was with his films."

Raj Khosla was introduced to Guru Dutt by Dev Anand. Khosla wanted to be a singer but Dev asked him to assist Guru in Baazi. When Khosla accepted the job, it changed his life.

After having worked with Guru, Khosla remarked, "You couldn't read through Guru, but I read one thing about him, in those days also…that he was *lost*. Lost in film-making, but lost to life."

Somehow, Raj Khosla observed, "You see, it's one thing to love somebody, it's another thing to say I love you. He was not a man who could not say I love you. He used to love but could not express himself. That was the enigma, so the whole thing came out in the films, that loving he put through in his movies."

The three of them, Raj Khosla, Dev Anand and Guru Dutt were good friends. Sometimes Dev would take Khosla on a trip out of town and sometimes Guru would do the same. Although all three of them worked together in C.I.D., Khosla always treated Guru as his mentor and guide. Khosla had been keen to become a singer like his idol KL Saigal. He would sometimes find his way to Dev's home and sit down on the floor with the harmonium and sing a few songs for Dev who, not impressed, found his voice, 'grainy.' Dev connected him with Guru who was busy working on Nav Ketan's Baazi at the time. Guru took him on as Assistant Director, after which there was no looking back for him. In time, Khosla became an outstanding director, but he would give full credit for what he had learnt about cinema to Guru. For example, Guru taught him to focus his camera on the eyes of the character portraying a role.

"Guru Dutt told me that 80 per cent of acting is done by the eyes of the actor, the rest is 20 per cent. The eyes are the most expressive part."

However, there was one major problem which became a hurdle in their work together. That was Waheeda Rehman. Guru was besotted by Waheeda but sadly, there were issues between Khosla and Waheeda. He found Waheeda difficult to work with. While Khosla and Guru shared a wonderful rapport, when it came to Waheeda they had differences. Khosla, from the very start, felt that Guru was over-estimating Waheeda, who often put her foot down for the slightest of reasons. She knew she could get away with it because Guru had a weakness for her and he could not refuse her what she wanted.

But the feelings were mutual. Talking about Raj Khosla at the 2015 Jaipur Lit Fest, Waheeda, too, on her part, complained about him. Firstly she objected to his wanting her name changed. She said that both Guru and Khosla had said her name was too long but she refused to change it. They gave her examples of Dilip Kumar, Meena Kumari, and Madhubala, but she would not budge. She said she was not like everyone else who changed their names. She stuck to her guns and 'Waheeda Rehman' stayed.

Again, during the shooting of her debut Hindi film, C.I.D., she had to dance to composer Nayyar's Kahin pe nigaahen, kahin pe nishaana. When she saw the costume meant for the song, she had a major argument with both Zohra Sehgal and director Khosla, complaining about it being too revealing. She wanted a change in her blouse, or at least an additional lining added to it because she felt what they wanted her to wear was a see-through blouse and she was uncomfortable with it. The costume designer Bhanu Athaiya and the Production Executive Guruswamy, in vain, tried to persuade her. The agitated Khosla made a long-distance call to Guru who was in Khandala working on the script of Pyaasa with Abrar Alvi. Khosla told him that time was running out, that Dev had to leave (his wife was pregnant and was due to deliver their son Suneil in Switzerland in June 1956), but Waheeda had stopped work because of her costume. Guru drove to Bombay and found that Khosla was right. He, too, could not see anything revealing about the blouse. However, since they were short of time, he acceded to her wishes, and they added a layer of a dupatta to the blouse and thus, Waheeda got her way.

Khosla then told Dutt, "None of her movies have been released yet and she is already difficult. If she becomes successful, you will be in big trouble." Prophetic and ironic words! Later when they worked together for Solva Saal, Khosla and Waheeda again argued over her dress. Khosla had to surrender again. Yet again, Waheeda had her way with Dev who was considering Khosla as a replacement for Chetan Anand for Guide: she refused to accept Khosla as the director of the film and Dev had to drop the idea. He then handed over the film's direction to Vijay Anand. But Vijay, too, found Waheeda difficult. He was very unhappy with Waheeda's stiffness and difficult behaviour, especially in some scenes in Kaanton se kheench ke ye aanchal. Because Waheeda was such a committed and brilliant actress, she managed to get her way.

Khosla and Guru worked together in Baazi, Jaal, Baaz, Aar Paar and C.I.D. When Khosla became successful they did not work together. Khosla came to be known as a 'women's director' because he understood how to bring out the best in his actresses.

Khosla directed several hit films including Kala Pani (1958), Woh Kaun Thi (1964), Mera Saaya (1966), Do Badan (1966), Do Raaste (1969), and Main Tulsi Tere Aangan Ki (1978) which received the Filmfare award for Best Film. Once his films stopped doing well, Khosla was disappointed and disillusioned with the film world and took to drinking. He died in 1991 when he was 66 years old.

Raj Khosla never stopped praising Guru Dutt for his guidance. He recalled what he had observed about Guru when they worked together. "For Guru Dutt, characters were not merely talking and acting — what worried him was: "What is my artist thinking at the moment in the story?" Perhaps, with such a genius as mentor, Raj Khosla had no choice but to be a very successful film director.

9

Johnny Walker

(November 11, 1926-July 29, 2003)

Guru Dutt knew that when he added Johnny Walker to his films, they would become hits. In an interview online on YouTube, Johnny Walker said that for Guru Dutt, Johnny's being in the film was a must, so much so that he would create a role for him, weaving his part into the narrative even if it was not part of the original story. Abrar Alvi and Guru Dutt would narrate to him the kind of character he was to play, whether he was a Parsi or a maalish waala and give him the language he had to speak, which would be consistent with the language in the song's lyrics as well. And Johnny would take the baton from them and run to the finish line!

Johnny Walker offered comic relief in Guru Dutt's films but their relationship went beyond their work on the sets. The camaraderie between them was great, both professionally and personally. Johnny seemed like a lucky mascot to Guru Dutt; even so, in Kaagaz Ke Phool his magic failed to enhance the film and its theme. The film flopped because Johnny's comedy took away from the seriousness of the film which was not a masala film but a classic of a very different kind. The tragedy that Kaagaz Ke Phool was, it needed no comic relief. It was only in Sahib Bibi Aur Ghulam that Guru Dutt understood that he was making a serious film again and Johnny's comedy would get in the way. Thus, while in the Muslim social Chaudhvin Ka Chand, Johnny Walker even got to lip sync two songs, in Saheb Bibi Aur Ghulam he had no role.

Johnny's brilliant performances kept the audience amused and provided a refreshing break from the main plot. He was even thrown into a scene as a confidante where all he did was respond in dismay at the mad friend who had fallen in love and could not stop talking about her, like in the song in Aeji dil par hua aisa jaadu in Mr. & Mrs. '55. Johnny would make the scene funny with just his facial expressions or his very presence. He was just what the doctor prescribed for Aar Paar, Mr. & Mrs.'55, and C.I.D.

When Guru was shooting a serious scene in the studio and if Johnny was around, Guru would say to him, "Johnny, chalo baahar!"

This was because he was so funny that even his very presence was sufficiently funny to distract a crew or cast member. He had the innate ability to dilute the serious atmosphere and change the mood of everyone around him. Nobody could keep a straight face or even think straight when Johnny was around! So when Guru commanded, "Johnny, chalo baahar," it was the unsparing perfectionist Guru Dutt talking.

In the same YouTube interview, Johnny Walker mentioned that once Guru had taken Johnny along with him to Calcutta. Johnny, who had never seen the city before, was fascinated. They were casually sitting in an open restaurant eating puchki when Guru saw a maalish waala do a head massage on a man sitting in front of him. Guru Dutt immediately asked Johnny to observe the man carefully: the way his hands moved, the way he worked, etc. Guru decided he would introduce the character of a maalish waala in Pyaasa and Johnny would do the role of Abdul Sattar, the masseur. Guru also asked Johnny to produce the same voice which he did for mosquitoes or machars. It was a strange high-pitched crow's caw kind of sound. The song 'maalish tel maalish, champi! Sar jo tera chakraaye' begins with Johnny's voice which is then followed by Rafi's singing.

Guru Dutt was extremely observant, so he would observe life and employ it in his films the way he observed the maalish waala and used that idea in Pyaasa. Johnny was present in almost all the films Guru directed or produced; Baazi, Jaal, Baaz, Aar Paar, Mr. & Mrs. '55, Pyaasa, Kaagaz Ke Phool, C.I.D., Chaudhvin Ka Chand and finally in Guru's posthumous film Baharen Phir Bhi Aayengi.

Johnny's character was often shown as the opposite of the character projected by Guru Dutt. Somehow, in his films, although Johnny, too, was facing challenges in his life, his spirit of positivity made him take life lightly. He appeared to be the answer in a tragic, materialistic universe, a man who overcame life's challenges with a spring in his step and a joke on his lips. His roles showed us that his poverty didn't bog him down, because he glided through grave situations and sorrows. It was as if Johnny, through the characters he portrayed, was offering Guru the answer to life's tough issues. Guru knew he ought not to take life seriously, yet, given his inherent moroseness, he realised he could not face life the way Johnny did. Guru had to get emotional when he saw injustice and unfair rejections, while Johnny was the laughing Buddha, albeit a thin laughing Buddha!

Johnny was Balraj Sahni's discovery. It was Balraj Sahni who recommended the comic Johnny to Guru Dutt. Johnny's real name was Badruddin Kazi, and he was hired to play the role of a drunkard in Baazi. Guru Dutt renamed him Johnny Walker because he was brilliant as a drunkard. In his personal life, however, Johnny was a teetotaller. He met actress Noor, Shakila's sister on the sets of Aar Paar, they fell in love during the shoots and they got married.

Because of his innate sense of timing, rhythm and comedy, Johnny Walker sang some brilliant songs in Guru Dutt's films. Although he acted in Baazi, Jaal, and Baaz, the first film in which he got a song to sing was in Aar Paar.

All the songs he sang in Guru Dutt's films were in Rafi's voice. They were:

Arrey na na na tauba tauba—Aar Paar

Jaane kahaan mera jigar gaya jee—Mr. & Mrs. '55

Ae dil hai mushkil jeena yahaan—C.I.D.

Sar jo tera chakraaye—Pyaasa

Dekh idhar, ae haseena—12 O'Clock

Hum tum jise kehte hain shaadi—Kaagaz Ke Phool

Mera yaar bana hai dulha—Chaudhvin Ka Chand

Ye duniya gol hai—Chaudhvin Ka Chand

Suno, suno, Miss Chatterjee—Baharen Phir Bhi Aayengi

10

Rehman

(June 23, 1921-November 5, 1984)

Guru Dutt and Dev Anand made friends with Rehman during their stint at Prabhat in Pune, and it was Guru Dutt who decided to cast him in most of his films in the character of the villain who nearly succeeded in defeating the protagonist.

Rehman began to work with Guru Dutt in the latter's more serious phase of film-making which began with Pyaasa. Thus, he acted in Pyaasa, Chaudhvin Ka Chand, Sahib Bibi Aur Ghulam, and Baharen Phir Bhi Aayengi. They worked together in 12 O' Clock, but it was not a Guru Dutt production. Just as Johnny Walker was required for comic relief, Guru Dutt, almost as if to balance the extremes in his films, would include Rehman for his menacing villainy too. Rehman was the hateful counterpoint to the protagonist, the other man in almost all cases, except in Baharen Phir Bhi Aayengi where his role was not villainous.

Rehman, the actor par excellence, specialised in projecting understated villainy towards either or both of the film's protagonists and while one hated actors Pran and Madan Puri for their crooked machinations, one could not but respect the subtle evil and criminality of Rehman. Rehman's character in his films was like that of a lizard waiting for its prey, pouncing on it when it was at its most vulnerable.

Rehman as the older man, the cold and ruthless jealous husband of Meena (Mala Sinha) in Pyaasa, was simply astounding. Cast as Ghosh, the corrupt publisher, Rehman was the best counterpoint to the idealist Vijay (Guru Dutt), the frustrated and homeless poet. They were like black is to white: one was clever, successful, wealthy, full of menace, the man who got a young and beautiful woman to marry him because he offered her security, comforts and wealth, while the other was the failed poet, who was brilliant, idealistic, poor, and unable to deal with the harsh realities of life. Vijay's anger and despair were in inverse proportion to Ghosh's devilishly macabre sadism. Only Rehman could have done what he did in Pyaasa as a counterpoint to the mercurial but idealistic temperament of the protagonist.

For example, in the film, Ghosh's suspicion, jealousy, and cruel sadism forced the poet Vijay to serve drinks to his party guests. His motive was to demean his rival and squash him underfoot because his wife Meena had not forgotten her college love and still pined for him. Vijay was a reminder to Ghosh of the fact that money could not buy love, so Ghosh wanted to destroy him.

In the song of despair, Jaane woh kaise log the jinke pyaar ko pyaar mila, cinematographer VK Murthy brilliantly shifted his camera from Ghosh's face to Vijay's to Meena's and to the general audience, showing us the different emotions on each of them. The question in the song, Jaane woh kaise log the jinke pyaar ko pyaar mila, was not a question, it was a statement of cynical despair, moaning the fact that those with empty pockets dare not dream of requited love but those with full pockets, like Ghosh, get beautiful women like Meena because of their wealth. The irony of the situation was brought out brilliantly by Ghosh's book-lined living room, proving the fact that education does not necessarily make one kind. Education, in the wrong hands, can prove to be deadly, killing careers, dreams, and Man's will to live. It can often be worse than illiteracy. Education was wasted on Ghosh; it had, in fact, made him worse.

But Rehman went on to get an even bigger role with Guru Dutt in Sahib Bibi Aur Ghulam where he played the womanising feudal lord who had his priorities twisted, where he was shown as someone who respected prostitutes and had contempt for his faithful wife. His portrayal of Chhote Babu can be regarded as one of the best roles of his career. His contempt for a faithful and beautiful wife, his wilful neglect and arrogance, it was a brilliant performance!

For his performance in this film, Rehman was nominated as Best Supporting Actor by Filmfare.

Rehman had exceptional roles in several films outside the Guru Dutt ambit as well. Badi Behen was one. Chhoti Behen, Phir Subah Hogi, Dharmputra, Yeh Raste Hain Pyaar Ke, Dil Ne Phir Yaad Kiya, and Waqt also had some of his best performances.

Later, he became a heavy drinker and because of his chain-smoking, he developed throat cancer and lost his voice. He died in 1984 when he was 63 years of age.

SECTION THREE

Guru Dutt's 'S Magical Music

1. OP Nayyar and Majrooh Sultanpuri

2. SD Burman, Sahir Ludhianvi and Kaifi Azmi

3. Ravi, Shakeel Badayuni and Guru Dutt

4. Hemant Kumar and Shakeel Badayuni

5. Themes of Guru Dutt's Songs

6. Singers of Guru Dutt's Films

1

OP Nayyar and
Majrooh Sultanpuri

When one studies the films that Guru Dutt produced, one can see three distinct phases in his career. Phase 1 is filled with upbeat and optimistic music, which I label as his Happy Phase, then comes Phase 2, the Crossover Phase with Pyaasa and its pessimism, and finally comes Phase 3, or the Failure Phase, which includes Kaagaz Ke Phool and Sahib Bibi Aur Ghulam.

The Happy Phase

Phase 1 of Guru Dutt's films is completely identified by OP Nayyar's music. The credit for writing the lyrics for the highest number of Guru Dutt-produced films goes to Majrooh Sultanpuri, who was not only the most prolific lyricist for Guru Dutt with 32 songs, he was also the most prolific lyricist for OP Nayyar for whom he wrote a whopping 127 poems! The euphoria and joie de vivre these compositions expressed were unmatched. But what made this team of Dutt, Nayyar and Majrooh work so well was the fact that although all three were geniuses in their respective fields, it was the more sanguine Majrooh who adjusted to the other two.

The eccentric genius OP Nayyar would compose the music and Majrooh would come up with the best lyrics for the melody, and this harmonious sync became invaluable to Guru Dutt. Majrooh kept the bigger picture in his mind and never let his ego get in the way of his work. He sensed that if he was the most mature of the three, they could create the most unforgettable melodies.

Majrooh Sultanpuri was jailed for over a year in 1951, by the then Congress government for a poem in which he had criticised Prime Minister Jawaharlal Nehru. But despite being in the lockup, his standing in the industry remained unchanged. Work was waiting for him. As soon as he was set free, he landed a few assignments; Guru Dutt's Baaz was amongst the first Majrooh signed.

OP Nayyar was such a genius that he would compose a melody within minutes of Guru Dutt telling him of the situation for which a song was needed. Majrooh, too, was equally adept at writing lyrics on demand! Majrooh would spend a few minutes in thought, put pen to paper, and voila, the song was ready!

Of the three, Majrooh Sultanpuri had the greatest challenge because he was working with the unsparing Nayyar. Majrooh was a brilliant poet, but pragmatism was also in his blood. He knew how to work around Nayyar's moods and temperament.

OP Nayyar and Majrooh Sultanpuri worked together in Phase 1 of Guru Dutt's career for 32 of the 34 songs in films that were produced by Guru Dutt. Theses being: Baaz, all 9 songs; Aar Paar, all 8 songs; Mr. & Mrs. '55, 8 songs (1 song was written by Saroj Mohini Nayyar, OP Nayyar's wife); and C.I.D. 7 songs (one song was written by Jan Nissar Akhtar). OP Nayyar, on his part, composed the music for all the 34 songs in these films of Guru Dutt's Phase 1 in cinema.

Geeta Roy and OP Nayyar had worked together in Aasmaan (1952). She introduced OP Nayyar to her beau Guru Dutt; it was Geeta again who brought Nayyar and Majrooh together. Geeta had enjoyed working with both of them and she knew talent when she saw it. After Nayyar and Dutt met, they hit it off and became great friends. That is how the invincible team of Guru Dutt, Geeta Roy, Majrooh Sultanpuri and OP Nayyar was formed.

They first worked together in Baaz (1953), Dutt's joint production with Geeta Bali's sister, Haridarshan Kaur. Baaz was, for all intents and purposes, Guru Dutt's first risky venture, since his earlier two films, Baazi and Jaal, had been with other producers. Incidentally, Geeta and Guru, who had been in love since 1951, got married in May 1953, a month before the release of Baaz.

Smarting from the failure of his first two films, Aasmaan and Chham Chhama Chham, Nayyar experimented with the voices of Rafi and Talat in Baaz. Although the last film flopped, there was a rare ghazal sung by Talat in the film. A sad song, it is one of Talat's best songs ever:

> Mujhe dekho hasrat ki tasveer hoon main
>
> Jo ban-ban ke bigdi woh taqdeer hoon main…
>
> Gira jo zameen par main hoon ek wo aansoo
>
> Mili khaak mein aisi tadbeer hoon main!

This is the first song to be filmed on Guru Dutt. It becomes ironic when you consider that he directed and co-produced the film, since he was unhappy in his last days. Talat's rendition of Majrooh's lyrics seems to come from his soul. Incidentally, this is the only Talat song Guru has ever lip synced for a Guru Dutt production. The last song Guru lip-synched under his own production was in Chaudhvin Ka Chand; Mili khaak mein muhabbat, which makes one wonder if it was a coincidence that both his first and last song are linked with each other through the painful words, 'mili khaak mein.'

This ghazal, in Raag Kedar, is set in a 10-beat cycle. In the film, Guru Dutt plays the character who is part of an uprising against the Portuguese. He is caught, after which he is humiliated by being paraded around town on a mule, hands tied behind his back, in punishment for his rebellion. Majrooh's words pierce the soul with the poignant lines of a man who supports the cause of freedom,

Chala main to ahl-e-watan khush raho tum

Na baittha nishaane pe wo teer hoon main

OP Nayyar used violins and the sitar to enhance the pathos of the situation. The film was a commercial flop and is seen by many as Guru Dutt's worst film. As a director, this was Dutt's third film, after Baazi and Jaal, but he made his debut in this film as an actor and co-producer.

Sadly, this was the third consecutive flop film for OP Nayyar. After this debacle, he decided to leave Bombay for good but first, he had to pay his bills. He went to collect his pending dues from Dutt. The filmmaker was unable to pay him thanks to Baaz being a flop, and also thanks to his recent high-profile marriage to the famous Geeta Roy. Instead, Guru Dutt offered him the opportunity to compose the music for his next film Aar Paar. And this decision was the turning point in their lives!

Nayyar was over the moon, he had one more chance! Majrooh Sultanpuri was taken on board too, since he had already proved his class in Baaz. Both Nayyar and Majrooh understood Guru Dutt and knew what he expected of them. Majrooh's mastery of poetry assured Nayyar that he could count on him. Aar Paar was the "make or break" film for the composer.

Some lyricist-composer combos have a handful of albums that depend on just one or two songs to carry the film to the box office. But with this deadly pair of geniuses, there are several albums where at least four songs are super hits! The very first proof of this came with Aar Paar in which each of the eight songs was a hit. These spectacular songs were,

Mohabbat kar lo jee bhar lo

Sun sun sun sun zaalima

Arrey na na na na na na tauba tauba

Babujee dheere chalna

Ye lo main haari piya, Hoon abhi main jawaan

Ja ja ja ja bewafa

Kabhi aar kabhi paar

Incidentally, the song Sun sun sun sun zaalima was inspired by Bing Crosby's Sing Sing Sing a Song for Me, while Babujee dheere chalna was inspired by the Spanish melody Quizas quizas quizas.

The audience was thrilled, the film had exhilarating, foot-tapping music. Cinema halls were crowded, and people saw the film not once but several times, mostly for the songs. The story was interesting, sure, but it was the music that was the magnet.

In my OP Nayyar biography, I have detailed how, after the incredible success of Aar Paar, other film producers signed him on for films for which they had already paid advances to other composers. The five films that came to him this way were Mehbooba (1954), in which Nayyar shared credits with Roshan; Mangu (1954), credits shared with Mohammed Shafi; Baap Re Baap (1955) credits shared with C Ramchandra; Sabse Bada Rupaiya (1955), credits shared with Naashaad; and Dhake Ki Malmal (1956), credits shared with Robin Chatterjee. Some songs in these films were by OP Nayyar while other songs belong to the other composers. In an interview, OP Nayyar said, "Is mein bhi bada lafda pad gaya…is mein Lata Mangeshkar, Naushad Ali, Anil Biswas, mere ko mile aake, ke bhai, ye tum kya kar rahe ho, ye to already composer signed hai. Maine kaha, Saahab, mera qasoor bataaiye, mera qasoor kuchh nahin hai, maine to kisi ko kaata nahin, na kisi ko katwaaaya hai. Ab ye reh gaya ke mujhe paise ki sakht zaroorat hai is waqt, to aap apni pocket se paise bhar dijiye to main picture chhod deta hoon…ab ye sab khaamosh ho gaye, na Latabai boli, na Naushad bole, na Anil Biswas sahab bole, to yahaan se Nayyar Saahab ki taqdeer khulti hai!"

But let's turn to Majrooh, who revealed their way of functioning. "When we worked together, Guru Dutt would sit with me and OP Nayyar, and he would start by explaining the story to us. Then he would describe the situation in which the song would appear. The music director would give me the tune. Guru Dutt also had a great sense of music. He would always make sure that the songs that I wrote would correspond to the vocabulary his character used. He would answer all my questions patiently. I would argue and if he wanted to win me over he would laugh and say, "Come on, stop arguing!" Majrooh observed that Guru Dutt did not want preludes to his songs but he wanted the song to be interesting. "His songs were always on a higher level, they had an impact. He gave them much thought, he would spend nights thinking of song situations."

I have chosen the Johnny Walker song as an example to show the Majrooh magic. The song is Arrey na na na na na na tauba tauba. Majrooh knew he had to create some impish moments in this light song. Keeping Johnny Walker in mind, he intentionally used repetitive words to make it catchy and easy for the common man. Majrooh also kept Guru Dutt's penchant for Western music in mind while writing the lyrics, and so he wove in English words. With Guru and Nayyar in mind, the wordsmith in Majrooh navigated his song to move the film up the musical charts. Not only did he make English words hold hands with chaste Urdu words here, he also used delicious tapori mispronunciations to this heady mix. In the same line, look how Majrooh stitches up Hindi-Urdu and English:

Dard-e-jigar se main weak hoon bahut, karo aisa na julam,

Ho jaayega fail abhi heart hamaara, tere sar ki kasam…

Words like "heart-fail" and "weak" are English words and they are woven in so beautifully by Majrooh. But then let's listen to the powerful imagery used in this comical song:

Tu jo kahe dharti mein kooaan khod daaloon,
doon ye duniya ujaad,

Tu jo kahe chadh jaoon lambe lambe ped, oonche
oonche ye pahaad!

Not to be beaten by his wild promises, the lady doth say no in her funny way too. She, too, uses English words to express her fake contempt for him:

Reechh ka tu uncle, bandar ka tu baap

Thoko nahin bandal, raho jee chup-chaap!

Look at Majrooh's mastery in the song, he combined the dehaati, "julam" in place of "zulm", and he used tapori slang words like "maara baap", "bandal", repetitive words, "na na", "wah wah", "chhee chhee" and "dekho dekho". Delicious creativity, and all this to embroider a song given to the comedian, not even to the hero of the film! Majrooh chiselled this chhed-chhad genre into an art since we saw him repeat his magic in later songs as well.

Aar Paar skyrocketed both Majrooh and Nayyar to the top. The failed team of Baaz sprinted to the top of the box office. Aar Paar was as much a game-changer for Guru Dutt as it was for Nayyar and Majrooh. Its intoxicating ebullience in music was a major disruption in the music industry. The film was a happy experience for all concerned in the theatre, but it was wonderful also for the newly wedded couple, Geeta and Guru Dutt, and, of course, for Nayyar and Majrooh.

The brief from Guru Dutt to this dynamic team of composer and lyricist was to push the envelope, to be fresh, breezy and different. The risk taker in Guru Dutt not only wanted to be different, he wanted to be ahead of his peers. One day he gave Nayyar English music LP records to listen to, to use them as a foundation for what he needed: Westernised tunes merged with Indian instruments and music. And so it was that Aar Paar was what it was, a brilliant musical with an unexceptional storyline, with great direction and acting and cinematography. But the cherry on the cake was its exhilarating music.

During the working of Mr. & Mrs. '55, there was a discussion on the language used in a song. Majrooh said, "Guru Dutt was particular that the language spoken in the film is also carried in the song. He wanted the vocabulary to be authentic." So if the person singing the song is a roadside ruffian, the vocabulary has to be in harmony with his street language as well." Once there was a difference of opinion between Majrooh and Dutt. The line in the song was, Sun sun sun sun zaalima, pyaar humko tumse ho gaya. Majrooh, being concerned with grammar, held that 'humko' was incorrect, and that 'mujhko' was correct grammatically. He held that if the word was 'humko', then the line should be 'Suno suno suno suno zaalima', so he wanted 'mujhko' to be used instead of 'humko'. Guru Dutt scoffed at his objection with a dismissive observation, done half in jest, "Arrey bhai, hatao, tumhaara wahaan audience mein ye kaun dekhega, grammar!" So it was decided that 'humko' would stay.

Of course, the melody was so enticing that the audience didn't even realise there was a grammatical error. After all, Nayyar's melodious magic carpet was enough! If the music was intoxicating, why would grammar matter?

In an interview with music historian Manek Premchand, Majrooh told him that Guru Dutt felt that a song should be used to take the narrative forward, so he was averse to preludes. Preludes were not this filmmaker's cup of tea because they slowed down the excitement of the film. He didn't want his films to become boring, since entertainment was his goal in Phase 1. Majrooh also said that he never had difficulty working with Guru Dutt because the filmmaker knew exactly what he wanted, and this made work easy.

Incidentally, in the four OP Nayyar-Guru Dutt films in which Guru Dutt acted, the latter had the following ten Nayyar songs filmed on him,

Mujhe dekho hasrat ki tasveer hoon main (Baaz)

Ghata mein chupke (Baaz)

Sun sun sun sun zaalima (Aar Paar)

Mohabbat kar lo jee bhar lo (Aar Paar)

Aeji dil par hua aisa jaadoo (Mr. & Mrs. '55)

Chal diye banda nawaaz (Mr. & Mrs. '55)

Udhar tum haseen ho (Mr. & Mrs. '55)

Main kho yahin kahin (12 O'Clock)

Tum jo hue mere humsafar (12 O'Clock)

The song which became the Bombay anthem, Ae dil hai mushkil, was also created by this brilliant team:

Ae dil hai mushkil jeena yahaan

Zara hatke, zara bachke, yeh hai Bombay meri jaan!

The magic of Nayyar with Majrooh in combination with the husband-wife team of Guru and Geeta only needed Rafi and Johnny Walker to come together to make this song a super hit.

The major reason for the success of this song is not only because of its melody, it is also because of its mischievous lyrics that share Bombay's karmic philosophy. Majrooh has offered us two points of view about the city of Bombay. The first voice in the song projects the opinion of the contemptuous outsider, reflected by Rafi/Johnny, and the second voice is the opinion of the insider, expressed by Geeta/Kum Kum. All of Johnny Walker's grouses highlight

Bombay's negatives: the hypocrisy, the crookedness, the paradox and the chaos of Bombay. On her part, Geeta is given only one stanza to shut him up but she does it brilliantly. Her master stroke is the law of karma. She explains that Bombay is all about cause and effect, good deeds and bad deeds result in similar good or bad outcomes. Through Geeta Dutt, Majrooh explains that Bombay wants you to earn its respect. It wastes no time on people who want to exploit you. In short, Geeta advises Rafi to know that there is no free lunch in Bombay! Majrooh projects both sides of the argument but delivers them with such delicious words that one cannot but love the song!

Let's see how Johnny critiques Bombay:

Kahin building, kahin tramen, kahin motor, kahin mill

Milta hai yahaan sab kuch ik milta nahin dil!

Then he runs down the material values of Bombayites…

Be-ghar ko awaara yahaan kehte hans hans

Khud kaaten gale sab ke kahen usko business!

Kum Kum, in her nine-yard Maharashtrian saree, represents Bombay and its mindset perfectly. Here's how she responds to him, in her only stanza in the song:

Bura duniya ko hai kehta, aisa bhola to na ban

Jo hai karta, woh hai bharta, hai yahaan ka ye chalan,

Dadagiri nahin chalne ki yahaan

Yeh hai Bombay yeh hai Bombay, ye hai Bombay, meri jaan!

Ae dil hai aasaan jeena yahaan

Suno mister, suno bandhu

Ye hai Bombay, meri jaan!

Majrooh follows Guru Dutt's advice to use English words, but he gives them a Hindi twist, like with "Tramen". Notice also how the genius of Nayyar employs the local ghoda-gaadi beat to combine it with the Western waltz! This blending of English words with Hindustani words is as much Majrooh's strength as is the merging of the clip-clop beat with the waltz an example of Nayyar's genius. East and West meet in the song, and by doing so, they fulfil Guru Dutt's wish to Indianise a Western tune, i.e., the English song Oh My Darling Clementine.

For a few years, the magic formula of this team worked wonders as they raked in the moolah, one box office hit after another.

Incidentally, the Guru-Geeta-Majrooh-Nayyar was a formidable team which gave us so many songs: Baaz (7 songs), Aar Paar (7 songs), 12 O'Clock (4 songs), Mr. & Mrs. '55 (6 songs) and C.I.D. (2 songs).

When the writer Dr. Mandar Bichhu interviewed OP Nayyar, the composer told him, "I personally never felt Guru Dutt knew a great deal about music. I still remember his initial reaction to Babuji Dheere chalna. He told me, "The mukhda (the opening) is excellent but the antara (stanza) lacks something." I asked, "What exactly is that 'something'?" He said, "I don't know—just do something with it". I just waited for two weeks. I didn't change a single note but after that, Guru accepted the same tune on my assurance that I have done 'something'!" "Later", he added to Bichhu, "After Mr. & Mrs. '55, I parted ways with Guru Dutt. We both were too egoistic to be compatible. But after many years, for Baharen Phir Bhi Aayengi, he pleaded with me to do the music."

A few years after they tied the knot, Guru and Geeta's marriage began to fail. In consonance with his unhappy moods, Guru moved towards sombre and pessimistic themes. Since Nayyar and Majrooh were identified with optimism and romance, they were replaced by SD Burman and Sahir with whom Dutt had previously worked in two films, Baazi, and Jaal. Sadly, even Geeta's work with her husband was reduced. Her two sons were born in this period and required her attention as well.

Romance, Majrooh, Nayyar and Dutt

Films that were weak both in plot and direction leaned heavily on the scintillating, romantic numbers offered by this team; this was exactly what producers and financiers were seeking, and so who better than Nayyar, the eternal romantic, to understand and express love through melody, and who better than Majrooh to give words to his enchanting melodies?

As a matter of interest, the song Jaata kahaan hai deewaane was snipped out of the film by the censors who objected to the nonsensical Majrooh word 'fiffy'; someone important felt it had sexual overtones, so the song was dropped.

If you are ready for a sumptuous buffet of romantic numbers, do run through a few of these delectable romantic numbers:

Aar Paar: Sun sun sun sun zaalima, and Ye lo main haari piya

Mr. & Mrs. '55: Udhar tum haseen ho

12 O'Clock: Dekh idhar ae haseena, Main kho gaya yahin kahin, and Tum jo hue mere humsafar

CID: Leke pehla pehla pyaar.

Repeated Lyrics

Majrooh had a penchant for repeating a certain word to make the song catchy, and of course, people relished this repetition! Here are a few examples:

12 O'Clock: Arrey tauba aarey tauba (Saari saari mehfil se nazrein uljhana seekho, aadhi-aadhi raaton ko zulfein bikhraana dekho).

Aar Paar: Sun sun sun sun zaalima, and Ye lo main haari piya (naye naye do nain mile hain).

Baaz: Chham chham ghunghroo baaje, and Har zabaan ruki ruki.

CID: Jaata kahaan hai deewaane (Fi-fi, kuchh tere dil mein fi-fi, kuchh mere dil mein fifi), and Leke pehla pehla pyaar.

Mr. & Mrs. '55: Ab to jee hone laga (gori gori goriyon ko pade na kaheen dil thaamna), and Jaane kahaan mera jigar gaya ji (sachchi sachchi keh do).

Ghazals

Let's not forget some beautiful ghazals created by this Nayyar-Majrooh team. Just listen to these stunning beauties, Mujhe dekho hasrat ki tasweer hoon main (Baaz) and Mohabbat kar lo jee bhar lo (Aar Paar)! As an aside, outside of Guru Dutt films too, this pair offered a few ghazals, for instance: Aanchal mein saja lena kaliyaan, from Phir Wohi Dil Laaya Hoon (1963), and Jhuka jhuka ke nigaahen milaaye jaate hain from Miss Coca Cola (1955).

Songs Based on Ragas

As a matter of interest, quite a few songs of this team were based on Raags. Here are a few examples:

Based on Raag Piloo:

Kabhi aar, kabhi paar (Aar Paar)

Jaata kahaan hai deewaane (C.I D.)

Boojh mera kya naao re (C.I D.)

Leke pehla pehla pyaar (C.I D.)

Kahin pe nigaahen (C.I D.)

Kaisa jaadoo balam tu ne daara (12 O'Clock)

Raag Yaman:

Woh hanske mile humse (Baharen Phir Bhi Aayengi)

Aapke haseen rukh pe (Baharen Phir Bhi Aayengi),

Dil to pehle hi se (Baharen Phir Bhi Aayengi)

Raag Madhuvanti:

Neele Aasmaani (Mr. & Mrs. '55)

Raag Pahadi:

Dekh idhar ae haseena (12 O'Clock),

Ab to jee hone laga (Mr. & Mrs. '55)

In the End...

When OP Nayyar was interviewed about Guru Dutt's death, he was very upset. He said, "Talking of Guru Dutt, I always feel a pang of guilt. He used to confide his problems in me. His wife Geeta and his flame Waheeda, both had deserted him in the end and he was pretty disturbed. At around two a.m. the same night that he committed suicide, my wife told me, "Raj Kapoor has phoned for you. He is saying that Guru Dutt is inebriated and is crying inconsolably, repeatedly calling for Nayyar Saab!" I was too tired and sleepy to go. I just told my wife to give some excuse. I had an appointment with Guru at his residence anyway the next morning at 10. I reached there the next morning and Abrar Alvi, his dialogue writer told me, "Guru has gone." Incredulously, I asked, "Where?" He said, "Guru Dutt is dead! His dead body is inside!" True to my straight-talking nature, I just blasted those two women for ruining Guru's life—Geeta, right there in front of Guru's dead body in the drawing room and Waheeda at the time of the funeral!"

In the end, Guru Dutt and OP Nayyar did work together in Baharen Phir Bhi Aayengi but Majrooh was not part of their team at this time. And while Nayyar was alive to see the film released in the cinema-halls, Guru Dutt, sadly, was not.

2

SD Burman

A) SD BURMAN AND SAHIR LUDHIANVI

Sahir Ludhianvi's poems with SD Burman's music dominated three of Guru Dutt's films, but this team is recognised most for its brilliance in Pyaasa. They worked together in Baazi (1951), Jaal (1952), and Pyaasa (1957). Although directed by Guru Dutt, the first two films were not Guru Dutt productions since they were produced by Navketan and Filmarts respectively. Pyaasa is the only film in which this team came together under the Guru Dutt banner.

The story of Pyaasa deals with darkness, failure and homelessness. It showcases the tragic lives led by the dark underbelly of a heartless city. Since the film is about an impoverished poet and focuses on social injustices, Guru Dutt remembered SD Burman, whose songs, especially folk songs, had been his favourites when he had been young. He signed on SD Burman and dropped OP Nayyar who was identified more with joyous melodies.

Phase One of Guru Dutt's career in films consisted of light romances which were hits, but he was moving towards serious cinema. Pyaasa belongs to Phase 2, which was the crossover phase of Guru Dutt's career. But even in this second phase, he wanted to retain the comedy element that had been successful in his previous films. Johnny Walker, in the voice of Rafi, had been a hit with Nayyar's Arrey na na na na na na tauba tauba (Aar Paar), Jaane kahaan mera jigar gaya jee (Mr. & Mrs. '55) and Ae dil hai mushkil jeena yahaan (C.I.D.). This is why he wove in Burman's Sar jo tera chakraaye in Pyaasa. It is said that when the financiers saw the rushes of Pyaasa, they felt the film was too dry and serious so they wanted Guru Dutt to add a romantic song to soften the mood. Guru Dutt then turned to SD Burman who prepared a beautiful foxtrot, Hum aap ki aankhon mein, which became an instant hit with the audience.

Sahir would have worked with Guru Dutt and SD Burman again had it not been reported to SD Burman that Sahir was bragging all over town, taking full credit for the success of Pyaasa because of his poems. This enraged the genius composer. Both friends, OP Nayyar and SD Burman, then decided that they would never work with Sahir again. Nayyar handed over the rest of the songs of Tumsa Nahin Dekha (except the title song which was already recorded with Sahir's lyrics) to Majrooh.

For his part, SD Burman signed up Kaifi Azmi for Kaagaz Ke Phool. Guru Dutt later moved to Ravi and Shakeel for Chaudhvin Ka Chand and to Hemant Kumar and Shakeel for Sahib Bibi Aur Ghulam. Of course, whether it was Kaifi Azmi or Shakeel, they also created magic for Guru Dutt.

But back to Burman, Sahir and Pyaasa.

Some reviewers regard Pyaasa not as a mere film but as a poem. The Sahir poems, whether in song or spoken verse, dominate the narrative and give the film the depth it merits. Some regard the film as much the success of Sahir as of Guru Dutt. While this is open to debate, there is no denying the fact that Sahir's poetry did its bit to elevate the film to incredible heights.

Let's examine the songs of Pyaasa. The several poetry recitations in the film are mentioned next.

1. Aaj sajan mohe ang laga-lo—Geeta

2. Ho laakh museebat raste mein—Rafi, Geeta and the chorus

3. Hum aap ki aankhon mein—Rafi and Geeta

4. Jaane kya tu ne kahi—Geeta

5. Jaane woh kaise log the jinke—Hemant

6. Rut phiri par din hamaare—Geeta (deleted song)

7. Sar jo tera chakraaye—Rafi and Johnny Walker

8. Ye kooche ye neelam ghar dilkashi ke (Jinhen naaz hai Hind par)—Rafi

9. Ye mehlon, ye takhton (Ye duniya agar mil bhi jaaye)—Rafi

Running down this list of stunning songs, with the bitter and cynical Ye kooche, ye neelam-ghar, and the Jaane woh kaise log the, one realises that the film depended as much on its lyrics as it depended on Guru Dutt's angst-ridden performance as the protagonist.

Pyaasa also had a few poetry recitations composed by SD Burman and written mostly by Sahir. These were:

1. Rafi's recitation of Sahir's poetry for Guru Dutt:

    Gham is qadar bade ke main ghabra ke pi gaya

    Is dil ki bebasi pe taras kha ke pi gaya

    Thukra raha tha mujhko badi der se jahaan

    Main aaj sab jahaan ko thukra ke pi gaya

2. Guru Dutt's recitation of Jaleel Manikpuri's modified couplet for himself:

    Jab hum chalen to saaya bhi apna na saath de

    Jab tum chalo, zameen chale, aasmaan chale

    (The original couplet by Jaleel Manikpuri was Jab main chaloon to saaya bhi apna na saath de, Jab tum chalo zameen chale, aasmaan chale)

3. A second couplet written by Sahir then followed this couplet:

   Jab hum ruken, to saath ruke shaam-e-bekasi

   Jab tum ruko, bahaar ruke, chaandni ruke

4. Geeta Dutt's recitation of Sahir's couplet as a prelude to the song Jaane kya tu ne kahi filmed on Waheeda Rehman:

   Phir na kijiye meri gustaakh nigaahee ka gila

   Dekhiye aap ne phir pyaar se dekha mujhko

5. Rafi's recitation of Sahir's poem for Guru Dutt:

   Tang aa chuke hain kashmakash-e-zindagi se hum

   Thukra na dein jahaan ko kahin be-dili se hum

   Hum ghumzada hain laayen kahaan se khushi ke geet

   Kahaan se khushi ke geet

   Denge wohi jo paayenge is zindagi se hum

   Ubhrenge ek baar abhi dil ke valvale, abhi dil ke valvale

   Maana ke dab gaye hain gham-e-zindagi se hum

   Lo aaj humne tod diya, lo aaj humne tod diya rishta-e-umeed

   Rishta-e- umeed

   Lo ab kabhi gila na karenge kisi se hum

6. Rafi's rendition of Sahir's poem for Guru Dutt:

   Ye hanste hue phool, ye mehka hua gulshan

   Ye rang mein aur noor mein doobi hui raahen

Ye phoolon ka ras peeke machalte hue bhanwre

Main doon bhi to kya doon tumhen ae shokh nazaaro

Le-de ke mere paas kuchh aansoo hain, kuchh aahein

The fragrance of Sahir's poems is spread through the film and offers it the necessary depth and emotional seriousness that it required.

Abrar Alvi, in a candid interview with Sathya Saran, explained how much Guru Dutt insisted on copying Western tunes. For example, he debunked the fact that the song Sar jo tera chakraaye was composed by RD Burman. He said that for years, "Only lies have come out. I am sorry to disappoint RDB fans, but the truth is different. Guru Dutt had picked up a bunch of 78 rpm records of English songs during his visit to England. There was one tune he liked a lot, and he decided to graft it onto Pyaasa. It was from the film Harry Black and the Tiger, which, though Guru Dutt did not know it then, would be released later in India. SD Burman, who was composing the music for the film, was asked to copy the song note for note. Of course, Dada Burman was disturbed by the instruction. He came to me and said, 'What is this that Guru is asking of me, public mujhe maarega. Please explain to him, he listens to you, let me put in a little of my tune into the song… change it a bit…' But Guru was adamant—the tune would have to be copied hundred per cent in the mukhda at least. 'Let him do what he wants in the antara,' he decreed and Burman Dada had to be content with that. However, the genius music director waved his baton effectively enough to blend the tune with his melody so that no one noticed the surgery, and the song remains a hit even today. Interestingly, much later, when the producer of Harry Black and the Tiger visited India, he heard the song and not only failed to recognise the tune but commended Dada on it." Abrar laughed.

For some of us, the most outstanding song of *Pyaasa* is this Hemant Kumar beauty:

Jaane woh kaise log the jinke pyaar ko pyaar mila

Humne to jab kaliyaan maangi kaanton ka haar mila…

How important a song is depends on so many factors. The visualisation by MR Achrekar, Guru Dutt and VK Murthy was critical. In an interview, Murthy said that the background of the song was intentionally uncluttered, there are only books behind Vijay when he sings this song of betrayal. He stands at one corner of the room, and Meena, who is also in the room, is across from him as if they are in a boxing ring; he persistently hits her with his veiled accusations, and she is shown visibly distressed by his attack.

In a conversation with lyricist Pulak Bandyopadhyay, Burman had mentioned that the second line of the national anthem— Punjab Sindh Gujarat Maratha Dravid Utkal Banga—had inspired the line, "Humne to jab kaliyaan maangi…The reference to the national anthem is so subtle that unless someone points it out, it is next to impossible to spot a similarity."

Vijay (Guru Dutt) is wearing a white shawl in this song. His body language, with his face wearing a semi-wry, semi-sad smile, with his arms stretched out, says he is defenceless and has nothing to hide. He stands alone, facing a room full of strangers. He appears to be assaulting all of them with his words, rebuking the rich for their superficiality. When he arrives, he is shocked to discover that his employer, Ghosh (Rehman), is also the husband of his ex-girlfriend Meena (Mala Sinha). She had betrayed the impoverished

Vijay because she wanted life's comforts and had gone on to marry the wealthy Ghosh.

The song has soft piano notes playing in the background, offering minimal support to the Hemant Kumar rendition. The light background music is almost self-effacing; SD Burman once explained that he had done this so that the Sahir poem becomes the hero of the song. Sadly, while it did immortalise the song, this was their last album together.

Guru Dutt had wanted this song to be rendered by Rafi but SD Burman, supported by Geeta, had insisted on Hemant Kumar. After arguing about it for a while, both Abrar Alvi and Guru Dutt reluctantly acceded to their wishes. Burman was proven right. The pristine song has a philosophical and sad tone, and Hemant Kumar's thoughtful tone raises the song to a sublime level.

Bichhad gaya, bichhad gaya

Bichhad gaya har saathi de kar pal do pal ka saath

Kisko fursat hai jo thaame deewaano ka haath

Humko apna saaya tak aksar bezaar mila

Humne to jab kaliyaan maangi…

Isko hi jeena kehte hain to yoon hi jee lenge

Uf na karenge, lab see lenge, aansoo pee lenge

Ghum se ab ghabraana kaisa, ghum sao baar mila

Humne to jab kaliyaan maangi…

Some people believe Pyaasa is Sahir's biopic, but the facts tell a different tale. The story was written by a depressed Guru Dutt much before Sahir and he met. Soon after his Prabhat days were over,

Guru Dutt was unemployed and living with his family in their tiny home in Matunga, Bombay. He wrote the story Kashmakash then, and later, the film based on it was titled Pyaas, and even later Guru Dutt changed it to Pyaasa. Kashmakash's protagonist, however, was a painter and not a poet. It was for narrative convenience that the protagonist was changed from painter to poet.

B) SD BURMAN AND KAIFI AZMI

Kaifi Azmi's role in Kaagaz ke Phool's immortality is, by all accounts, very significant. Born into a zamindar family, Kaifi Azmi was born as Syed Athar Hussain Rizvi, on Jan 14, 1919, in the village of Mizwaan in Uttar Pradesh. He wrote his first poem, a ghazal, when he was just eleven. Always deeply concerned with the underdog, he joined the Communist Party of India when he was 19. He was the co-lyricist, along with Shailendra, in his first film song, Rote rote guzar gayi raat re, for Buzdil (1951).

Kaifi Azmi stepped in after the falling out between SD Burman and Sahir. Since this was to be Guru Dutt's magnum opus, a deeply sensitive poet was required. Kaifi's poems in Kaagaz Ke Phool were brilliant and certainly did everything to enhance the film's magic quotient. It's another matter that the film flopped because it was ahead of its time and the audience was not ready for such stark realism in cinema.

I have chosen a song that is regarded as a classic by many Hindi film music lovers: the leitmotif song Dekhi zamaane ki yaari, bichhde sabhi baari baari is at the start, middle and end of the film. It represents the feelings of Suresh Sinha (Guru Dutt) and runs in the background to repeatedly comment on his life and emotional state.

In Guru Dutt's cinema, backing vocals were mostly used to echo the protagonist's emotions and thoughts. When it echoed what the character was going through, it repeated lines to stress and reaffirm his or her state. The choral singers in Guru Dutt's movies are heard but sometimes their performers are not seen. In this epic melody of Kaagaz Ke Phool, the chorus is a vital device to move us away from Suresh Sinha's impoverished current reality to its opposite, his successful past. The song begins with a slow Rafi line, Dekhi zamaane ki yaari. When the first stanza is over, the music is lifted and we go waltzing in flashback into the beautiful past with the chorus expressing its adoration and applause of his success. It keeps emphasizing the line:

Daur ye chalta rahe, rang uchhalta rahe

Roop machalta rahe, jaam badalta rahe…

These lines are sung, not once or twice but six times! How wonderful it is, stresses the chorus, to be acclaimed and famous; let the good times roll, let beauty flourish, let the rounds of drinks continue! The excitement is emphasised through these repeated lines. The heady period that Suresh Sinha is going through must consist of colours, beauty and intoxication. The chorus is representing Suresh Sinha and how exhilarated he is thanks to his success.

But Guru Dutt shows us two contrasting realities in the same song; he exhibits to us both the rise and the fall of the protagonist. This song also examines the human predicament: Who is mine, and is there anyone who belongs to anyone? Do true friendship and love exist? The answer to all these questions is offered by a cynical Kaifi Azmi through this divine melody of SD Burman. Azmi concludes his argument by telling us that there is no such thing as love or friendship, that it's all a giant farce, that everyone is yours as long as you are of some use to them and, finally, that the world is full of opportunists and materialists:

> Matlab ki duniya hai saari, bichhde sabhi, bichhde
> sabhi baari baari…

This refrain emphasises the sense of isolation and becomes almost compulsive:

> Arrey, dekhi zamaane ki yaari
>
> Bichhde sabhi bichhde sabhi baari baari

This background song laments that nothing and nobody lasts in your life, and that, sooner or later, everyone leaves you. These thoughts run through the mind of the old protagonist, the shabbily clothed film director Sinha. When he is recognised by his discovery Shanti, he flees from her. His running away from her is his way of denying the truth of his impoverished reality. Guru Dutt, through

Kaifi and SD Burman, shows us how it is easier for Sinha to live with himself if nobody recognises him. Kaifi's lyrics express the thought process of a man who, after having once touched the stars, is now down in the dumps. Under no circumstances does he crave recognition; he prefers anonymity. Why would he seek pity from the shallow *kaagaz ke phool* that applaud none but the successful? And yet, there is Shanti, who tries hard to help him out of his distress. But his pride cannot accept her intervention.

Kaifi Azmi excels when his thoughts are showcased in the high-pitched Rafi voice

Ud ja, ud ja, pyaase bhanwre, ras na milega khaaron mein

Kaagaz ke phool jahaan khilte hain, baith na un gulzaaron mein

Naadaan tamanna reti mein, umeed ki kashti kheti hai

Ik haath se deti hai duniya, sau haathon se le leti hai…

The world gives to us with one hand but takes with a hundred hands! Can it get more agonising than that? The words are painful and Kaifi represents Suresh Sinha's pessimism beautifully. Shanti tries to stop him, to rescue him, but the scene is symbolically sketched at this point. The crowd that throngs to her for her autograph blocks her from reaching out to him. Once again, society blocks their union. While Kaifi can certainly take full credit for the beauty of the song and its enchanting lyrics, the mastery of Guru Dutt, both as an actor and as a director, completes the outstanding scene with the brilliant cinematography of Murthy. The crowd of fans, symbolising the fickle society we live in, this time recognises and idolises Shanti. As for Sinha, once it had recognised him too, but now it cannot recall him. Therein lies the tragedy that Guru Dutt was showcasing as the harsh reality of showbiz.

Again, the innocent amongst us are metaphorically presented in this song. A bhanwra or bumble bee is blissfully ignorant of the fact that the flower that he is attracted to is a paper flower. He does not know he is approaching a fake object with no life or nectar in it. In vain, the bee expects nectar from the flower, when what the paper flower will offer him instead is the pain of failure. Guru Dutt wanted to portray how contact with those with false materialistic values can be destructive, and thus, he warns the bhanwra to fly away from the dead souls around him.

While the sad part of this song plays on in the background, we see Guru in his dry, bearded condition. He is now an old man empty of hope and with a lifeless look in his eyes. We are taken back to his pleasant past, his earlier days when crowds wanted his autograph, when he was mobbed by fans and when every studio hand stopped to salute him. At that time he felt on top of the world. He had arrived and he could do no wrong. But this extraordinary man who was shown to be successful and calling the shots once, is now reduced and brought down to zero. He is now a nonentity, someone who is finished with the business of creation.

At the end of the song, he is unrecognisable and dies quietly seated in the director's chair. They are told to move his dead body from the studio where he had once been king because his body is holding up their shoots. Such is life, it can be so unfair. But then, the show must go on.

Pal bhar ki khushiyaan hain saari…

When the audience watched Kaagaz Ke Phool, many viewers found it difficult to recover from the tragic impact of the film. Especially this song, the film's piece de resistance. As a song that encapsulates the director's success and failure, as well as his life and death, it is an epic commentary on Suresh Sinha and others like him who experience such vicissitudes. There is no doubt that Waqt ne kiya kya haseen sitam is a brilliantly visualised song (for which full marks to all three, Art Director M R Achrekar, DoP VK Murthy and of course to Guru Dutt), but by every yardstick, as a song, Dekhi zamaane ki yaari goes past it to the finish line. The song plumbs the depths of despair, taking us into the mind of the utterly bereft Sinha. The tragedy of Suresh Sinha is intensified by the fact that the world that he once held in the palm of his hand has slipped away from him, leaving him alone with a handful of painful memories.

The song and sequence are perfect, but the scene stealer is the actor-director of this song. Guru Dutt and his portrayal of the defeated director's life is par excellence, it is the best character sketch one has seen in Hindi cinema. When everything becomes zero, he sings,

Aansoo ke siva kuchh paas nahin, kaanton ki bhi aas nahin

Matlab ki duniya hai saari, bichhde sabhi baari baari...

Not words, only tears can adequately respond to this sequence and song. Rafi has the distinction of having presented some of the greatest cinematic moments in Hindi films, and this song is one of those that belong to the great cinematic moments in the history of Indian cinema. A rich texture of authenticity runs through its filming at every stage, when the highs and the lows are beautifully visualised, and the grandeur perfectly contrasted with the penury. The cynical tone over-arching the life and death of the director is beyond compare. The film rises because it is not only about Suresh Sinha and his rise and fall, it is about Guru Dutt predicting his own success and failure as well. During the making of Pyaasa, he had attempted suicide for the first time and he had seen reality with bleak and disappointed eyes. He had seen failure waiting in the wings. He projected this in Kaagaz Ke Phool, having seen death at his door only recently.

The title of the film speaks for the subject in three words: Kaagaz Ke Phool, three words that are to be found deep inside the song:

Kaagaz ke phool jahaan khilte hain,
baith na un gulzaaron mein…

In the words of a friend, the late writer MV Devraj, "The song reinforces an ultimate truism: Life is like a long journey; we meet several fellow passengers en route, but each one parts from us sooner or later. And then, finally, there are none."

Finally, Rafi utters the most significant sigh he has ever uttered in Hindi songs when he completes his profound, unanswerable question:

Ik haath se deti hai duniya, sau haathon se le leti hai…

Ye khel hai kab se jaari?

Haaye…

That question, followed by that Haaye, leads us to the end of the song and the end of Suresh Sinha. The protagonist appears to finally understand and he comes to a point of resignation. He accepts the bitter truth of life and decides to stop fighting it. His sighing indicates two things at once: on the one hand, it expresses his resignation and, on the other hand, his moment of decision. He has made his choice. His every hope remains unfulfilled, his every desire dashed. He has sought 'shanti' all through his life, and the only way he can have this peace is by surrendering his body and yielding to nothingness. Nothingness is pain-free, existence is painful…

And while SD Burman and Kaifi Azmi take this song to supreme heights, the singer par excellence Mohammad Rafi is batting on the front foot, hitting the ball out of the cricket stadium for a magnificent six. Yes, Sinha becomes a corpse, a mere inconvenience for the new filmmaker in the studio who asks that the dead body be removed urgently so that work may continue.

The show must go on…

> Ud ja, ud ja, pyaase bhanwre, ras na milega
> khaaron mein

> Kaagaz ke phool jahaan khilte hain, baith na un
> gulzaaron mein…

Ravi, Shakeel Badayuni and Guru Dutt

In the October 13, 1989 issue of Screen, composer Ravi spoke about his association with Guru Dutt and poet Shakeel when they worked together for the film Chaudhvin Ka Chand. Titled, 'He Was a Very Generous Man', he spoke to the journalist Farida Tyebkhan at length about the genius he had the good fortune to work with. Ravi told her how shocked and miserable he had been when he had heard that Guru Dutt had suddenly passed away. He was truly perplexed, "One somehow felt that such a great genius did not deserve to go like this. When it came to his films, he always knew what was to be done next. He had his priorities right. I sometimes wonder why he was so baffled about life!"

Ravi and Guru Dutt worked on only one film for Guru Dutt Films Pvt. Ltd. That film, Chaudhvin Ka Chand, was Guru Dutt's biggest money-spinner. Although Ravi was comparatively new in the film world as a composer, he was thrilled when Guru Dutt invited him to create the music for that film. Like many others in the industry, he was in awe of Guru Dutt. When they met, he was pleasantly surprised to discover that the filmmaker had no airs and that, "he was so simple and straightforward." Others had forewarned him that Guru Dutt was a tough taskmaster, but Ravi's experience with Guru Dutt had turned out to be quite the opposite. In fact, Ravi was astonished when the soft-spoken Guru Dutt asked him which lyricist he would like to work with for the film's music. He had expected that Guru Dutt would assign the lyricist and ask him to accept his choice. Ravi admired Shakeel from the days his guru Hemant Kumar had sung for that lyricist in Shabab (1954). He thought Shakeel's poetry would fit the Lucknowi nawab theme, so he hesitantly mentioned the name of the already-established Shakeel Badayuni. Interestingly, Chaudhvin's director was going to be M Sadiq, who too had worked very happily with Shakeel, having directed the same Shabab just mentioned. Guru Dutt accepted his choice immediately. Now Ravi was in for another pleasant surprise. They were to meet one day, and instead of the comparative newcomer Ravi going up to talk to Shakeel, the lyric writer walked up to him and spoke in a very polite and friendly manner. Ravi found him, like Guru Dutt, so down to earth! Shakeel then requested Ravi in a humble tone, "Mujhe sambhaalna!" The composer couldn't believe his ears!

There were to be two mujras in the film, so Shakti Samanta, SH Bihari and Ravi accompanied Guru Dutt to attend an authentic mujra singer in Bombay. "Guru Dutt wanted the typical style and manner of the original mujras and not something filmy…The next day we composed a tune and I played it to him. He asked me very gently if Geeta could sing it. I said I would do riyaaz with her and then I called her up. It was a difficult tune…she tried it, then she herself realised this and she rang up Guru Dutt and told him that it was a difficult classical number which she could not do justice to. The song was Bedardi mere saiyaan, and Asha Bhosle was finally taken to render it."

The Shakeel-Ravi team had a great understanding because the perfectionist that Guru Dutt was, he was not interested in anything but in getting magic out of the film's music. He was keen to have the right lyrics for each melody consistent with the storyline and the characters in the film.

Ravi also shared a story behind the existence of the song Dil ki kahaani rang laayi hai. Shakeel and Ravi had originally worded a song with the lyrics Jiyara uljhan mein mora, which Lata Mangeshkar sang. However, it seemed as if it was jinxed. It first kept getting cancelled; then when it was finally recorded, Ravi was uncomfortable with it. He felt something was off in the song's lyrics. It made him uneasy. The situation was that the hero was down in the dumps and had gone to watch a mujra because he wanted to change his mood. In such a situation, a soulful song with such lyrics was most inappropriate and would make the hero even more depressed. Unable to keep this to himself, the disturbed Ravi picked up the courage and called up Guru Dutt. He shared these misgivings with him, that the lyrics were inappropriate for the situation. Guru Dutt understood exactly what he was saying and they then called upon Shakeel, who, too, immediately understood and agreed. Quickly, they changed the whole song and the singer. A new song was created and it became a big hit, the song was Dil ki kahaani rang laayi hai and the singer was Asha Bhosle.

Ravi made this point through these anecdotes: he found that Guru Dutt listened to everyone. "Suggestions were welcome. Never did he discourage anyone from coming up with new ideas, even if they opposed his conception. That was a great thing. He always meant what he said…" On the same night that they composed Dil ki kahaani rang laayi hai, they tuned two other songs, Ye duniya gol hai and Mili khaak mein mohabbat.

"Dutt liked Mili khaak mein mohabbat so much (which was created that same night), that we sat up the whole night. I must have sung it at least five hundred times then…Coming to the title song, Chaudhvin Ka Chand ho, Guru Dutt complimented me and said it was a sure hit. I could not quite believe him but he said he meant it. When Rafi rendered it, I felt he used that slightly drunken tone at times, typically his style. I wanted it removed and asked Guru Dutt who agreed immediately. But no time or opportunity came up for this. Rafi had liked the song so much that he had recited it at some functions. By the end of it, the song was so popular that when I finally asked Guru Dutt, a few days before the release of the movie, to revise it, he laughed and asked me in return, 'Do you think it will be more popular than it already is?' I had no answer and the song remained as originally recorded."

Ravi also observed that he found Guru Dutt a very generous man who easily parted with his money to all around him. "When we were in Calcutta for the film's premiere, he gave away money generously to his workers. But he was not keeping well and he had started taking drugs…Clad in a crumpled kurta pyjama, he was unable to speak on the premiere day. We dressed him in a sherwani and requested the public that since he was not well, he would not speak. The public was craving just to have a glimpse of him and he came on stage during the interval for a few minutes, that's all. He said to me the next day that the music was a definite winner to make the film such a hit and told me to ask for anything I wanted. I made him promise to give up drugs and asked him for his bottle of drugs. He smiled and promised he would give it to me and stop taking them."

Of course, in time Ravi learnt that he had done no such thing. But he never stopped admiring the genius. When they worked together again for Bharosa where Guru Dutt was only the actor, he found that Guru Dutt would never interfere with the director's work. Although he was a director of a much higher calibre, he would keep his ideas to himself and never bother the Madras directors with his unsolicited advice. He refrained from offering his inputs; instead, he would obey their instructions like any ordinary film actor would.

The songs Shakeel, Ravi and Guru Dutt did together for Chaudhvin Ka Chand were:

1. Baalam se milan hoga—Geeta and chorus

2. Badle badle mere sarkaar nazar aate hain—Lata

3. Bedardi mere saiyaan—Asha

4. Chaudhvin ka chaand ho—Rafi

5. Dil ki kahaani rang layee hai—Asha

6. Mili khaak mein mohabbat—Rafi

7. Ye Lucknow ki sarzameen—Rafi

8. Ye duniya gol hai—Rafi

This film made history for Guru Dutt. Chaudhvin Ka Chand won two Filmfare awards, one for Shakeel for Best Lyrics, and the other for Mohammed Rafi for Best Singer. For both of them, this was a first, since they had never won a Filmfare award before.

Of course, the title song Chaudhvin ka chaand ho was the most loved one of the film, but for several critics and connoisseurs, the winner was the Rafi beauty, Mili khaak mein mohabbat. The song had the magic of Shakeel, Rafi and Ravi all together. Guru Dutt ensured they combined their strengths to create a song for a despondent Guru Dutt whose universe is collapsing around him. Such songs remain with us and surface in our minds in our darkest periods. They remind us of life's harsh realities, taking us from the heights of intense love to the depths of utter loneliness, from the joys of trust to the agony of mistrust. Here is that sensational Shakeel, Rafi and Ravi ghazal in the Guru Dutt blockbuster:

Mili khaak mein mohabbat, jala dil ka aashiyaana

Jo thi aaj tak haqeeqat, wohi ban gay fasaana…

Ye bahaar kaisi aayi jo khizaan bhi saath layee

Main kahaan rahoon chaman mein, mera lut gaya thikaana

Mili khaak mein mohabbat…

Mujhe raasta dikha kar, mere kaarvaan ko loota

Idhar aa, gale laga loon tujhe gardish-e-zamaana

Mili khaak mein mohabbat…

Happiness is so often about getting lost in the music, poetry, and sublime expression of the beauty and pathos of the human condition. And this song comes after the dark and sombre Kaagaz Ke Phool's Dekhi zamaane ki yaari, bichhde sabhi baari baari. It's the same thought process, the same pathos, the same Rafi and, of course, the very same Guru Dutt.

One cannot write a chapter on this film without mentioning its most popular song, the beautiful Chaudhvin ka chand ho, sung by Rafi in his most gentle and caressing voice. This wedding night song is so melodious and sensual, it has no equals. For this, of course, full marks to Ravi who made Rafi sing it with the depth and range he was capable of in romantic songs.

Chehra hai jaise jheel mein hansta hua kamal

Ya zindagi ke saaz pe chhedi hui ghazal

Jaan-e-bahaar tum kisi shair ka khwaab ho

Chaudhvin ka chaand ho…

4

Hemant Kumar & Shakeel Badayuni

Sahib Bibi Aur Ghulam was the only film in which Hemant Kumar offered music for a Guru Dutt Production. They worked together for the first time in Jaal, a film which Guru Dutt directed. There, under composer SD Burman's music direction, Hemant Kumar had rendered the two brilliant tandem versions of Ye raat ye chaandni phir kahaan (one as a solo and the other as a duet with Lata Mangeshkar). Then, later they worked together for the first time in a Guru Dutt production, where Hemant Kumar sang the SD Burman-Sahir classic Jaane woh kaise log the jinke.

Guru Dutt, who had lived in Bengal for many years and was deeply steeped in its culture, wanted a Bengali composer for his film Sahib Bibi Aur Ghulam. Hemant Kumar fitted the bill perfectly. Even more fortuitous was that Geeta Dutt, his wife, was extremely close to the Hemant Kumar family; they even regularly socialised together. Their friendship was only natural since they were all

Bengalis who shared the same culture and language, and, what was even more important, they were both passionate about music.

Since Sahib Bibi Aur Ghulam was about a decadent feudal family that consisted of debauched Bengali men and suffering wives, Guru Dutt knew Hemant Kumar would be perfect. But Hemant Kumar, on his part, was hesitant. In an interview with Quint, Hemant Kumar was asked several questions by their journalist Mrityunjoy Kumar Jha. When he was asked about Lata Mangeshkar and why there was not a single song of Lata Mangeshkar in his album for Sahib Bibi Aur Ghulam, he answered, "That was Guru Dutt's film. For his films, he used to pick the best. He was ruthless about choosing music and songs for his own films. When Guru Dutt asked me for Sahib Bibi Aur Ghulam, I said you have a reputation for discarding music directors if you don't like their music. I told Guru, 'Gadbad mat karna… tum ek gaana record karoge, phir bologe, no'. But Guru Dutt told me, 'This won't happen. Only you can do justice to Sahib Bibi Aur Ghulam. Since the background of the film is set in Bengal, only you can do its music best because you understand the culture of Bengal.' If you hear the songs, there was no place for Lata there. Geeta Dutt, Guru Dutt's wife, was a great singer and Asha Bhosle's youthful voice was fit for Bhanwara bada naadaan…In my films (however), I always go for Lata first, then for others."

There were 8 songs in this film. Asha Bhosle sang 4 solos, Geeta Dutt sang 3 solos and Hemant Kumar sang 1 solo which unfortunately got deleted a couple of days after the release of the film.

1. Bhanwra bada naadaan haaye—Asha

2. Koi duur se aawaaz de chale aao—Geeta

3. Meri baat rahi mere man mein—Asha

4. Meri jaan, o meri jaan—Asha

5. Na jao saiyaan chhuda ke baiyaan—Geeta

6. Piya aiso jeeya mein samaaye gayo re—Geeta

7. Saaqiya aaj mujhe neend nahin ayegi—Asha and chorus

8. Saahil ki taraf kashti le—Hemant Kumar (deleted song)

This movie had quite a few firsts! For the first time in a Guru Dutt film there was no Johnny Walker song because there was no Johnny Walker! Guru Dutt had learnt his lesson when Kaagaz Ke Phool flopped. Johnny Walker, in that very serious Guru Dutt film, had diluted the film's power. Guru Dutt had understood that Johnny's presence could be counterproductive again in this serious Bengal story. Secondly, it didn't make sense to have promiscuous drunkards (Rehman and Sapru in breathtaking portrayals) singing songs either. Bhootnath (Guru Dutt himself) was too shy to sing songs, so that left only women who could sing in the film. Meena Kumari, Waheeda Rehman and Minoo Mumtaz did their bit in carrying the musical load of the film. Dhumal provided a bit of comic relief but he was in a minor capacity. This is, again, the first film from Guru Dutt where the male protagonist, i.e., Guru Dutt himself, has no song.

Incidentally, as mentioned elsewhere in this book, it has been proven that a few scenes involving Waheeda Rehman as also all the songs were directed by Guru Dutt, while the rest of the film was directed by Abrar Alvi. In an interview with Filmfare, Guru Dutt's brother Devi Dutt, revealed, "Abrar Alvi did direct Sahib Bibi Aur Ghulam. Only the songs were shot by Guru Dutt as he was particular about them. Once, when Guru Dutt was away, Abrar shot the song Bhanwra bada naadaan. When Guru Dutt returned, he watched the reel almost 10 times and then said, "What have you done!" Abrar was hurt. Guru Dutt then reshot it, adding elements of comedy."

Manek Premchand, in his biography of Hemant Kumar, The Unforgettable Music of Hemant Kumar, wrote at length about this song, Bhanwra bada naadaan haaye. Jaba (Waheeda Rehman) is using the bhanwra as a metaphor for Bhootnath, and while she sings, she is unaware that the subject in question is secretly listening to her teasing song. Manek Premchand observes, "Towards the end of the song, she suddenly finds him in the scene, approaching her for what certainly looks like a promising conversation. With her Saamne aaye nain milaaye mukh dekhe kuchh bole na claim suddenly turning out to be wrong, she is stunned, her singing arrested by a sharp intake of breath, after Bhanwra bada. That's how this song ends, mid-sentence with originality of a high order, indeed…Again in another song, Meri Jaan, O meri Jaan, it has the exemplary use of the cabasa, the rattle which makes a pleasant swishing sound. It is chiefly the rhythm that compellingly drives the song forward to make it so foot-tapping. The film had the great VK Murthy's cinematography, but everyone, including Hemant Kumar, achieved high levels of excellence in the film."

Out of the film's eight Hemant Kumar composed songs, seven were sung by females. All three by Geeta Dutt were filmed on Meena Kumari as Chhoti Bahu, and were superlative: Koi duur se aawaaz de chale aao; Piya also jeeya mein samaaye gayo re; and Na jao saiyaan chhuda ke baiyaan. Both the tawaif songs were rendered by Asha Bhosle: Meri jaan, o meri jaan sung to Manjhle Babu, and Saaqiya aaj mujhe neend nahin aayegi sung to Chhote Babu. As Jaba, Waheeda Rehman lip-synched two Asha Bhosle songs, Bhanwra bada naadaan haaye and Meri baat rahi mere man mein.

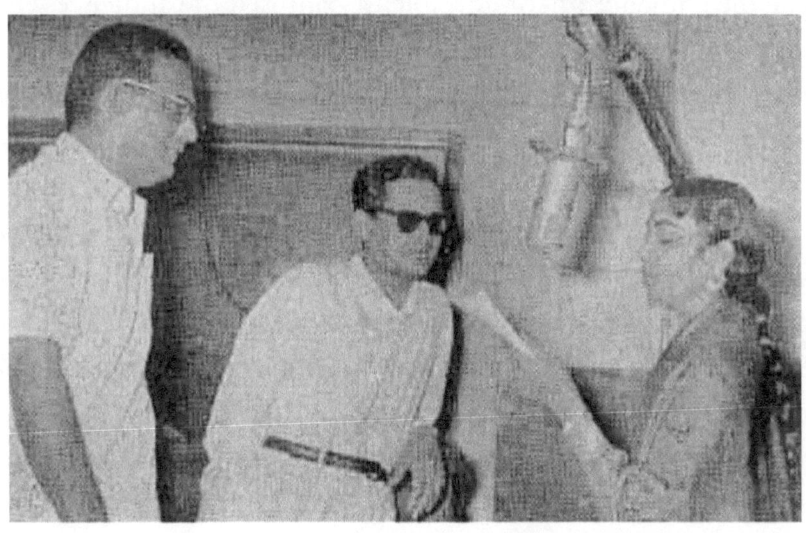

Since Hemant Kumar was close to the Dutts, he knew of their domestic squabbles and, quite intentionally, he may have used the voice of Geeta Dutt for the faithful, kind woman Chhoti Bahu, while Asha Bhosle was the voice of Jaba and the nautch girls. One wonders if, through this film, Guru Dutt was equating himself with the villainous Rehman; he, too, neglected his wife Geeta and paid attention to a single woman, the dancing actress Waheeda. When Guru Dutt first saw Waheeda she was acting as a dancer in a Telugu film. The similarity is so obvious. According to Bimal Mitra, Geeta Dutt told Guru Dutt that he should not do the film since it was portraying their life. But Guru Dutt was headstrong and heeded nobody once his mind was made up.

The only male song in the film, rendered by the composer himself, was deleted because the scene was dropped from the film. The story behind this is interesting.

The day the film was released, Guru Dutt went to watch the film and observed that the last scene between Chhoti Bahu and Bhootnath made the audience uncomfortable. It confused the audience which found the physical proximity between them unacceptable. In the scene, while the song was playing in the background, Meena Kumari was shown resting her head on Guru Dutt's lap before she got killed. The relationship between them was shown as intimate, although not sexual. But the audience wondered what the director was trying to say. Was the scene showing their amorous feelings for each other or was it like a mother-son relationship? When Dutt went to K Asif's home that night, the latter complimented him on the film but he advised him to change the ending. Asif told him on two consecutive days that he should change the ending and make it a comedy. He advised him to show that Rehman mends his ways and the husband and wife give up alcohol and live happily ever after. While Guru Dutt didn't exactly subscribe to Asif's formula, he did realise his mistake and eliminated the controversial scene and replaced it with a more acceptable one where there was no physical proximity between Chhoti Bahu and Bhootnath. The sets were put up again, and the cast and crew were called back once more. In other words, Meena Kumari and Rehman were brought back a couple of days later after the film's release. They shot the last scene once again as well as the scene before it where Chhote Babu's condition was shown. The public was relieved and the film, while it did not do as well as they expected, was at least not a flop like Kaagaz Ke Phool.

Incidentally, in the Long Play record of the film, the Hemant Kumar song is not even there. Only the other seven songs show on the album cover!

The deleted Hemant Kumar song had beautiful lyrics:

Saahil ki taraf kashti le chal, toofaan ke thapade sehna kya…

Tu aap hi apna maanjhi ban, maujon ke sahaare behna kya

Saahil ki taraf kashti le chal…

Ye beech safar mein kaisi thakan, manzil bhi teri jab duur nahin

Soye hue raahi jaag zara, khwaabon mein ulajh kar rehna kya

Saahil ki taraf kashti le chal…

Kuchh neend bhi hai, kuchh hosh bhi hai

Na jaane ye aalam kaunsa hai, ya doob ja ya chal saahil par

Tinke ke sahaare behna kya…

Saahil ki taraf kashti le chal, toofaan ke thapade sehna kya

Tu aap hi apna maanjhi ban, maujon ke sahaare behna kya

Saahil ki taraf kashti le chal…

Since this song was dropped from the film, Hemant Kumar later used the same tune for the film Anupama (1966) for the very popular song Ya dil ki suno duniya waalon. The lyrics for Anupama were not by Shakeel but by Kaifi Azmi.

The mujras composed by Hemant Kumar with Shakeel's lyrics are outstanding, they are sung by Asha Bhosle since she had a more enticing voice. Asha also sang for Waheeda, since Geeta did not want to have her lip sync her voice. Geeta was the voice of the hapless victim Meena Kumari. Since both Meena and Geeta were going through their own personal crises with their husbands, Geeta could do full justice to the sad songs she sang.

Hemant Kumar's music has a certain ethereal quality about it which, to date, is unmatched. When Chhoti Bahu sings Na jao saiyaan, we, in the audience, empathise with her because Hemant Kumar got the best out of his friend Geeta Dutt in the song. The ghostly song Koi duur se aawaz de has a haunting echo in it to make us sense the supernatural in the song. When Chhoti Bahu is happy, singing Piya aise jeeya mein, we are happy for her too, even though we know her husband is a disgusting human being.

Sahib Bibi Aur Ghulam is one of the best albums in Hemant Kumar's career as a composer.

5

Some Themes of Guru Dutt's Songs

Imitation, it is said, is the best form of flattery. Soon after Guru Dutt's films succeeded at the box office, a few other filmmakers began to throw in similar songs and scenes in their films. Some trivia about the songs of Guru Dutt's films follows.

Mistaken Identity Songs

Mistakes are made by humans, and misunderstandings too! For example, the song from Baazi (1951), Ye kaun aaya ke mere dil, was rendered by Geeta for Kalpana Kartik who fell in love with Dev Anand and was singing a romantic solo in the presence of her father KN Singh. Her beau, Krishan Dhawan, was deluded into believing that the song was for him, whereas she was expressing her love for the absent Dev Anand. Two years later, in Sangdil (1953), Dilip Kumar was shown singing a song with Madhubala in mind but the delighted actress Shammi believed he was serenading her with the song Ye hawa ye raat ye chaandni. Another viral song showed up fourteen years later in BR Chopra's Waqt (1965), in which Sadhana lip-synched her love for Sunil Dutt but Raaj Kumar believed the song's message was for him. That song was Kaun aaya ke nigaahon mein chamak jaag uthi, with the kaun aaya part offering a similar feel to the Baazi song. Guru Dutt's last film as producer, Baharen Phir Bhi Aayengi, had the Rafi charmer Aap ke haseen rukh pe aaj naya noor hai, in which Dharmendra was romancing Tanuja but her elder sister Mala Sinha believed he was singing for her! Such songs assured producers of box-office returns.

Surrogate Songs

Songs were sometimes sung by minor actors to express the feelings of the lead actors of the film. These melodies enhanced the element of mischief and joy since the audience could imagine the protagonists' feelings. Quite often the impish lyrics expressed the lead pair's hidden feelings and brought them to the surface, thus forcing them to face their feelings.

Baaz, Guru Dutt's first film as co-producer, had a song sung onscreen by Yashodhara Katju to express Geeta Bali's hidden feelings of love for Guru Dutt. The Geeta Roy rendered song was Maanjhi albele. There was another song in the same film, Ghata mein chupke that was sung by Rafi, a teasing song that expressed Geeta Bali's emotions. Such songs heightened the drama quotient of the film, with the heroine pretending to be indifferent to the hero, while the hero was in hot pursuit of her. Then in Aar Paar, we had the melodious title song Kabhi aar kabhi paar, sung by Shamshad Begum for Kum Kum who lip-synched the song to express the feelings of the two lead stars. Incidentally, the song was a lucky break for Kum Kum since the song became hugely popular and it was her first film!

Next, look at these songs from Mr. & Mrs. '55. Ab to jee hone laga by Shamshad Begum was performed onscreen by the minor actress Rooplaxmi who was selling a musical instrument and had a woven basket on her head but the song was meant for Guru Dutt and Madhubala who were falling in love. Then, in the same film, there was the qawwali Meri duniya lut rahi thi aur main khaamosh tha, sung by Mohammed Rafi and chorus, which was filmed on Rasheed Khan and others to reflect the sadness of Guru Dutt. Again, the Geeta Dutt rendered Neele aasmaani was filmed on Cuckoo to express Madhubala's emotions when the latter was deliberately dancing with someone else to make Guru Dutt jealous. The drama of the situation was, of course, aced by the camera of VK Murthy who captured the tension beautifully.

In Kaagaz Ke Phool, a film which is often associated with silent communication, songs were used to express the deep feelings of a couple that was not inclined to be very vocal or demonstrative. When Suresh Sinha (Guru Dutt) began to fall in love with Shanti (Waheeda Rehman), the two were shown seated in a moving convertible, while a group of merry-makers was travelling behind them in an open truck. In the voices of Mohammed Rafi, Asha Bhosle and Sudha Malhotra they sang the stunning, chorus-laden San san san woh chali hawa to heighten the intoxication of the scene. They were expressing the couple's emotions while the two were shown exchanging shy, knowing glances with each other. Later, when Suresh Sinha was shooting a scene in the studio, he was shown forgetting himself and mistaking some other actress for Shanti and disrupting the scene because of it. It was not Shanti who was singing and dancing to the song Ulte seedhe dao lagaaye sung by Asha Bhosle; however, since he was so obsessed with Shanti he saw her everywhere and the lyrics spoke for his life. The short song made him realise he was losing his grip on reality, thanks to his obsession with Shanti. In C. I. D., there is the hugely popular song Leke pehla pehla pyaar with street singers expressing the emotions of the lead actors, Dev Anand and Shakila. While Shakila had yet to fall in love with Dev, the singers predicted that she would! In Pyaasa too, there was a surrogate song, Aaj sajan mohe ang laga lo, which was sung by Geeta Dutt for the actress Ashita who was performing to a Baul song for the Almighty, but Waheeda internalised the song as an expression of her deep, almost divine, love for Guru Dutt.

Chetavani Songs

These are songs that warn or guide. Guru Dutt and Dev Anand loved adding such songs to their films to heighten the suspense and drama of the plot. For example, Suno gajar kya gaaye from Baazi was a warning song filmed on Geeta Bali who was warning Dev Anand about the danger around him. Then in Aar Paar, the Geeta Dutt song Babujee dheere chalna was filmed on Shakila to warn Guru Dutt. In C.I. D., the super popular song Kahin pe nigaahen kahin pe nishaana, was a lucky break for Waheeda because she made her maiden appearance in Hindi films with this song. The song warned Dev Anand, through veiled words, that the villain was nearby and he ought to hide.

Background Songs

Quite a few important songs in Guru Dutt's films were background songs. Listed below are a few significant ones.

First, in Kaagaz Ke Phool, the most significant Geeta Dutt song, Waqt ne kiya from Kaagaz Ke Phool was a background song expressing the feelings of the lead pair. Again, in the same movie, there was Dekhi zamaane ki yaari, an epic song sung by Mohammed Rafi and chorus to reflect the rise and fall of the protagonist Suresh Sinha. Yet again, in the same film, in continuation of the earlier song, Dekhi zamaane ki yaari came its sequel, Ud ja ud ja pyaase bhanwre which, through its melodrama, intensified the loneliness, the sense of shame and agony of the failed Sinha who ran away from Shanti, his lady love.

OP Nayyar had a hit even before he entered the Hindi film industry. That was a song rendered by CH Atma and it was Preetam aan milo. Guru Dutt liked that song so much that in Mr. & Mrs. '55 he named his character Preetam just so he could use the song. However, he used Geeta Dutt's voice for the number and placed it as a background song in the final scene. The film ended on a happy note. The song's lyrics were written by OP Nayyar's wife, Saroj Mohini Nayyar.

The film Chaudhvin Ka Chand began with the song Ye Lucknow ki sarzameen, a Rafi song in the background, with the titles playing out.

Waltzing Tunes

There is nothing quite like the waltzing melody to express romance, and Guru Dutt understood this so well! Yet it was sometimes used in other situations as well. In C. I. D., listen to a musical argument in which Rafi and Geeta speak about Bombay in Ae dil hai mushkil jeena yahaan. This Bombay anthem owes its existence to the inimitable team of OP Nayyar and Majrooh Sultanpuri. Another beautiful waltz is Udhar tum haseen ho in Mr. & Mrs. '55. Geeta Dutt and Mohammed Rafi excel in this beautiful waltz, once again created by Nayyar and Majrooh. Let's not forget the outstanding Aap ke haseen rukh pe from Baharen Phir Bhi Aayengi with Mohammed Rafi doing the honours for a Nayyar- Anjaan dream of a song! In Pyaasa we have the whoosh and sweep of the waltz again when, in his imagination, the poet Vijay waltzes with his sweetheart Meena in Hum aap ki aankhon mein. Incidentally, this song is the only imaginary dream song that has ever appeared in a Guru Dutt production. An unlikely waltz is this song sung by Johnny Walker in Kaagaz Ke Phool, O Peter O Harry, Hum tum jisse kehta hai shaadi. Burman and Kaifi come together to mock marriages in this waltz!

English Hinglish!

Some songs had quite a few delicious English words in them. From Aar Paar comes, Jaane kahaan mera jigar gaya jee which has English words jumbled in the songs, like

Dard-e-jigar se main weak hoon bahut karo aisa na julam

Arrey, ho jaayenga fail abhi heart hamaara, tere sar ki kasam!

Or then

Reechh ka tu uncle, bandar ka tu baap

Thoko nahin bundle, raho jee chup-chaap!

Listen to the mischief in Baharen Phir Bhi Aayengi through the Johnny Walker song:

Suno, suno Miss Chatterjee, mere dil ka matter jee

Calcutte waali rooth gayi kyun, baat nahin ye better jee!

The second stanza continues in the same vein:

Ban-than ke kahaan chali ho fifty ki raftaar se

Dil waala koi kood na jaaye chalti motor-car se!

Chalte chalte padhti jao dil ka open letter jee!

Not to be out-done by the pesky flirt, she replies,

Phaad de apne dil ka letter, kisko fool banaata hai

Tu hi keh de kaise nibhaayega tera mera matter jee?

But he won't give up, will he?

Hoye, hoye, marte marte likh jaoonga Government ko letter jee!

6

The Singers of Guru Dutt's Music

FEMALE SINGERS

Geeta Dutt

Of the female singers who sang for Guru Dutt Films Pvt. Ltd., Geeta Dutt, with 42 songs (solos and duets), was at the top. The break-up:

Baaz, 7 songs: Ae dil ae deewane, Chham chham chham (Jaago jaago savera), Har zabaan ruki ruki (Ae watan ke naujawan)-1&2, Maanjhi albele, Taare chaandni, and Zara saamne aa.

Aar Paar, 7 songs: Arrey na na na na na na tauba tauba, Babujee dheere chalna, Hoon abhi main jawaan, Ja ja ja ja bewafa, Mohabbat kar lo, Sun, sun, sun sun zaalima, and Ae lo main haari piya.

Mr. & Mrs. '55, 6 songs: Chal diye banda-nawaaz, Jaane kahaan mera jigar gaya ji, Neele aasmaani, Preetam aan milo, Thandi hawa kaali ghata, and Udhar tum haseen ho.

Sailaab, 7 songs: Aa gayi aa gayi, Chaand ke aansoo, Hai ye duniya kaun si, Jiyara baat nahin maane, Om Hari om Hari, Tan pe rang, sakhi, and Ye rut ye raat jawaan.

C. I. D., 3 songs: Aankhon hi aankhon mein, Ae dil hai mushkil, and Jaata kahaan hai deewaane.

Gouri, 1 solo: Jaani, bhromora kaino katha koy na.

Pyaasa, 5 songs: Aaj sajan mohe ang laga lo, Ho laakh museebat raste mein, Hum aap ki aankhon mein, Jaane kya tu ne kahi, and Rut phiri par din hamaare.

Kaagaz Ke Phool, 2 songs: Ek do teen chaar, and Waqt ne kiya kya haseen sitam.

Chaudhvin Ka Chand, 1 solo: Baalam se milan hoga.

Sahib Bibi Aur Ghulam, 3 solos: Koi duur se aawaaz de, Na jaao saiyaan, and Piya aiso jeeya mein.

Asha Bhosle sang 15 songs (solos, duets, and triets) for Guru Dutt Films:

C.I.D., 2 songs: O Leke pehla pehla pyaar (2 versions)

Kaagaz ke Phool, 2 songs: San san san woh chali hawa, and Ulte seedhe dao lagaaye (Haar kabhi jeet kabhi).

Chaudhvin Ka Chand, 3 songs: Bedardi more saiyaan, Dil ki kahaani, and Sharma ke yoon sab pardanasheen.

Sahib Bibi Aur Ghulam, 4 songs: Bhanwra bada naadaan haaye, Meri baat rahi mere man mein, Meri jaan o meri jaan, and Saaqiya aaj mujhe neend nahin aayegi.

Baharen Phir Bhi Aayengi, 4 songs: Dil to pehle hi se, Koi keh de keh de, Suno suno Miss Chatterjee, and Woh hanske mile humse.

Shamshad Begum sang a total of 7 songs (solos or duets) for Guru Dutt:

Aar Paar, 1 song: Kabhi aar, kabhi paar.

Mr. & Mrs. '55, 1 song: Ab to jee hone laga.

C.I.D., 4 songs: Boojh mera kya nao re, Kahin pe nigaahen, and Leke pehla pehla pyaar (both versions).

Chaudhvin Ka Chand, I song: Sharma ke kyun sab pardanasheen.

Sudha Malhotra, 1 song in Kaagaz Ke Phool: San san san woh chali hawa

Lata Mangeshkar, 1 song in Chaudhvin Ka Chand: Badle badle mere sarkaar.

Suman Kalyanpur, 1 song in Aar Paar: Mohabbat kar lo jee bhar lo.

MALE SINGERS

Mohammed Rafi

Mohammed Rafi was Guru Dutt's playback singer in almost all the films he produced. Only three songs belonged to other singers, 2 to Hemant Kumar and 1 to Talat Mehmood. Rafi had the distinction of not only being Guru Dutt's voice in these films, he even sang for others in Dutt's films, whether for Johnny Walker or someone else. Rafi sang a total of 32 songs for Guru Dutt's films.

He also rendered 3 spoken verses in Pyaasa. Rafi and Nayyar were great friends. Rafi's daughter-in-law Yasmin Khalid Rafi wrote in her biography of Rafi, "Music director O P Nayyar was the only one in the entire film industry with whom Rafi Saheb was really friendly." Since the majority of Guru Dutt songs belong to the Nayyar stable, Rafi got to represent Guru Dutt and Johnny Walker in them. Incidentally, Rafi was an extremely generous person who would silently help others from the industry. He was known to anonymously leave cash envelopes around film industry singers who had fallen on bad days just to help them out (anonymously) of their financial crisis. His 32 songs are:

Baaz, 1 song: Ghata mein chhupke

Aar Paar, 3 songs: Arrey na na na na na na tauba tauba, Mohabbat kar lo, and Sun sun sun sun zaalima.

Mr. & Mrs. '55, 5 songs: Aeji dil par hua aisa jaadu, Chal diye banda-nawaaz, Jaane kahaan mera jigar gaya jee, Meri duniya lut rahi thi, and Udhar tum haseen ho.

C.I.D., 5 songs: Aankhon hi aankhon mein, Ae dil hai mushkil, and Leke pehla pehla pyaar (all 3 versions).

Pyaasa, 5 songs: Ho laakh museebat, Hum aap ki aankhon mein, Sar jo tera chakraaye, Ye kooche ye neelam ghar, and Ye mehlon ye takhton ye tajon ki duniya.

Kaagaz Ke Phool, 5 songs: Dekhi zamaane ki yaari, Hum tum jise kehte hain, San san san woh chali hawa, Ud ja ud ja pyaase bhawnre (Dekhi zamaane ki yaari), and Ulte seedhe dao lagaaye (Haar kabhi jeet kabhi).

Chaudhvin Ka Chand, 5 songs: Chaudhvin ka chaand ho, Mera yaar bana hai doolha, Mili khaak mein mohabbat, Ye Lucknow ki sarzameen, and Ye duniya gol hai.

Baharen Phir Bhi Aayengi, 3 songs: Aap ke haseen rukh pe, Dil to pehle hi se madhosh hai, and Suno suno Miss Chatterjee.

As an aside, the composer originally signed up for Baharen Phir Bhi Aayengi was SD Burman. In that SD Burman had Rafi sing a song with the words Koi na tera saathi ho, based on the title tune of the film The Bridge On The River Kwai. However, due to SD Burman's illness, Guru Dutt reverted to OP Nayyar who went on to compose all the songs for the film. The SD Burman song was later redone, with Burman giving a new avatar to the song and using it for Jewel Thief with the same tune but with different lyrics, i.e., Ye dil na hota bechaara. The song is available on YouTube under the heading Koi na tera saathi ho. When OP Nayyar was signed on as the composer for the film, he replaced the Rafi song with the Mahendra Kapoor song, Badal jaaye agar maali, for the same situation.

The other male singers who sang for Guru Dutt's production and banner were as follows:

Talat Mehmood, 1 song in Baaz: Mujhe dekho hasrat ki tasveer hoon main.

Hemant Kumar, 2 songs. One in Pyaasa: Jaane woh kaise log the jinke, and the other in Sahib Bibi Aur Ghulam: Saahil ki taraf.

Mahendra Kapoor, 1 song in Baharen Phir Bhi Aayengi: Badal jaaye agar maali.

SD Burman, 1 song in Gouri: Jaani, bhromora kaino katha koy na.

SINGER STATISTICS

The totals are as follows:

Geeta Dutt: 42

Mohammed Rafi: 32

Asha Bhosle: 15

Shamshad Begum: 6

Hemant Kumar: 2

Lata Mangeshkar: 1

Mahendra Kapoor: 1

Sudha Malhotra: 1

Suman Kalyanpur: 1

Talat Mehmood: 1

SD Burman: 1

In Conclusion

The Last Word

'The more I see of other countries, the more I love my own.'
– Guru Dutt

Immediately after his return from a much-deserved holiday abroad, Guru Dutt wrote an article which appeared in the Filmfare of June 7, 1957, titled, 'No Place Like Home'. Accompanied by their friends, KK Kapoor and his wife, Geeta and Guru had gone on a six-week holiday to the Middle East and Europe. Kapoor was Guru Dutt's close friend and film distributor. The foursome had travelled to several places including Teheran, which Guru Dutt called 'the land of Omar Khayyam and Hafiz'. But he was sorely disappointed to find the locals not dressed in their traditional Iranian clothes since they were attired like Europeans. In that article, he observed, "In the costumes of its people, it is no different from Marseilles or Boston." The cab driver, too, shocked him, for he drove fast, at 70 miles an hour! When the tense Guru Dutt asked him to slow down, the cabbie laughed at him. "I wondered if Iran had not lost her ancient soul." This cultural shock was somewhat compensated by one discovery: he learnt that Iranians, although they didn't understand Hindi, loved the comedy and the music of Raj Kapoor's films.

In Beirut, too, he was disappointed, but here again, he found that Mehboob Khan's film Aan had run for many weeks and there was now an interest in importing Hindi cinema to Lebanon. Flying out of Beirut, the foursome went to Rome and then to Paris. In Paris, Geeta was mobbed because she was a known celebrity while he wasn't. The crowds also loved her beautiful sarees but also because she was 'unusual'. Guru Dutt began to see the plus points of India and wrote, "In Paris, I felt that the more I see of other countries, the more I love my own..."

They left Paris for London where for several reasons he felt most at home on this international journey, mainly because he said he got "further evidence of the appreciation of our film music when my film Pyaasa was shown in a mixed audience of Europeans and Indians. This information may come as a surprise to many highbrows in our country who frown upon our film music and are critical of the number of songs and dances in our pictures. They wonder why film songs are so popular with our masses; they would wonder all the more if they saw how foreign audiences enjoy our film music."

Music was evidently working as a bridge between different parts of the world where nothing else was in common. And Guru Dutt had always known this, because for all his films he would sit in and explain the situation, then work with the singers, lyricists and composers to ensure the songs were created in accordance with the way he planned to film them with his meticulous direction. Although he gave up direction after Kaagaz Ke Phool, he never gave up directing his film's song sequences.

His observations mentioned above came after he visited the Middle East and Europe. But what happened before this vacation?

The overwork, tension, late nights, quarrels, and insomnia, and several other concerns had led him to attempt suicide during the shooting of Pyaasa. This holiday was taken after Pyaasa had become a big hit. In the Filmfare article, he described himself as a gypsy, "Even in boyhood the wanderlust was in me. Lured by the fascination of far-off places, I longed to be a gypsy. But it was only during my school days that I was able to travel to many places in India. When I joined films, the wanderer in me was put into solitary confinement and the door of my 'prison' was opened only after the release of my film Pyaasa. Never before had I worked as hard on a film. Tired in body and mind, I wanted a rest— a holiday and a change of surroundings."

Since both Geeta and Guru were now parents of two children, and since both were working in films in different capacities, they took the holiday to get away from it all. They now had the world at their feet. Even so, Guru was as restless as he had been before the film's success. His quest was never done. His insatiable appetite for trouble and tension has been perfectly described by author Bimal Mitra in his study of the giant.

Guru Dutt had taken Bimal Mitra with him to Mahabalipuram for a few days because he was shooting there as an actor. Mitra wrote, "Mahabalipuram mein maine pehli baar dekha ke Guru man-pran se ashanti chahta hai. Ashanti na mile to usse shanti nahin milti thi, ya isse hi agar ghoom kar kaha jaaye, to woh ashanti duur karne ke liye ashanti ko bulaava deta tha."

So, if Dutt's desire for peace could only be obtained through more turmoil, one can see the vicious circle he was in. Guru Dutt was averse to sameness, so he constantly sought activity, tension, and trouble. Tension and stress led to forgetfulness. He could live with tension, but not with boredom and sameness.

While his thirst for knowledge was insatiable, his driving force was to create world-class cinema. He was possessed by his creative urge, so he relentlessly thought out of the box. His restless soul demanded that he keep awake so that he could do something aesthetically different. Perhaps at that time science had not yet shone a light on the importance of sleep for the creation of better art. Ironically, he would take sleeping pills too, because this constant staying awake would zap him. But still sleep eluded him. His genius was embedded in a super-intelligent brain, besides which he was so well-read that many in the industry envied him. They could see that he was a leader, not a follower. He was perceptive about gifted people and recognised talent before anyone else could. And he hated partying. He said that when he went to them, people would talk to him about his films but he didn't want to indulge in this kind of small talk and meaningless chitchat. Leaders like him are so ahead of the pack, they simply cannot blend in a group. They need to stand alone.

Bimal Mitra said that he found two things that engrossed Guru Dutt constantly. Alcohol and books. This actor and filmmaker could read several languages and there was always a book at his bedside. On his last day, too, there was a half-opened Hindi book at his bedside. He had drunk himself to sleep, but he had done so after reading some pages from a book. The genius of Guru Dutt, his insatiable curiosity, his desire to understand and then portray through cinema, his engrossing work, all these made his blood rush to his brain. They were his reason for living. They kept him alive.

But then there was his emotional self, the part of him that magnified a situation several times. He took things to heart very easily. When VK Murthy decided to shift to Bangalore, he met Guru Dutt along with Abrar Alvi. Guru Dutt told him, "I have become an orphan now. Gharwale nahin hain, tum Bangalore ja rahe ho, Abrar doosra film likhne ke liye Madras ja raha hai. I have become an orphan. Kya karoon main?"

He felt his team was deserting him just as his family had. His mind became filled with gloom and sadness. He could not handle change well any more. He was no longer living with Geeta and their three children. Colour cinema had come but he still had not understood that medium, Raj Kapoor's Sangam had been super successful, making him wonder if his mastery of black and white cinema was soon going to become redundant. He had stopped directing films and his work was no longer motivating him, so one imagines that he was experiencing a burnout of a massive kind. What was worse was that he would not eat properly, even as he went into excessive drinking and smoking. His health went spiralling down so he was in constant need of medical advice and attention. Dev Anand, who met Dutt five or six days before he passed away, observed that he was losing his looks, his hair was thinning, his face seemed pale, and he seemed disheartened as well. He developed anxiety, for which he took medicines, but they did not help. He became such a disturbed human being that, in the end, people stopped visiting him. Introverts seek aloneness, but here was an introvert seeking company to keep his anxiety at bay. He sought company but when he found it, he found it inadequate, because he was way past them intellectually. These emotional conflicts deepened his frustration and made his life hell. These contradictory pulls and pushes took their toll on his health. A few hours before he died he was excitedly making plans about his new home. He prepared omelettes for his brother, an activity that indicates he was optimistic. But then, he was told about the income tax department being on the verge of raiding his home and office. And he had one more argument with Geeta. Such things took him down into the dark abyss of his mind. He went from hopefulness and euphoria to despair and gloom. He might have already guessed that he was becoming like his fictional character Suresh Sinha, his protagonist in Kaagaz Ke Phool, who ended his life quietly when nobody was around.

I am rather spiritual by nature, so I am inclined to see his brief presence on this planet as a divine gift to us in this world. All of us seek a friend who truly understands us. He had, perhaps, been sent to earth for us to understand, through his cinema, that we are not alone in our sorrows; that there was a Guru Dutt who understood it all, and that this was the human condition. It was as if he had been sent to this world, not to exist for himself, but to serve us and also to serve, with unconditional love, his mistress Art.

Raj Khosla found him lost on most days. Chhaya Arya found that while working with him, he would wander off, deep in his thoughts. Abrar Alvi felt that even though he was closest to Guru, he was never Guru's confidante. His sister Lalita Lajmi said he would never open up to anyone; he was that private. Sometimes, they they could see that he was in pain, but nobody could help him, since he was too proud to accept anyone's help. But sadly, due to his internalised anxiety, he would often magnify small things and give them the importance they didn't deserve. This is how his romantic melodrama came into being, through his stories that kept getting darker with time.

VK Murthy observed that both he and Guru Dutt were into art, so they got along well. They experimented with serious, intellectual types of work. They were both keen to be innovative. "He would never compromise on the way the film turned out, the way each scene linked with the other. He was an obsessive director, and until the shot came out just as he wanted he would continue with as many takes as he needed, without a break. He never said, 'Okay, jaane do.' Even with himself, for the famous Pyaasa scene, he shot 104 takes! He kept forgetting the dialogues as it was a very lengthy shot, but he wanted it just right. We started the shot at 5 pm, and it went on till 10:30 pm. When I asked him to stop for the day and try it afresh later, he was adamant. We finally packed up at 11:30 pm. Finally, the next morning we canned it perfectly on the very first take!"

But then there was Guru Dutt and his despair. One day, when VK Murthy and Guru Dutt were in Baroda to look for locations for Chaudhvin Ka Chand, Guru Dutt, who was feeling depressed, remarked, with a line from Pyaasa, "Agar yeh duniya mujhe mil bhi jaaye to kya hai." Murthy asked him why he was saying this, to which he replied, "Mujhe waise hi lag raha hai. Dekho na, mujhe director banna tha, director ban gaya; actor banna tha, actor ban gaya; picture achche bannane the, achche bane. Paisa hai, sab kuchh hai, par kuchh bhi nahi raha..."

His commitment to cinema made Guru Dutt obsessed with the art of creation. Yet, underneath it all, he was dissatisfied with himself. As a perfectionist, it wasn't only the world he was unhappy with, he was a self-analytical genius too. Unlike so many others who were leading double lives in the quiet, he, like his two friends, OP Nayyar and Dev Anand, was leading a fast life in the public's glare. Fast cars, throwing money around, creating magic through cinema and its music, all three brilliant men were unstoppable. Yet, they were so unlike each other. Nayyar was a gutsy, honest human being who acknowledged that he found himself homeless in the end because it was his doing. Till his last day, his face was peaceful and showed him to be a realist. He had been thrown out of his home by his wife and children. He was living with a middle-class family in Thane, paying for one room in their home. His reverses made him blame himself and also his past karma. On his part, when Dev Anand failed, he would spend zero minutes in introspection or brooding, he would zip towards the next project, breathless to move on. He was positivity personified. Dutt, on the other hand, had none of Dev Anand's irrepressible energy and optimism. He had a great belief in destiny and, somehow, it made him morose. He would internalise whatever happened to him and then his agonising thoughts would overpower him.

A few images drawn by Bimal Mitra never leave my mind.

—An astrologer told him that Tuesdays were very bad for him. Guru Dutt told Bimal Mitra that he avoided doing anything on Tuesdays.

—He would order his staff to prepare a fabulous spread to be laid out at the dining table, but he would be found away from his guests, seated in another room eating a spartan meal that was as simple as dal chawal.

—He would keep repeating to Bimal Mitra that he felt as if he was going mad. Genius, it is said, is akin to madness, I wonder if he felt his brain could not handle the millions of thoughts he was generating and it would collapse out of information overload.

—Suddenly one April afternoon, when they were together, it began to rain. Guru Dutt said to Bimal Mitra, "Chaliye, Bimal Babu, uth jaaiye, barsaat ho rahi hai. Ab kaam karne ka man nahin hai"…Bimal Mitra wrote, "Woh bachchon ki tarah maare khushi ke uchalta raha. Hum sab Guru ki gaadi mein savaar ho gaye. Guru gaadi chala raha tha…"

Here was a man who understood Hafiz and knew Shakespeare, who saw the best of international cinema, who was a voracious reader, and who experienced life in all its hues. It boggles many that such a man had to end in such a tragic manner. It reminds me of the conversation between Bimal Mitra and him when he observed, "Bimal babu, mrityu se main nahin darta, lekin zindagi ke liye hi bhaybheet rehta hoon."

The man who could dance in the rain like a gleeful child, the man who had everything, the genius who created world-class cinema, such a man was sleepless.

When Suresh Sinha of Kaagaz Ke Phool finished with his memories and was done with his creative best, he heaved his last sigh:

Ik haath se deti hai duniya, sau haathon se le leti hai…

Ye khel hai kab se jaari?

Haaye…

Bichde sabhi baari baari…

Dekhi zamaane ki yaari…

Bichde sabhi baari baari…

Approximately 80 miles away from Bombay, Guru Dutt owned a farmhouse that had several acres of land. Grain was grown there with the help of some local farmers. The land had a huge water well, some chicken and a few ducks too.

On this land, there was a small cottage with a verandah out in the front. The hovel, consisting of one and a half tiny rooms, got electricity with the help of a dynamo which Guru Dutt had installed. In the bedroom, there was a bed, some pillows, a fridge, a telephone and a few chairs. The view from the cottage was beautiful. On rainy days, one could see the clouds descending on the nearby hills and on his cottage too. Guru Dutt loved the rain.

One day when Bimal Mitra and the writing team were working on the script of Sahib Bibi Aur Ghulam in his Lonavala bungalow, Guru Dutt got up and informed them that he was leaving for his farmhouse. Bimal Mitra wrote that he understood what Guru Dutt was in the habit of doing when he reached the farm. "Wahaan jaakar, apne kamre ke saamne, kursi lekar, akele akele baitha rehta tha, ya koi kitab padta rehta tha, ya gehu ke khet mein ghoomta -tehelta rehta tha. Wahan kuch-ek ghante akele hi pada rehta tha. Shaam ghir aati thi, woh kamre ke baramde mein apni kursi par jama rehta. Kabhi kabhi mere man mein sawaal uthta tha ke Guru adda chodhkar, wahaan us andhere mein akele kyun baitha rehta tha?"

This final image of Guru Dutt does not leave me. Although this is not a scene from a Guru Dutt film, I want to re-create what would happen once he reached his farmhouse.

He enters his tiny cottage, puts his bag down, takes a book and a pen out of his bag, then takes a chair out to the verandah of his dimly lit cottage, sits on the chair and begins to read a book. From time to time he looks around at the acres of land he owns and at a few hills nearby.

It begins to rain, he puts his book down and smiles, his brow wrinkling, his eyes soft with love. He is remembering something and is lost in his thoughts. The rolling mists descend on his cottage, the fog dims everything around him. When the fog envelopes him, he stretches out his hands, cups the raindrops, and then takes his wet hands to his lips to give the rain a kiss. He continues to sit there for an eternity. He cannot see anyone, and nobody can see him either. Even if he is completely enveloped by the blanket of fog, somehow we know he is there, happy in his simple down-to-earth Indian home, away from the crowds, away from it all.

He has reached his home.

He is happy because there is no place like home.

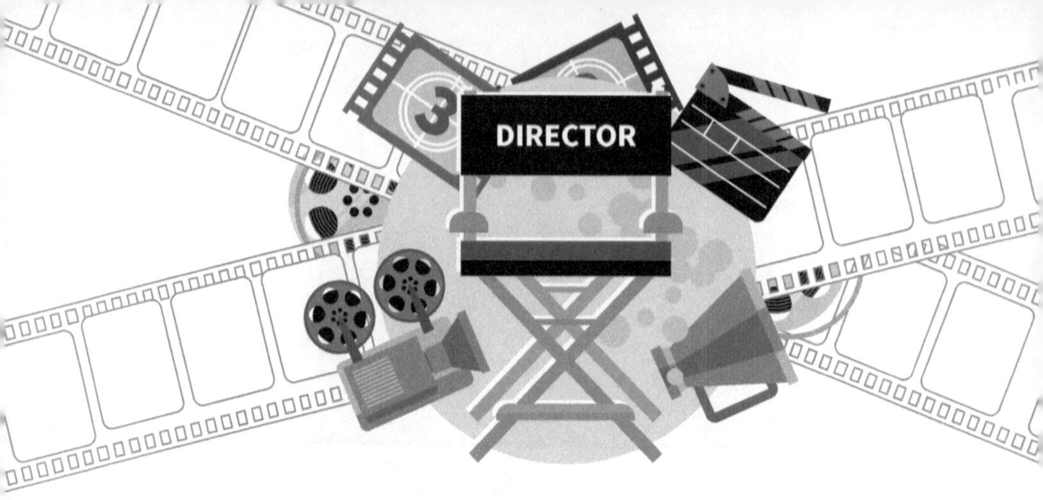

Bibliography and References

- A Treasure Trove of Urdu Couplets, compiled by Rajesh Sharma
- Bichhde Sabhi Bari-Bari, authored by Bimal Mitra (originally in Bengali published as Binidra
- Bollywood, A History, authored by Mihir Bose
- Bonding, Vyjayanthimala's autobiography
- Conversations with Waheeda Rehman, authored by Nasreen Munni Kabir
- Dilip Kumar, the Substance and the Shadow, authored by Dilip Kumar
- Director's Chair, authored by Manek Premchand
- Follywood Flashback, authored by Bunny Reuben
- Guide, the Film Perspectives, authored by Lata Jagtiani

- Guru Dutt a Tragedy in Three Acts, by Arun Khopkar

- Guru Dutt, a Life in Cinema by Nasreen Munni Kabir

- Guru Dutt, an Unfinished Story authored by Yasser Usman

- Guru Dutt, authored by Rashmi Doraiswamy

- Hindi Cinema and its Unforgettable Icons, authored by BM Malhotra

- Housefull, the Golden Age of Hindi Cinema, Edited by Ziya Us Salam

- In Black and White, authored by Darius Cooper

- Incomparable Sachin Dev Burman, authored by HQ Chowdhury

- Lata Mangeshkar in her own Voice, authored by Nasreen Munni Kabir

- Majrooh Sultanpuri, the Poet for all Reasons by Manek Premchand

- Melodies, Movies and Memories, authored by Nalin Shah

- Mohammed Rafi, Golden Voice of the Silver Screen authored by Sujata Dev

- Mohammed Rafi, My Abba authored by Yasmin Khalid Rafi

- My Son Guru Dutt, authored by Vasanthi Padukone in Kannada translated to English and published by Screen and Imprint magazine, April 1979. Originally titled Nanna Maga Guru Dutt published in 1976.

- OP Nayyar King of Melody, authored by Lata Jagtiani

- Our Films Their Films, Essays authored by Satyajit Ray

- Prefaces by Bernard Shaw—A compilation.

- Raj Kapoor, the One and Only Showman, authored by Ritu Nanda

- Romancing the Song, authored by Manek Premchand

- Romancing with Life, authored by Dev Anand

- Sahir Ludhianvi The People's Poet, authored by Akshay Manwani

- Satyajit Ray, the Inner Eye by Andrew Robinson

- Shailendra A love Lyric in Print authored by Amla Shailendra Mazumdar

- Short Stories of Guy de Maupassant

- Take2—50 Films That Deserve a New Audience by Deepa Gehlot

- Ten Years With Guru Dutt Abrar Alvi's Journey authored by Sathya Saran

- The Hundred Luminaries of Hindi Cinema, authored by Dinesh Raheja and Jitendra Kothari

- The Stars of Yesterday, authored by Nand Kishore

- The Summing Up, authored by Somerset Maugham

- The Unforgettable Music of Hemant Kumar, by Manek Premchand

- Wuthering Heights—Emily Bronte

- Yesterday's Melodies, Today's Memories, authored by Manek Premchand

- Yours Guru Dutt, compiled and presented by Nasreen Munni Kabir

Online and offine references:

- Ajay Chandravanshi on Pyaasa in Deshbandu of July 9, 1923, page 6.

- Arun Dutt's online interviews with India Abroad in Oct 2004, which are available on YouTube

- Avijit Pathak's essay, Why Guru Dutt's Black and White Existential Poetry is Relevant in the Glossy India of Today, published in The Wire on October 10, 2017.

- Ayn Rand's novel The Fountainhead

- Dr Mandar Bichhu's interview of the composer OP Nayyar, An Intimate Interview, published in Cinemasangeet of June 6, 2003. Available on a web portal named after the composer.

- Edgar Cochran on web portal Letterbox.com

- Filmfare's interview of Shyama by Farhana Farook on November 15, 2017.

- Filmfare's interview with Devi Dutt titled, Women Were Ready to do Anything for Guru Dutt.

- FilmIndia July 1954 issue.

- Firoze Rangoonwalla's monograph for National Film Archives of India 1973, where he has published an article in the special issue of Journal of Film Industry, with reference to Waheeda Rehman.

- Gobind Nihalani's documentary showcased by him to honour VK Murthy at the Bangalore Film Festival in 2023

- Guide ke Pehle by Ashalata in Madhuri magazine

- Guruswamy's essay, 'There was a certain nobility about him' in Screen dated Oct 13, 1989.

- Har Mandir Singh Hamraaz's Geet Kosh Volume 3.

- Henrik Ibsen's play A Doll's House

- Karan Bali's critique of C.I.D. on May 2015 available on his website Upperstall.

- Lalitha Lajmi's several interviews on YouTube, her interview with Sushmita Bhattrai in 2020 on Seniorstoday, "Guru Dutt Introvert and Genius."

- Listener's Bulletin, April 2010 issue on Guru Dutt

- Manisha Mandal's write-up Suicide or Drug Overdose, published in Indiatimes.com on July 9, 2021

- Many online interviews of VK Murthy on YouTube on his mentor Guru Dutt, where he spoke on Baazi and his freedom to create as he wished.

- Nabendu Ghosh's essay on Guru Dutt Of Incomplete Tales, my Friendship with Guru Dutt available on Learningandcreativity. com

- Online web portal Harveypam.com

- Rahul Jayaram's essay Guru Dutt and Me, an interview with VK Murthy on the web portal of Open magazine.

- Raj Khosla's online interviews available on YouTube titled Raj Khosla Talks About Life.

- Roshmila Bhattacharya's write-up in Mumbai Mirror dated 13.7.2019, titled Guru Dutt and the Sands of Time

- Sanjit Narwekar's online essay The Incomplete Films of Guru Dutt published in Screen on October 13, 1989.

- Shishir Krishna Sharma's essay Koi Door Se Awaaz De Chale Aao on his webportal.

- Vandana Kumar's essay in IndiaCurrents, Never Say Goodbye.

- Waheeda Rehman's write-up Under Foreign Skies in Filmfare 1963.

- WildfilmsIndia's web portal where Arun Dutt was interviewed.

Other films viewed for reference:

- Gilda (1946)
- Bitter Rice (1949)
- Late Spring (1949)
- A Star Is Born (1954)
- Devdas (1955)
- The Apu Trilogy (1955, 1956, 1959)
- Jalsaghar (1958)
- Gumrah (1963)
- Zorba the Greek (1964)
- Guide (1965)
- Nayak (1966)
- Ek Din Achanak (1988)
- Force Majeure (2014)
- Anatomy of A Fall (2023)

www.ingramcontent.com/pod-product-compliance
Lightning Source LLC
Chambersburg PA
CBHW031520150726
47990CB00001B/19